Poetry in the N

For my angels

# Poetry in the Mind

## The Cognition of Contemporary Poetic Style

JOANNA GAVINS

EDINBURGH
University Press

Edinburgh University Press is one of the leading university presses in the UK. We publish academic books and journals in our selected subject areas across the humanities and social sciences, combining cutting-edge scholarship with high editorial and production values to produce academic works of lasting importance. For more information visit our website: edinburghuniversitypress.com

Edinburgh University Press Ltd
The Tun – Holyrood Road, 12(2f) Jackson's Entry, Edinburgh EH8 8PJ

First published in hardback by Edinburgh University Press 2020

Typeset in 10/12 Times New Roman by
Servis Filmsetting Ltd, Stockport, Cheshire
and printed and bound by CPI Group (UK) Ltd,
Croydon, CR0 4YY

A CIP record for this book is available from the British Library

ISBN 978 1 4744 2070 9 (hardback)
ISBN 978 1 4744 9246 1 (Paperback)
ISBN 978 1 4744 2071 6 (webready PDF)
ISBN 978 1 4744 2072 3 (epub)

Grateful acknowledgement is made for permission to reproduce material previously published elsewhere. Every effort has been made to trace the copyright holders, but if any have been inadvertently overlooked, the publisher will be pleased to make the necessary arrangements at the first opportunity.

# Contents

# List of Figures

# Acknowledgements

I am grateful to the friends and colleagues who read parts of this manuscript and offered constructive and helpful feedback at various stages of its production, particularly Jessica Mason, Peter Stockwell, Peter Verdonk and Sara Whiteley. My thanks, too, to Jon Daughtry of DED Associates who designed the cover, and to Paul Scott (aka Lippy Kid) whose music accompanied much of my writing. Thank you to my family for their love and support throughout this project, and to my friends Alice Bell, Sam Browse, Julian Church, David Ewing, David Forrest, Rachel Hughes, Shaun Lawrence, Emma Moore and Sophie Maxwell for the same. I am also grateful to the poets who generously agreed to me reproducing their work in the coming chapters free of charge – Simon Armitage, Jo Bell, John Burnside, Sinéad Morrissey and Kate Tempest. In Chapter 6, the poem 'Song of a Stone', by Alice Oswald, is taken from *Woods Etc.* (Oswald 2005a) and is reproduced by permission of Faber and Faber Ltd.

# 1 Reading Poetry

## Approaching poetic discourse

Academic research which seeks to define and examine the nature of poetry already exists in significant abundance. Critical works on poetic texts number in their thousands and students of literature regularly spend months, or even years, attempting to get to the heart of what poetry is and how it functions as a phenomenon in the world; entire careers, as well as countless books, articles and courses have been dedicated to these questions alone in scholarship dating back as far as Ancient Greece. The present book is inevitably positioned within this extensive critical context and it aims, too, to engage in a productive and meaningful dialogue with as much preceding opinion on poetry as is practicably possible within its limited pages. Over the course of the coming chapters, I will be exploring many of the same aspects of poetic text which have preoccupied innumerable critics and theorists before me and which can be seen, in many ways, to underpin the foundations of the contemporary understanding of poetry. This book is structured around some of the key dimensions of poetic style which have engrossed those critics and delineated the majority of their ideas on the subject for hundreds of years: time and space; intertextuality; absence; performance; and metaphor. However, it is important to note from the outset that I approach these facets of poetry from a perspective that differs significantly from a great deal of previous research on the subject.

First and foremost, I do not attempt in this book to forge a novel definition of the genre of poetry, nor is it my interest to frame poetry around a distinct or original theoretical metaphor. These kinds of imaginative hermeneutic activities tend to form the focus of literary criticism and theory, a field of study of which I do not consider myself to be centrally a part. It is, however, a field which has provided a rich and highly inventive seam of ideas about and interpretations of poetry over many decades. This book will seek to converse with and be provoked by those existing ideas, rather than aiming primarily to contribute further to what is already a substantial body of work. My own disciplinary home is in linguistics. This means that I am chiefly interested in poetry as a form of naturally occurring discourse and in what its multitudinous manifestations in the world can tell us about human beings, the ways in which they communicate with each other and express themselves creatively. It also means that, like the majority of linguists whose research focuses on literary language, my core concern is to try to explain *how* and *why* certain readings of literature might come into being, both in the academic sphere and beyond it, rather than formulating unique or formative readings of my own. I am interested in poetry as a shared cultural and artistic language event and in the broadly consensual interpretations that occur in response to it.

The second dimension along which my investigation of poetry differs from those of a good number of literary critics, and from many literary-linguists too, is that I do not view poetry here as a fixed or stable object in the world. Although much of my discussion is based around the examination of formal features of poetic language, I do not view these forms and structures as existing in material isolation, nor do I consider them in a way that might give rise to a similarly fixed or immutable analysis. This is because I am specifically and fundamentally a *cognitive* linguist by both background and approach. Cognitive linguistics is founded upon an essential commitment to making one's account of language accord with what is known about the human mind and brain by drawing on scholarly work in disciplines other than linguistics (see Lakoff 1990: 40). Research across the cognitive sciences has shown that language is a direct reflection of the principal properties of human thought and of the basis of this thought in our everyday, embodied experience of the world around us. As Lakoff and Johnson (1999: 19) explain, 'the peculiar nature of our bodies shapes our very possibilities for conceptualization and categorization'. This means that there are basic features of our physicality which directly forge and control how we interact with our surroundings: we are vertically upright beings, for example; we inhabit bodies which have a front and a back; and we perceive the world mainly from the upper part of those bodies. In consequence, this physicality regulates how we express our day-to-day experiences and perceptions through language. My central focus as a cognitive-literary-linguist, therefore, is on poetic discourse as a particular expression of our physical relationships with the world. My account of poetry – at its core – strives to recognise that poetic language, although it is often especially complex and creative, is at the same time like all other forms of human communication, and in two important ways. First of all, it is a spontaneous phenomenon derived from embodied everyday experience, and its nature and design features are directly reflective of those of the human mind. Secondly, poetry occurs in a specific context, the potential impact of which on the actuality of poetic language is so great that it must form the foundation of any coherent account of this or any other type of discourse. Although poetry obviously has material substance in the world, as printed or spoken text, its materiality is the product of complex human cognition and it is also fundamentally situated in both time and space. That spatio-temporal situation shapes both the creation and the reception of poetic discourse in profound ways. Furthermore, the situated nature of poetry transforms it beyond the concrete boundaries of text alone. Recognising the importance of the physical, historical and cultural context in which poetic discourse occurs means also recognising that poetry is much more than a tangible art object, receptive to analytical dissection; it is a dynamic, embodied and conceptual human experience, which requires a fully context-sensitive approach if its cognitive complexity is to be properly understood. My focus throughout this book is therefore not simply on poetic text alone, but on the reading of poetic text in a specific context and on the effects this produces in the mind.

## Understanding poetic worlds

The account of the cognition of poetic discourse which I develop over the coming chapters recruits and deploys a range of concepts and analytical apparatus from the cognitive sciences, especially cognitive linguistics and cognitive psychology. It also engages with a variety of ideas about poetry put forward in literary criticism and in literary and cultural theory. However, it is primarily framed, like all my research, through the lens of Text World Theory (see Gavins 2007; Gavins and Lahey 2016; and Werth 1999, for a comprehensive overview), a cognitive-linguistic framework designed to enable the rigorous and systematic examination of all forms of human discourse. Although each of the chapters of this book focuses on a different aspect of poetic discourse, or pursues a particular idea about poetry, Text World Theory forms the overarching explanatory structure through which each of these individual discussions is principally facilitated. Even though I employ an assortment of concepts from a diversity of disciplinary perspectives over the course of the book, the notion that all poetry constructs a 'world' in the minds of its readers forms the essential bedrock of my understanding of how poetic discourse works linguistically and conceptually.

The text-world approach to the analysis of language views all discourse as fundamentally grounded in a context of use. That context is known as the *discourse-world* in Text World Theory terms (see Gavins 2007: 18–33). It consists of the physical environment in which a discourse takes place and it includes the human participants who make the discourse happen in the first place. Crucially, the discourse-world contains not just the participants themselves, but all the cultural, perceptual, experiential and linguistic knowledge they bring with them to a language event. This knowledge is drawn not only from the immediate circumstances surrounding the participants as they communicate with one another, but also from all their previous experiences, their memories, opinions, beliefs, and so on. Text World Theory recognises that this knowledge has the potential to influence the ways in which the participants produce and understand discourse at any point in

---

their communication. In the case of discourses which happen face to face, participants may gesture or refer to elements of their surroundings, as well as reacting and responding to the verbal and physical behaviour of their co-participant(s), their facial expressions, body language and intonation. They will also need to access other forms of knowledge in order to understand the language they encounter and to produce understandable language of their own. In the case of written discourses, where the author and the reader of a text are most often separated in time and space, this wider knowledge becomes of paramount importance. Situations such as these are common in literary discourse, but they also occur in telephone communication and in many other forms of written language; they are known as *split discourse-worlds* in Text World Theory (see Gavins 2007: 26). Without the additional comprehension clues that a shared immediate environment can supply, the participants in a split discourse-world must draw much more heavily on their cultural and experiential knowledge in order to comprehend the discourse. The majority of poetic discourses examined over the course of this book take place in a split discourse-world, where poet and reader do not occupy the same spatio-temporal environment. However, in Chapters 3 and 5 I also consider the face-to-face discourse-worlds in which poetry can take place in the form of poetic performance or live poetry reading.

Obviously, the individual knowledge stores which human beings carry with them through their everyday lives are considerable and practically unmappable within the confines of a single, coherent linguistic theory. However, from a Text World Theory perspective, the potentially unwieldy nature of participant knowledge is regulated by the text the participants produce. In other words, the text-world framework views the deployment of knowledge during communication as essentially *text-driven* (see Gavins 2007: 33). This means that, from the vast body of knowledge participants have available to them in their discourse-worlds, the language of the text itself will define which aspects of that knowledge are needed in order to comprehend the discourse at hand. When reading John Keats's famous poem, 'Ode on a Grecian Urn', for example, the reader will first of all need to access the linguistic knowledge necessary to understand that the words of the poem and their connected experiential knowledge of trees, heifers, priests, spring, music, and so on, will all come into play in the processing of the discourse. Readers might also activate knowledge about Keats himself, as their co-participant in the discourse-world, about previous works by Keats they may also have read, about nineteenth-century poetry more broadly, or about Ancient Greek art and mythology, all of which are cued by linguistic elements in the text. They will not, however, need their knowledge of baking, or basketball, or the rules of chess. The basic principle of text-drivenness narrows the scope of Text World Theory to the much more manageable field of the text, its immediate and relevant context, and the conceptual effects of these two things combined.

As the participants in the discourse-world communicate they create mental representations of the discourse in their minds, known as *text-worlds* (see Gavins 2007: 35–72). These conceptual spaces are constructed primarily from information contained in the text, but they are fleshed out by inferences and additional details drawn from the participants' discourse-world knowledge. This means that, for the participants, the text-worlds they build in their minds have the potential to become as richly detailed and as immersive as the real-world environment from which they originate. It also means that all text-worlds are unique and individual to each participant, evolving, as they do, as a mixture of the textual information shared in the discourse-world and private, internal knowledge. Text-worlds are assembled and organised around a subjective point of view, known as the *origo* in linguistic theory (see Bühler 1982; Jarvella and Klein 1982; Rauh 1983). Just as our own interactions with the everyday world are perceived from the zero-point of reference around which our embodied sense of self is organised, so the text-worlds we establish in our minds from language represent the perspective of a particular experiencing centre. Some of the linguistic features of a text which shape how that perspective is represented and conceptualised are known as *deictic expressions* in linguistics. This is a closed set of grammatical terms which includes such items as personal and demonstrative pronouns, certain adverbials and definite referring expressions, among other things. As Green (1992) notes, however, deixis is fundamentally dependent on the context of its use, which means that a much wider range of textual features can often be seen to function deictically in discourse. Green goes on to explain:

> If I say one morning while looking out of my window, *The sky is blue*, then I am using this sentence deictically. If, however, I mean *The sky is blue* as a general statement – a proposition about a general state of affairs – then I do not use it deictically (I use it generically). Tense, therefore, can be deictic inasmuch as it can be used to encode specific temporal relations with respect to the encoder [. . .] Deixis has a powerful pragmatic base as most deictic elements and terms can be used non-deictically. Pronouns, for instance, can be used anaphorically and demonstratives can be used in a non-demonstrative way, for example the expressions *here and there* and *this and that*. Despite being a closed set of terms linked with a number of functioning elements, deixis lacks a taxonomy of occurrences because of its pragmatic base. Context and use are vital to our understanding of deixis, and this is why the investigation of its behaviour in a particular discourse is relevant.
>
> (Green 1992: 122–3)

In other words, many linguistic items change their deictic function depending on how they are used and in what circumstance. For this reason, in Text World Theory all the deictically functioning components of a particular text are known collectively as its *world-building elements* (see Gavins 2007: 36).

The primary purpose of these textual elements is to construct the spatial and temporal parameters of our mental representations of discourse in a way that is essentially dependent on their context of use. One of the defining attributes of literary discourse specifically is its capacity to use such world-building features to create viewpoints representing fictional minds and experiences other than our own. Likewise, it is a defining aspect of our humanity that we are able to project ourselves into such remote deictic centres and to develop empathetic relationships with literary characters as a consequence.

## Poetry in the mind

Perhaps the easiest way to demonstrate how the construction of a text-world takes place in poetic discourse is through the analysis of an example text. Below is a poem by the British poet, Jo Bell (2015), which can be seen in many ways to enact much of the linguistic theory discussed so far in this chapter. The poem is reproduced here in full by kind permission of the poet.

### Crates

Observe that when I speak of crates
your mind supplies one straight away.

Likely you are thinking of the fruiterer's crate:
a shallow slatted box of rain-napped pine,
the archetype of apples stencilled on the side,
a cartouche slot above it for the grocer's hand.

Your crate may be the sturdy plastic tub
of the eco-minded council, waiting at the gate
with all its rinsed tomato cans
and in this case a drowned frog;

or then again the solid, beer-smooth wood
hefted by the publican
with its hangover slump of bottles
to the yard, the morning after.

Your crate exists as soon as it is thought.
Its shape is shown in speaking of it.
Now, let us speak of love.

This poem provides a neat first example with which to begin my investigation of the language and cognition of poetry, since it represents a linguistic performance of precisely the sort of conceptual world-building I have been describing up to this point and which will form the focus of much of the rest of this book. 'Crates' operates very much as a dynamic and shifting poetic reading experience, which evolves through the interaction of the text itself with the reader's individual context and background knowledge.

The poem addresses the reader in their half of a split discourse-world directly from the first word of its first line: 'Observe'. This imperative verb creates a particular linguistic and conceptual position for the reader in the text-world of the poem from the outset, a position which may also cause specific effects – psychological, emotional, aesthetic – to be experienced by that reader over the course of their interaction with the poem. In order to understand how these effects occur, it is useful at this point to add a little more detail to our understanding of the ontological structure which under-pins the communicative situation of literary discourses. Some of the most helpful theorising of this aspect of literary language comes from the field of narratology and has been formulated to account for narrative prose fiction specifically. However, much of it is more broadly applicable to non-narrative literary texts, such as drama and poetry, too. For example, Rabinowitz (1977) provides an easily generalisable account of how different types of readers, authors and audiences communicate through and are constructed by narrative fiction. He distinguishes 'the actual audience' of flesh-and-blood people in the real world from 'the authorial audience', a hypothetical con-struct for whom the author rhetorically designs the text (Rabinowitz 1977: 126). Rabinowitz goes on to point out that there always exists some degree of distance between these two audiences, but that the actual audience must come to share at least some of the authorial audience's characteristics if they are to understand the text, since it has been specially structured and com-posed for this imaginary set of people. He further notes that authors have a range of approaches to the actual audience: some write to minimise the distance between their real readers and the authorial audience; some write without an apparent care for the actual audience's real-world knowledge and expectations; and some even seem to write deliberately in order to make the actual audience feel inferior to an 'ethically superior' authorial audience (Rabinowitz 1977: 126), equipped with greater understanding and intellect, at whom the text is aimed.

Rabinowitz identifies a further type of audience, which he terms 'the narrative audience', a concept which he explains as follows:

> One way to determine the characteristics of the narrative audience is to ask, 'What sort of reader would be implied if this work of fiction were real?' or, even better, 'What sort of person would I have to pretend to be – what would I have to know and believe – if I wanted to take this work of fiction as real?' Normally, it is a fairly simple task to pretend to be a member of the narrative audience: we temporarily take on certain minimal beliefs in addition to those we already hold. Thus, for a while, we believe that a woman named Anna Karenina really exists, and

thinks and acts in a certain way; or, on a broader scale, that Yoknapat
County and its inhabitants really exist.

(Rabinowitz 1977: 128)

The narrative audience, then, is the audience implicitly addressed by the
narrator of a text. This audience is afforded an observing position on the
text-world and temporarily adopts the information, beliefs, knowledge and
opinions that the author assumes it has. Phelan (1996) offers a further exten-
sion of Rabinowitz's ideas and a useful way of thinking about the effects of
this kind of reader positioning, which again he sets out in relation to nar-
rative fiction but which can be extended to poetic text-worlds too. Phelan's
work is particularly appealing to anyone interested in the cognition of literary
texts, since it both recognises the fundamentally situated and contextualised
nature of literary communication and focuses centrally on the consequences
for readers of certain linguistic choices made by authors. Phelan explains:

> Even as we participate in the authorial and narrative audiences, we
> never lose our identities as flesh-and-blood readers, and that fact adds a
> further layer to our experience. Just as the authorial audience evaluates
> the narrator's values, so too does the flesh-and-blood audience evalu-
> ate the author's. Entering the authorial audience allows us to recognize
> the ethical and ideological bases of the author's invitations. Comparing
> those values to the ones we bring to the text leads us into a dialogue
> about those values. Sometimes our values may be confined by those of
> the text, sometimes they may be challenged, and sometimes they may
> be ignored or insulted. When our values conflict with those of the text,
> we either will alter ours or resist those of the text (in whole or in part).
> The ethical dimension of the story involves the values upon which the
> authorial audience's judgments are based, the way those values are
> deployed in the narrative, and, finally, the values and beliefs implicit in
> the thematizing of the character's experience.
>
> (Phelan 1996: 100)

All of these ideas can be translated into a poetic context if we consider the
concept of the authorial audience as remaining the same and the narrative
audience as being better described as 'the poetic audience' in poetic dis-
courses. Poems have an author just as narrative texts do, and poetic texts are
constructed around the same relationships between authors and readers as
Phelan and Rabinowitz both describe. That said, Phelan is careful to outline
what he sees as crucial differences between narrative and poetic – specifically
lyrical – literary forms. For example, in his discussion of some of the lyrical
qualities of Virginia Woolf's narrative, *The Waves*, he notes that preceding
theories have tended to differentiate between narrative and lyric on the basis
that narrative focuses on dynamic sequence, where lyric focuses on state of

mind, most often presented in stasis. He notes, however, that these are tendencies rather than absolutes and that the temporal nature of reading itself means that lyric is as dependent on sequence as narrative is. Phelan suggests instead that it is more accurate to focus on the differing attitudes readers are asked to take towards the content of the text. Where narrative texts encourage readers to develop hypotheses about characters, assign motivations, hopes for resolution, and so on, Phelan argues that in lyric poetry 'we are asked to see the world through the speaker's eyes without making a judgement on that vision' (Phelan 1996: 36).

It is possible to see 'Crates', then, as opening with a signalling of the existence of an authorial audience which has been imagined by the poet and which is directly addressed through the verb 'Observe'. The explicit and idealised role marked out for this authorial audience in the emerging text-world is sustained linguistically by the repeated use of the second-person pronoun 'you' throughout the poem. The use of the second person in literary discourse can have complex conceptual effects, which are also worth exploring a little further at this point. In first- and third-person texts, the proper names and pronouns used in a discourse nominate particular entities as present in the text-world. These entities are another component of the world-building elements of the discourse in Text World Theory terms and, under this approach, they are known as 'enactors' (see Gavins 2007: 41), in recognition of the fact that different variants of the same person can exist at different conceptual levels of any discourse (see also Emmott 1997). For example, as readers of Charles Dickens's novel, *Great Expectations*, we understand that there exists a single character, Pip, whose personality changes and evolves over the course of the entire novel. Pip as an adult and Pip as a child are both represented in the text and are connected yet temporally separate textual versions of the same person. Pip has different life experiences and consequently different knowledge at different points in the novel and the entire fiction revolves, in fact, around his contrasting views and responses to his situation at these discreet moments. The grown-up enactor of Pip who narrates *Great Expectations* has a reflective and contemplative view on an earlier enactor of himself, who he describes as helping Magwitch, falling in love with Estella, and so on, often with considerably critical self-evaluation.

When the second person is used in fictional discourse, it can refer to entities both inside and outside the text-world: the discourse-world participants and/or text-world enactors aligned to this form of address can vary in subtle degrees. Herman (1994, 2002) outlines no fewer than five different types of textual 'you', noting that in some cases the second person may have only a very generalised reference into the discourse-world. This kind of highly impersonal 'you' is commonly used in proverbs and sayings (such as 'a little of what you fancy does you good' or 'as you sow, so shall you reap'), in advertising and in instruction manuals. Other types of 'you' refer within what Herman terms 'the frame of the fiction' (2002: 342) and entail address to or by members of the same fictional world. In most of these cases of 'horizontal address', as Herman (2002: 341) calls it, it is immediately clear to the reader that the 'you' being picked out by this pronoun is a fictional entity which does not align with themselves or anyone else inhabiting the discourse-world level of the communication. However, Herman also identifies a further type of 'you', which is not limited to either the discourse-world or the text-world alone but which appears to refer across the ontological boundaries between these spaces. He terms this type of second-person reference 'double deixis' (Herman 2002: 341) and further explains as follows:

> the [doubly deictic] second person makes of the reader a fellow player, who is suspended between a fictive world and his own real world, and who stands simultaneously inside and outside the fiction [. . .] In doubly deictic contexts, in other words, the audience will find itself more or less subject to conflation with the fictional self addressed by you. The deictic force of you is double; or to put it another way, the scope of the discourse context embedding the description is indeterminate, as is the domain of participants in principle specified or picked out by you.
>
>                                                          (Herman 1994: 406)

The instances of 'you' and 'your' which are repeated four times over the course of 'Crates' fall into this category of second-person reference. In the opening stanza of the poem, both the imperative verb 'Observe' and the reference to 'your mind' which follows it in the second line can equally plausibly be interpreted as referring to an imagined entity in the text-world, thinking of a crate, and as reaching directly into the discourse-world to address the real reader at the same time. This cross-world ambiguity is further strengthened by the existence of the first-person pronoun 'I' alongside the textual 'you'. Although 'I' is only used once in the opening line of the text, this nevertheless creates a presence for an enactor of the author in the text-world. This fictionalised implied author logically exists as the addresser of the fictionalised enactor addressed by 'you'. The doubly deictic nature of that address not only extends to the real reader of the poem in the discourse-world, but also encourages them to implicate themselves in the addressee position 'you' creates in the text-world at the same time. As such, it makes apparent all three ethical positions involved in the discourse at once: the actual audience being addressed in their real-world situation; the idealised authorial audience around whom the address is imagined and constructed by the poet; and the poetic audience's viewing position on the text-world. As we have seen Phelan point out, individual members of the actual audience will have differing experiences of the tensions this creates in their 'dialogue', as he puts it, with the different invitations the poem offers.

The construction of a first-person poetic persona in the text-world is another typical feature of lyric poetry. Later on in his account of the deixis of poetic literary texts, Green (1992) argues that lyric poetry is a 'particular kind of universe of discourse' (Green 1992: 126). He puts forward the following as the defining stylistic features of the lyric, which we can consider as a more detailed linguistic extension of Phelan's (1996) exegesis, discussed above:

1. It mobilises a monologic 'I' figure.
2. There will often be a dramatisation of situation.
3. Because of the absence of extralinguistic elements, actual situation and emotional situation will be compounded [. . .].
4. Referring expressions will be introduced on the basis of assumed knowledge on the part of the reader.
5. Spatial and temporal deixis will be used to orientate the reader to an assumed context.
6. The poem will assume an addressee and a decoder.

(Green 1992: 125–6)

In further explanation of the third point in this list, Green uses these lines from William Wordsworth's poem, 'Nutting', as a typical example of the merging of 'an actual situation and emotional situation':

[. . .] Then up I rose,
And dragged to earth both branch and bough, with crash
And merciless ravage; and the shady nook
Of hazels, and the green and mossy bower,
Deformed and sullied, patiently gave up
Their quiet being: and unless I now
Confound my present feelings with the past,
Even then, when from the bower I turned away,
Exulting, rich beyond the wealth of kings
I felt a sense of pain when I beheld
The silent trees and the intruding sky.

In this poem, which Green argues is highly typical of the Romantic lyric more broadly, he points out that the 'experiencing mode' and the 'observing mode' of discourse are combined: a situation is dramatised in the text, while Wordsworth's sensibility in that dramatised situation is simultaneously represented. 'Crates', by contrast, operates in a slightly different way. Although the first-person pronoun in the poem nominates an implied-author enactor as present in the text-world, the poem's emphasis falls more heavily on the observing mode; instead of the implied author's sensibility forming its central focus in simultaneity with an unfolding scene, it is the addressee's emotional situation – the 'you' of the poem – that is most prominently represented in the language of the text. This does not mean that 'Crates' is not a lyric poem. We have already seen that it 'mobilises a monologic "I" figure', in Green's terms, and that it not only assumes but makes linguistically explicit an addressee and decoder in its use of the second-person pronoun and the imperative verb 'Observe'. As the remainder of this chapter will demonstrate, the poem also constructs its text-world through the referring expressions and spatial and temporal deixis it contains, all of which function using existing discourse-world knowledge on the part of the actual audience and all of which orient the reader to an assumed context.

It is the doubly deictic nature of the second-person pronoun in 'Crates' which makes the conceptual effect of the poem so markedly different from that of Wordsworth's and many other lyrical texts. Instead of depicting the situation and emotional state of the 'I' enactor, and thus confining its referring expressions to the ontological boundaries of the text-world, the poem blurs the distinction between the real-world situation of the actual audience and the imagined world of the poem. The second-person address appears to straddle these two realms, an effect which is further emphasised through the meta-textual theme of the poem. 'Crates' describes the process of reading itself and the conceptual activity of imagining which results from this, which is depicted, for example, in 'your mind supplies one', 'Likely you are thinking', and so on. However, it foregrounds the writing process too, with 'when I speak of crates' referring both anaphorically to the title of the poem and exophorically to the poet's act of writing (speaking) it and the rest of the text in her side of the split discourse-world. It is this consistent theme of literary writing and reading which leads the 'I' enactor to take the form of a counterpart of the real author of the poem, rather than some other, more vaguely anchored fictional voice in the text. The use of the present tense in 'I speak' is crucial here as well, since this acts first of all to heighten the immediacy the text-world, aligning its temporal parameters with those of the moment of its reading in the discourse-world. Both the double deixis in 'Crates' and its playful, self-aware, meta-textuality can be seen to be typical of postmodern literature, as Herman explains:

> Double deixis marks illocutionary overload, as it were, and instead of fostering strategic discriminations between specious and actual addressees, double deictic *you* is part of a (postmodern) discourse strategy that constructs addressee and audience, participant and nonparticipant, as deeply and irremediably interlinked.
>
> (Herman 2002: 363)

Herman is talking here of tendencies in postmodern narrative prose fiction. However, my own previous research has found similar muddying and manipulation of the ontological boundary between discourse-world and text-world to be commonplace in contemporary poetry (see Gavins 2015, 2016) and in contemporary absurdist poetry, in particular (see Gavins, 2013: 135–60). McHale (1987: 34) describes this boundary as the ontological 'epidermis' of the text and I have argued elsewhere (Gavins 2013: 144–5) that texts that manipulate it through the use of doubly deictic 'you' foreground their own fictionality as a consequence. Such texts not only include the actual audience in the scope of their second-person address, but they also simultaneously project a fictional entity into the text-world through the same linguistic item. This encourages a powerful empathetic connection between the reader in the discourse-world and the imagined content of the poem: the actual audience is not only able to observe the unfolding text-world scene but is pushed to experience it as though it were a first-hand real-world phenomenon.

The construction of the 'I' enactor in 'Crates' bears further examination alongside the second-person pronoun and its doubly deictic effects, since it too acts to destabilise the boundaries between the discourse-world and text-world for the reader of the poem in a number of ways. First of all, the first-person addresser of 'you' in 'Crates' initially appears commanding and authoritative as the result of the use of an imperative verb to open the poem. It is possible, too, to identify the same commanding tone in the final line of the text: 'Now, let us speak of love'. These verbs not only create the voice of the implied author in the text-world, but they also ensure that this voice is an assured and prominent one. There is an added sense of urgency to the instructions the implied-author enactor issues too, which arises from the inclusion of the temporal adverbial 'Now' in the closing line, as well as earlier in the poem in the second line with 'straight away'. It is worth noting, in fact, the number of verbs which appear in the poem in the present tense, present continuous tense or as present participles: 'supplies', 'you are thinking', 'exists' and 'speaking'. Each of these acts to emphasise the immediacy of the text-world and of the address being made from the first-person implied-author enactor to the second-person addressee.

However, the features of the poem which give the text-world its contiguous feel are balanced out by other linguistic choices that seem to present a more generalised and universal picture. For example, many of the world-building nouns 'Crates' contains are presented in a non-specific and/or indefinite form. The 'crates' themselves mentioned in both the title and the opening line are plural, non-specific and appear without a pre-modifying determiner. Similarly, 'a shallow slatted box' occurs in indefinite form, with a definite archetype stencilled on the side, but of plural and non-specific 'apples'. Above this is the indefinite 'a cartouche slot', and later 'a drowned frog' appears in indefinite form again at the bottom of a plastic tub. These types of reference are highly dependent on the discourse-world knowledge real readers bring with them to the poem. Instead of describing a specific text-world object in imaginary detail, they require the actual audience to access previous experiences of similar objects in their real world and to deploy this existing knowledge in their conceptualisation of the text. In 'Crates', non-specific, plural and indefinite references form a significant amount of the spatial world-building which is used 'to orient the reader to an assumed context', as Green (1992:

126) puts it. The assumption is, specifically, that the actual audience shares with the poet the background knowledge that is needed to mentally represent these items, that they have previous experience of cartouche slots, apples, boxes, and so on. It is at these points that the co-presence of the authorial audience is signalled most strongly by the text – the ideal audience for whom the poem is rhetorically constructed, which possesses the knowledge the poet assumes it to have, and which the actual audience must strive to emulate if a text-world for 'Crates' is to be built at all.

There are, of course, plenty of occurrences of definite reference in the poem too but, on closer inspection, many of these instances have a broad scope that is similar to that of the indefinite world-building in the poem. For example, note that 'the fruiterer's crate' in the second stanza refers not to a specific fruiterer and a specific crate, nominated as a definite entity and a definite object in this world. Rather, the noun phrase, although pre-modified with a definite article, refers to a typical person of a well-known occupation and a typical object associated with that role in the discourse-world. Once again, then, the mental representation of this part of the poem is highly dependent on a knowledge base to which the poet is assuming the reader has shared and equal access. A little further on in the same stanza, 'the archetype of apples' repeats the same kind of gesture to cultural norms and shared real-world experience. Note, too, that an alternative choice could have been made at this point: 'your archetype of apples' or even 'an archetype of apples' would have made this particular world-builder either much more personal to the reader, or so unspecific as to fit any conceptualisation of apples formulated by anyone and in any circumstance. The use of the definite article here, though, keeps this a generalised reference, but one which is still contained within cultural and experiential parameters shared between poet and reader: this is 'the typical fruiterer's crate jointly known to both you and me', not 'the fruiterer's crate you alone imagine', or 'any fruiterer's crate anyone could possibly imagine'.

The only other specific and definite references in this stanza operate as anaphoric reference back to the fruiterer's crate, providing further detail about items already established in that world. The first of these, 'the side', focuses in on a particular area of the crate, while the second, 'the grocer's hand', has the same zooming-in effect, this time on one of the fruiterer's body parts. Other stanzas follow a very similar pattern. In the third stanza, for example, 'the sturdy plastic tub / of the eco-minded council' introduces these two world-building elements in much the same way as 'the fruiterer's crate': as familiar and typical components in a shared cultural environment, knowledge of which must be accessed in order to conceptualise them. The mention here of 'the gate' where this tub waits, while not anaphoric reference exactly, is nevertheless an extension or a detail added to an already established scene, also indicated by its position in a subordinate clause. Even 'in this case', while deictically proximal and specific, is still a reference back to the scenario of the tub by the gate, which has already been sketched out. The third stanza contains more of the same type of reference and is presented in a similar way. Here, 'the solid, beer-smooth wood' and 'the publican' who carries it to 'the yard' are all reliant on the reader recognising these as commonplace discourse-world entities, objects and locations. In the final line of this stanza, 'the morning after' is a particularly discourse-world dependent term, as an idiomatic expression that cannot be understood without the real-world cultural knowledge of its reference to alcoholic over-indulgence. Interestingly, this phrase also entails a connected idiomatic expression, 'the night before', which, although not made linguistically manifest in the poem, is still inferred simply through the use of the typically collocating clause 'the morning after'.

The text-world of 'Crates', then, is inextricably linked to the discourse-world of its production and reception. Furthermore, it plays with this dependency through the foregrounding of that real-world situation in its consistent theme of reading and writing, and through the heavy reliance its world-building elements have on discourse-world knowledge shared between the poet and the reader. Although each of the middle three stanzas in the poem presents a different way of conceptualising a crate, and although each of these three different imaginary versions of a crate is descriptively distinct, they are also all presented as equally possible and equally unrealised. This is because, in Text World Theory terms, they are not actually positioned in a text-world at all. The text-world framework recognises that, once a discourse is progressing and the participants have begun to construct a mental representation of it in their minds from a combination of world-building information in the text and their own background knowledge, new mental representations can be created at any time. These new worlds can occur whenever the language of a text specifies a shift in the spatial or temporal parameters of the text-world. For example, a change in tense may signal that a new time-zone is being described, or a new location may be represented through the use of altered spatial locatives or other deictic items. The separate worlds created by these features are known as *world-switches* (Gavins 2007: 48) and an extended text, such as a novel, may contain many thousands of them. World-switches exist on the same ontological plane as the text-world from which they originate: they are simply movements in time and space away from their matrix world, and sometimes back again. Some of these temporal and spatial switches may be fleeting, while others may become extended in themselves and have the potential to become as detailed and immersive as any other type of text-world. Other kinds of worlds may also be constructed through discourse that involve a more complex shift in perception to a space that is positioned at a conceptual distance from the text-world level of the discourse. In Text World Theory, these worlds are known as *modal-worlds* (Gavins 2007: 91–125) and they occur whenever ontological or epistemic distance is expressed in language. This can happen through the use of conditional constructions, any instance of hypotheticality, or through the use of modalised expressions reflecting the speaker's or writer's attitude to a particular proposition.

Modality in English is most often divided into three main categories (see Simpson 1993 for an accessible overview). The first of these, boulomaic modality, cncompasses all expressions of desires, hopes and wishes through such syntactic items as modal lexical verbs (e.g. 'I *wish* I could go to the party tonight') and modal adverbs (e.g. '*Regrettably*, I can't make it to the party'). Secondly, deontic modality is used to express degrees of obligation and per-mission and includes deontic modal auxiliaries (e.g. 'You *must* come to the party') and participial and adjectival constructions (e.g. 'She *was forbidden* to go to the party by her parents'), as well as lexical verbs (e.g. 'I won't *allow* you to go to'). Finally, the epistemic modal system enables the articulation of all forms of knowledge, belief and opinion through similar syntactic means to the other two categories of modality (e.g. 'I *believe* she already left for the party', '*Supposedly*, she's not going', 'He's *unlikely* to turn up too'). Epistemic modality also contains a subsystem of expressions of knowledge and belief, known as perception modality, where a speaker's epistemic commitment is expressed through reference to one of the senses, most often sight (e.g. '*It's clear* they're not at the party'). In all of these cases, the modalised items in the sentence have the effect of constructing a conceptual space which is separate from its originating world. Crucially, the content of these modal-worlds, the situations they describe, are often unrealised at the time of their creation and have to be conceptualised by the hearer or reader as existing at some level of remoteness from their creator's reality.

We have already seen how the temporal and spatial boundaries of the initial text-world created by 'Crates' are set by the present tense of the verb 'Observe', which also indirectly nominates an addresser and an addressee as fictionalised enactors present in that world. However, this text-world does not develop much further before another world branches off from within its parameters. The imperative mood of the verb 'Observe' has the same effect as other forms of deontic modalisation and produces a distant and unre-alised possibility, a *deontic modal-world* (Gavins 2007: 99), which extends from the more stable and ontologically proximal text-world. As Portner explains, 'imperatives contribute to a To-Do list, in particular the To-Do list of the addressee' (2007: 352), and importantly this is a 'To-Do list' that has not yet been done or even acceded to by the reader of the text. The things to be observed, then, are sketched out in a modal-world which does not yet exist and may never do. Furthermore, the opening line of 'Crates' contains another linguistic marker of a shift in worlds. No sooner is a deontic modal-world constructed by the opening imperative verb in the poem, than a world-switch is caused by the temporal adverb in '*when* I speak'. In this clause of the first line, 'when' refers to a time-zone in which the speaking of crates is taking place, and this is a time-zone which is separate from that in which the instruction to 'Observe' is being uttered. Interestingly, the precise temporal

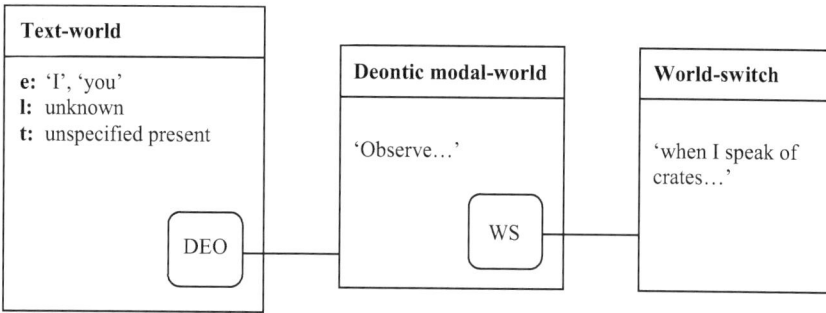

**Figure 1.1** The world structure of the opening line of 'Crates'

point picked out by this adverb is also ambiguous, since 'when' could refer to either a specific and singular instance or to all instances – past, present and future – in which the 'I' of the poem is or could be speaking of crates.

Figure 1.1 illustrates the world structure of the first stanza of 'Crates' using standard Text World Theory conventions (see Gavins 2007 for a full introduction). Diagrams such as this one are common in text-world analyses of discourse, as they enable often complicated configurations of text-worlds, world-switches and modal-worlds to be visualised more easily. To the far left of Figure 1.1 is the initial text-world of 'Crates', which contains the enactors (e) of the implied author 'I' and the fictionalised enactor of the real reader addressed by 'you' and the imperative verb 'Observe'. The location (l) of these text-world entities is never fully sketched out and, although the present tense of the verbs aligns the text-world with the discourse-world, the precise temporal parameters (t) of this world are not otherwise linguistically specified. Emerging from that first, under-defined text-world, then, is the deontic modal-world in which the action of observing can be conceptualised (marked 'DEO' in Figure 1.1). The figure makes clear that this exists at a distance from the world in which the imperative verb is issued. Embedded within this already remote and unrealised world is the further temporal world-switch (marked 'WS') created by 'when', which signals a shift in time to a point where the speaking of crates is taking place.

The poem goes on to make a further three shifts in worlds over the next three stanzas, as each different imaginary crate is described in turn in the text. At the beginning of the second stanza, the epistemic modal adverb 'likely' creates a corresponding *epistemic modal-world* (Gavins 2007: 110), in which a fruiterer's crate is conceptualised. This is only a possibility, however, a likelihood not a definite. The world containing the fruiterer's crate is only as possible as the sturdy plastic tub that replaces it in the third stanza, which is introduced through more epistemic modality in, 'Your crate *may be*'. Again, this modality creates a remote epistemic modal-world which is imagined, supposed and not necessarily realised. The fourth stanza is modal-world forming in the same way. The first line, 'or then again', although it does not contain a modalised linguistic item, is a hypothetical situation and signals a repeat of the same process of imagined possibility depicted in the preceding two stanzas. Each of these worlds exists at an ontological remove from the text-world of the poem in which the 'I' implied-author enactor is issuing the instruction to 'Observe' and, as each new hypothesised world replaces the last, the instability of the entire conceptual structure of the poem becomes more and more apparent. Rather than privileging any single possible conceptualisation of a crate, the text playfully explores the process of poetic cognition itself. The poem shifts continually between equally remote modalworlds, each one constructed by some form of epistemic modalisation and then fleshed out with world-building description.

Through this technique, 'Crates' enacts one of the most elemental ways in which human beings understand their physical existence and their conceptual selves. In cognitive linguistics, it is argued that our cognition is fundamentally shaped by a set of primary underlying *image schemas* (Johnson, 1987), mental patterns which arise from repeated physical interactions with and in the real world and which provide structured understanding of those experiences. There are various different types of image schemas, including Force, Path, Verticality and, crucially for our understanding of 'Crates', Containment. Our conceptualisation of the phenomenon of Containment is made up of a collection of fundamental notions, which we develop from birth through our embodied experience in our physical environment. These include notions of objects having tangible boundaries, of the inside and outside of those boundaries, and of the relatively fixed position of objects within a container. In 'Crates' this basic building block of human cognition becomes the vehicle for an extended metaphor that runs throughout the text, and through which the mind of the addressee of the poem is structured as a container to be filled with imaginary detail by the addressing 'I' of the text. This metaphor is made textually visible in the first two lines: 'when I speak of crates / your mind supplies one straight away' (Chapter 6 explores the cognition of metaphors such as this in more detail).

The fact that such image-schematic understanding of embodied experience has been shown to be a universal component of the human mind once again shifts 'Crates' beyond the limited scope of address that initially appears to be delineated through its second-person pronouns, its opening imperative verb, and the specific definite reference it contains. Once again, we can see here the tension the poems creates between the personal and specific, and the broad and generalised. It is the same tension which is also exploited in the poem's ontological transgressions between the discourse-world and the text-world and which are enabled by the double deixis in the poem, as well as by its overall dependence on shared discourse-world knowledge. All of these features of poetic style extend the representative and referential radius of 'Crates' to encompass not just this poem, this poet and this reader, but all poems, their poets and the multitudinous and diverse mental representations created in the minds of their audiences.

## The dynamics of poetic reading

It is clear, then, that 'Crates' leads its readers through something of a conceptual game. It is also clear that the position the poem affords the poetic audience is a complex and shifting one. Phelan (2007) discusses the effects such ethical positioning can have on readers in their interactions with narrative texts. He looks in particular at texts with unreliable narrators which, he argues, can show their unreliability through behaviours such as under-reporting or misreporting of facts and events, misinterpreting and misevaluating events and other characters, and so on. In some cases of unreliability, though, Phelan suggests that an 'estranging' effect can occur, where the distance between the narrator and the authorial audience is increased. In other cases, a 'bonding' takes place, reducing that distance. He explains:

> in estranging unreliability, the authorial audience recognizes that adopting the narrator's perspective would mean moving far away from the implied author's, and in that sense, the adoption would be a net loss for the author–audience relationship [. . .] In bonding unreliability, the discrepancies between the narrator's reports, interpretations, or evaluations and the inferences of the authorial audience have the paradoxical result of reducing the interpretive, affective, or ethical distance between the narrator and the authorial audience. In other words, although the authorial audience recognizes the narrator's unreliability, that unreliability includes some communication that the implied author – and thus the authorial audience – endorses.
>
> (Phelan 2007: 225)

'Crates' bears all the hallmarks of an unreliable text, and one which foregrounds its own fictionality through its meta-textual theme, its creation of a series of unrealised modal-worlds and its doubly deictic reference. The game which is being played by the poem, however, is one in which the authorial audience is willing to take part, in spite of being made aware of its essential artifice throughout the text. And if the actual audience is to construct any kind of mental representation of the text, then it is also a game in which they must strive to participate. Although the remoteness and instability of the worlds established over the course of 'Crates' is not only apparent but often foregrounded, the poem nevertheless sustains a bonding effect throughout. The effects of this bonding poetic unreliability are nowhere more keenly felt than in the closing stanza of the poem. Here, after moving through three modal-worlds depicting distant but possible manifestations of crates, the poem switches back to the text-world containing the 'I' enactor of the implied author and the addressee in an unspecified location and at an unspecified time. By this point, 'Crates' has shifted from its opening first-person pronoun, through numerous uses of the second person, which I have already shown extend doubly-deictically into both the text-world and the discourse-world. In these final lines of the text, a new pronoun, 'us', appears for the first time. This first-person plural might reasonably be assumed and expected to act as an inclusive form of textual address. However, in 'Crates' its use has a markedly different function and effect.

The final stanza of the poem opens with two statements – 'Your crate exists as soon as it is thought. / Its shape is shown in speaking of it' – both of which sustain the double deixis created elsewhere in the text and allow for a reading of both 'your' and 'its' as referring to objects and entities in either the text-world or the discourse-world. The final line of the poem, however, performs a sudden elimination of one of those interpretative possibilities. As I have pointed out already, the 'Now' of this line foregrounds the immediacy of the text-world here and aligns its temporal parameters with those of the actual audience in the discourse-world, further blurring the boundaries between the text-world and the real world. However, in 'let us speak of love' a distinct ontological shift occurs. Where elsewhere in the poem various verb phrases, such as 'I speak', 'your mind supplies' and 'you are thinking', describe activities that could equally plausibly be taking place in either discourse-world or text-world, it is not possible to conceptualise 'Now, let us speak' as operating in the same cross-world manner. While it is logically possible for the 'I' of the poem to speak in the text-world, and also for a fictional enactor to speak back, it is not possible for the reader in the discourse-world to participate in this conversation. It becomes immediately apparent in this line, then, that the 'us' here is not doubly deictic at all but can refer only to text-world entities. The address of 'Crates' becomes suddenly exclusive, a shift which is emphasised further by the switch in topic from the description of such mundane everyday objects as 'crates', to the profound and transcendent qualities of the abstract concept of 'love'. Having been encouraged both to observe and to self-implicate in all the worlds of the text throughout its preceding stanzas, the actual audience is now afforded the position of observer only, and, what is more, it is an observing position on a private exchange between lovers. Not only is the real reader excluded from the poem's pronominal address, they are put in the uncomfortable situation of an eavesdropper, as the curtains are abruptly snapped shut on an unfolding intimate scene.

## The cognition of contemporary poetic style

The experience of reading the shifting worlds of 'Crates' may be especially dynamic and one which plays obviously with themes of writing, reading and cognition. I have already admitted to choosing it as a text to open this book because of its synergy with the text-world approach to discourse analysis and its linguistic performance of many of the key concepts I wish to explore over the course of the coming chapters. However, the rest of this book will seek to demonstrate that Text World Theory, used in conjunction with complementary cognitivist and other theories, is not just well suited to the examination of this poetic text, but is ideally and uniquely situated to advance our understanding of the cognition of all poetic discourse.

There are a number of key reasons for this. Firstly, both by its nature and as a result of its evolution, the text-world approach is eclectic and interdisciplinary. It has its roots in cognitive linguistics, but it borrows elements of its structure and many of its most important concepts from a variety of other disciplines, including stylistics, sociolinguistics, pragmatics, cognitive psychology, philosophy, neuroscience and literary criticism. Text World Theory therefore has a nucleus of flexibility and an openness to new ideas built in. Since this book seeks to bring fresh perspectives to bear on the cognition of poetic style from outside literary-linguistics and to formulate a new understanding of how poetry is conceptualised in the mind, Text World Theory provides the ideal vehicle through which such a liberal and heterogeneous account might be achieved. Secondly, the analytical architecture of Text World Theory allows poetic discourse to be considered in a rigorous and systematic way and in all its communicative and cognitive complexity. The theory enables the examination of all aspects of discourse under a single, unified framework – from the environment surrounding the production and reception of language in the discourse-world; to the mental representations that language creates in the minds of readers and listeners; to the psychological and emotional responses that are their end result. Text World Theory thus provides the comprehensive and properly connected approach needed in order to understand fully how context, text and cognition interact with and interdepend on one another.

The ability Text World Theory has to develop and change in harmony with current thinking on cognition and language is another of its key assets. This ability has been amply demonstrated in the array of applications of the framework which have been made to an ever-widening multitude of different discourse types over the last twenty years or so (see Gavins and Lahey 2016 for an indicative contemporary selection). As well as presenting an original and multidisciplinary perspective on poetic discourse, this book also aims to continue the expansion and improvement of Text World Theory itself. It will do so through the ongoing engagement with other schools of thought, other methods of analysis, other prospects, approaches and beliefs, which have come to characterise contemporary text-world scholarship. I will not only be suggesting new ways of looking at and understanding poetry over the coming pages, but I will put Text World Theory into an innovative dialogue with contemporary ideas from beyond its immediate scope too, extending and augmenting its theoretical and explanatory capacity as a result.

As I explained at the beginning of the book, each of the remaining chapters examines a key aspect of poetic discourse. The constraints of time and space mean I have had to be selective about which poetic techniques I explore, so I have chosen those dimensions of poetic language that I believe firstly to be the most important in our cognition of poetic texts; secondly to be the most interesting to readers wishing to understand contemporary poetic style; and thirdly to be among the most prevalent stylistic features to be found across twenty-first-century poetry. These are to some extent subjective judgements, but subjectivity necessarily underscores all literary-linguistic enquiry and I am not afraid to admit my singular perspective, nor to offer it up for criticism from an alternative point of view. In this respect, then, *Poetry in the Mind* is specifically *my* view of the style of contemporary poetry. However, I present that view through practical, retrievable and replicable applications of contemporary cognitive and linguistic theories with the aim of making my methods and findings, at their heart, as open and accessible as possible.

I have further restricted the focus of my discussion of poetic style to the style that is used by a selection of British poets writing and publishing today: all of the poets whose work I analyse in this book were born in the UK and all of them have had at least one major poetry collection published since 2000. There are two main reasons for making this choice. The first and most important one is that I want this book on contemporary poetry to be truly contemporary. As I have already stated at the start of this chapter, and as I reiterate at various later points in the volume, I am committed to a view of literary discourse as a form of language that is fundamentally situated in nature. By this I mean that it is essential for any account of the cognition of any discourse to be properly sensitive to the context in which that discourse is produced and received and to pursue its exploration from this fundamental basis. One of the easiest ways for me to ensure that my own approach is attuned to the situatedness of poetic language is to write about poetry with which I share a cultural, temporal and geographical situation. I have therefore chosen poets whose work can be seen to be represent British writing at the beginning of the twenty-first century and whose poetry reflects the environment in which both they and I are, broadly speaking, co-located.

This brings me onto my second reason for restricting my focus to contemporary British poetry. I am centrally interested not just in how human beings conceptualise poetic discourse, but in the power that discourse possesses to move the people who read it psychologically and emotionally. One of my core aims in this book is to understand not just how poetry creates text-worlds in readers' minds, but the effects those text-worlds have beyond simple comprehension and in the real world. I have therefore chosen poets who are not just writing in the current moment, but who have been critically acclaimed for their work in the recent past. This means that the selection of texts I have chosen for analysis not only provides a snapshot of contemporary British poetry, but specifically of contemporary British poetry that has been culturally recognised and valued in some way. All of the poems I examine, and all of their authors, have received a major national or international poetry prize of one form or another within the last twenty years. Of course, the capacity to move readers is not limited to award-winning poetry alone and I recognise that poetry prizes are only one form of literary value, and a potentially problematic one at that. Nevertheless, exploring poetry which has been formally celebrated in some way still reveals something interesting to us about what kinds of literary expression are admired in twenty-first-century Britain and about the wider culture in which that admiration is located.

Each of the chapters which follows, then, takes the form of a poetic case study. I examine one poet per chapter, one poem in its entirety, and I work my analysis around one main stylistic feature or theme. I am deeply grateful to all of the poets who have generously agreed to let me reproduce their work in full in this volume. This has enabled me to explore their discourse in greater depth, with greater coherence, and in a much more naturalistic way than would ever have been possible had I been forced to piece together my argument through analyses of shorter extracts of text. The first case study to follow this chapter looks at the poem 'Evening', by Simon Armitage (2006). It begins my examination of the cognition of poetry by concentrating in particular on how the spatial and temporal parameters of poetic text-worlds are constructed through language. Specifically, this case study focuses on how time and space interact with and are dependent on one another in poetry, as well as in language in general.

The chapter starts with a more detailed look at how text-worlds are built around a central experiencing perspective, or deictic centre. It analyses how readers of Armitage's text are encouraged to project themselves into the imagined point of view of a young boy as he moves through a rural landscape. This point of view does not remain stable in the text but is one which varies and changes as the poem progresses. In order to understand the cognitive effects of this, I pick up the discussion of second-person pronouns begun here in Chapter 1. This is a key stylistic feature in Armitage's text too, yet one which functions in a markedly different way from the second person in Jo Bell's 'Crates'. The second-person pronouns in 'Evening' mainly describe the viewpoint of the young boy in the poem, but this enactor's perspective conflates at various points with that of the poetic persona who narrates the text. This creates a layering of worlds and of voices, which is repeated elsewhere in the poem as other enactors appear or are suggested to be present. My analysis also reveals how the spatial and temporal foundations of the text-worlds of 'Evening' do not remain stable either but are dynamic and shifting throughout the poem in much the same way as the poem's changing viewpoint. I look in detail at the slippages in time which the poem enacts and their relationships with the spatial dimensions of the text. To do this, I make use of research in cognitive psychology on the conceptualisation of time. I also draw on contemporary accounts of visual perception to understand how the temporal structure of 'Evening' becomes peculiarly distorted. Overall, the chapter is an exploration of how the text-worlds we construct from poetic discourse can sometimes be coherent and immersive but can equally possibly be volatile and disorienting.

In Chapter 3, my central concern is how the style of one text can be cognised by readers in their interaction with another, and how this cognition might affect their responses when it occurs in poetry. I examine the phenomenon of intertextuality here in an analysis of the poem '1801', by Sinéad Morrissey (2013). Intertextuality is another aspect of literary style which is so ubiquitous in the twenty-first century that neglecting to address it in this book would be a glaring omission; indeed, it has been described by Jameson (1991) as a defining feature not just of postmodern literature, but of the whole of postmodern culture. Morrissey's poem presents a perfect case study for this chapter, since it is based on Dorothy Wordsworth's journals and replicates a good deal of her diary-writing style in poetic form. My examination of Morrissey's use of intertextuality in '1801' begins by looking at how the poet herself often frames the text's connections with Wordsworth's writing in her live and recorded readings of the poem. I go on to discuss the discourse-world of poetry readings in general and how, along with Morrissey's paratextual preamble, the specialist nature of the audiences at such events might impact on their reception of intertextual references. I then employ one of the most recent cognitive-stylistic accounts of intertextuality, developed by Mason (2015, 2019), in a detailed analysis of the language of '1801'. This is the first extension of Mason's work on narrative textual interrelationships to be undertaken in the context of poetic discourse.

Alongside this, I make use of corpus-linguistic methods to reveal the aspects of Wordsworth's style which might be most conspicuous to readers of a contemporary reworking of her writing. These are the features of her language which are most unusual when compared with more modern written and spoken discourse. I then return to Morrissey's text to see whether any of these characteristics can be found in the text of '1801' and whether she captures the most singular aspects of Wordsworth's writing. In order to ensure that my account of the intertextual features of the poem is properly context-sensitive and engages with responses beyond my own experience of the text, I report on an empirical experiment I did with a group of twenty-nine students of English, aged between fifteen and sixteen years old, at a large comprehensive school in Sheffield in 2018. The reactions to '1801' provided by this group of much younger readers offer a useful counterpoint to my own, admittedly more specialist, reading. They also reveal a remarkable sensitivity among the students, both to the textual interrelations Morrissey makes with

Wordsworth's journals, and to the other techniques she employs to create a complex layering of poetic voices in her poem.

Chapter 4 examines John Burnside's poem, 'Hearsay' (2011). I approach this text with a particular interest in how it represents different forms of absence and near-presence through language and in its use of negation as a key means of achieving this. I show that Burnside's use of linguistic negation is not isolated, but that it becomes an extended theme running throughout the poem, made manifest in a number of different stylistic features. The extended and repeated use of negation and other negative tropes is a key characteristic of 'apophatic poetry' (see Gibbons 2007 for an overview), which seeks to address concepts that are present through their absence, or for which no adequate language exists. I discuss this concept at greater length in the chapter and, in my analysis of 'Hearsay', I build upon my previous explorations of the cognitive consequences of apophasis (Gavins 2016), using Text World Theory to understand how Burnside's poem uses this technique to create an accumulative and deeply disconcerting effect on its readers. Alongside the text's overall negativity, Burnside employs a number of other linguistic features which destabilise the textworlds of 'Hearsay'. The narrator of the poem, for example, appears to be highly unreliable and in a way that creates an estranging rather than bonding effect, to use Phelan's (2007) terms. The poetic voice seems to withhold information from the reader, and figures and objects in the poem appear and disappear or take on other ghostly characteristics. Burnside also creates a disturbing sub-text to his poem, through which the abduction and murder of a child are suggested to have taken place. 'Hearsay', however, is a poem full of absences and none of the implied gruesome undercurrents to the text is ever confirmed or fully fleshed out. Instead, the instinctive tendency for the human mind to fill in gaps in information and perception is consistently manipulated across the discourse, and the reader is encouraged to complete the incomplete picture the poem sketches out with their own inferences. On the whole, 'Hearsay' functions as a Gestalt – a partial representation which the mind seeks to finalise. What is more, the dark undertones of the poem lead that finalisation to take on a similarly sinister nature, as the absences in Burnside's text become filled with death, decay and fear.

In the fifth chapter of this book, I extend my consideration of the cognition of poetic style beyond the written word and turn to look at the live performance of poetry and its conceptual effects. My focus here is specifically on spoken word performances which play with the boundaries between poetry and music, particularly rap music. My aim is to understand the emotional impact and popularity of performed texts such as these in the twenty-first century. To this end, I analyse a performance of a poem called 'End Times' by Kate Tempest (2009) and I begin by exploring the discourse-world environment in which this text is delivered. Because Tempest is equally successful and well known as a rapper and a poet, I argue that it is likely that her audiences approach her performances in both of these contexts with a mixture of expectations drawn from both their music and poetry knowledge schemas. I examine how the staging of Tempest's performance, along with aspects of her delivery of her poem, encourage her listeners to access their understanding of both of these sides of her creative persona in their processing of the discourse. I look at how Tempest breaks down many of the barriers between poet and audience – physical, social and psychological – which often exist in more traditional poetry reading situations.

Tempest's intonation, her gestures and her other bodily movements all play a key role in the reception of her text too. My analysis of her poem considers how she uses these discourse-world cues to express her own emotions, to communicate authenticity and to heighten the emotional reactions of her audience. Tempest's expressions of embodied experience do not exist in isolation, however, and my consistent argument throughout Chapter 5 is that her physical behaviour and the style of her text are entirely co-dependent on one another. To use Gräbner's (2011) term, Tempest constructs a 'polysensual layering' throughout her performance of her poem, in which context and text are inextricably and multi-sensorily linked.

My analysis of 'End Times' continues to examine how stylistic features of the text – including the use of biblical register, personal pronouns and meta-textuality – all interact with elements of Tempest's performance to create a highly affecting language event. I show how Tempest uses various techniques from rap music to intensify this and how she employs rhyme and rhythm, in particular, to create a rap-like 'flow' in her performance. I show, too, how Tempest establishes a clear role for herself in both the discourse-world and the text-world as a prophet and a 'teller'. However, in much the same way as she dismantles the formality normally associated with traditional poetry readings, Tempest uses both her text and its context to reduce the social, psychological and epistemological distance that might normally exist between a religious preacher and a congregation. Tempest instead creates a discourse which is highly inclusive and communal, rather than private and exclusive, all the time grounding her prophetic text in her embodied experience in the discourse-world environment she inhabits with her listeners. I conclude the chapter by suggesting that the shared perception and emotion which Tempest constructs between herself and her audience constitutes an example of 'the extended mind' (see Clark 2008 for an overview). This view of cognition sees the environment and the human mind as integral components in our conceptualisation of the world and our cognitive processes as distributed beyond the brain and the individual.

In the final chapter of the book, I examine metaphor. Although this is the aspect of language and cognition which has received more academic attention than any other over recent years, I have deliberately left my own consideration of it as a feature of poetic discourse until last. This is because, in many respects, a coherent account of the cognition of poetic metaphor is dependent on many of the topics and features that form the focus of the chapters that precede it. The poem I have chosen as a concluding case study is 'Song of a Stone' (2005a), by Alice Oswald. Oswald is most often viewed by literary critics through the lens of eco-criticism and with good reason: she writes frequently about nature and landscape and, as I show in the chapter, has herself talked in detail about the natural elements and concerns that underpin much of her work.

From one perspective, Oswald creates strong stylistic coherence running throughout her poem and she uses sound patterning as one of her key cohesive devices. On the other hand, however, there are an equal number of features of 'Song of a Stone' which disrupt this cohesion and create a more fluid and shifting feel to the text. My analysis looks, for example, at how Oswald's use of metre fluctuates and how her use of imperfect sound patterning undermines any sense of stability in the poem. I also show how both the physical and temporal boundaries of the text-worlds of 'Song of a Stone' are difficult to pin down and conceptualise. I make use of Cognitive Grammar (c.f. Langacker 1987, 1991) to examine how Oswald makes repeated use of non-finite verb forms, which give the text a timeless quality, and intransitive verbs, which reduce the dynamism of the poem. Alongside this, inanimate objects and features of the natural landscape are given great potency and potential in 'Song of a Stone', as they are strongly profiled and personified as agents in the text.

My main focus, however, is on the chains of metaphor worlds Oswald constructs across the poem. I explore how the conceptual structure of these worlds presents a significant challenge to existing notions of how metaphor operates in cognitive terms. I show how all of the metaphor worlds Oswald creates are completely co-dependent on one another and how meaning is constantly deferred in the text through this interrelationship. I draw, in particular, on the work of Bate (2000) and Snyder (1980) in order to frame 'Song of a Stone' as a poetic version of a 'climax community', a natural system that achieves optimum diversity and a steady state through the process of ecological succession. I argue that Oswald's text can be seen as a kind of literary ecosystem, with all of its conceptual components existing in a delicate balance of synergetic interconnectedness.

Although I approach each of the poems I analyse in this book in turn and as complete case studies in their own right, I also seek to find stylistic and cognitive connections between them as my discussion progresses. In Chapter 7, I reflect on some of the patterns of creative expression which serendipitously emerge across all the chapters in this volume as by-products of my main analyses. I also consider some of the directions in which the cognitivist examination of poetic discourse might travel in the future. While the account of the cognition of contemporary poetic style I present over the coming pages is by no means comprehensive, it aims at its core to engage in an open and interdisciplinary dialogue with other perspectives on poetry and on the mind. It aims too to embark on that dialogue from a position which is fundamentally context-sensitive and centrally focused on the situated and embodied experience of reading poetry.

# 2 Time and Space

## Conceptualising poetic time and space

In Chapter 1, I outlined the cognitivist principles which underpin my approach to the investigation of discourse and which will form the foundations of each of the analyses of poetic texts presented in this book. I talked in that opening chapter about the importance of understanding poetic language as a dynamic and embodied communicative experience, just like any other form of discourse, and also of understanding its crucial situation in a context of production and reception. I gave an overview of the cognitive-linguistic framework of Text World Theory (Gavins 2007; Werth 1999), through which the majority of my previous research has been structured and enabled, and which also provides the central analytical lens through which some of the key aspects of the style of contemporary British poetry will be examined over the coming chapters. One of my main aims in Chapter 1 was to demonstrate that Text World Theory's unified and systematic approach to context, text and cognition makes it uniquely well suited to the analysis of poetry and its conceptual effects. My discussion of the poem 'Crates', by Jo Bell, facilitated an initial examination of the linguistic and conceptual means by which mental representations of literary texts are constructed in readers' minds. That chapter looked at the pragmatic situation which surrounds the creation and reception of poetic discourse, the different participant roles involved in poetic communication, and the different ways in which literary texts, both narrative and poetic, address and position their audiences. As a consequence, my analysis of 'Crates' did not stop with a simple examination of the multiple text-worlds created over the course of the poem; I made a broader argument alongside this for the greater integration of theories of narrative reading with theories of poetic reading, wherever this integration might prove practically workable and beneficial to our understanding of literary experience. Some theories which have developed within the discipline of narratology tend to retain a narrow focus on the structural components of narrative, which makes them difficult to employ in the analysis of other contexts and text types. However, where narrative theories extend to examine the relationships and interactions between authors, readers and reading situations more broadly, there seems to me little sense in not investigating their applicability to a wider range of literary discourses.

In the present chapter, I will be revisiting in more depth the notion of world-building which I introduced in Chapter 1, exploring in greater detail how poetic language creates conceptual spaces. I am particularly interested here in how time is represented linguistically in poetry, in how the temporal parameters of poetic text-worlds are established in readers' minds as a consequence, and in how these parameters may shift and change over the course of a single poem. The coming discussion focuses especially on how the temporal signature of a poem interacts with and is dependent upon its spatial dimensions. Once again, I will be drawing on theories and concepts from other disciplines in order to understand this interrelationship fully. I will look at research in cognitive linguistics and cognitive psychology which throws light on the human conceptualisation of time and space and its expression through language in general. As I outlined in Chapter 1, it is my firm opinion that such an interdisciplinary approach is essential if the complexity of poetic discourse and its experience by readers is to be properly appreciated and explained.

The poem which forms the case study for this chapter is 'Evening', by Simon Armitage, reproduced in full below, with the kind permission of the author:

### Evening

You're twelve. Thirteen at most.
You're leaving the house by the back door.
There's still time. You've promised
not to be long, not to go far.

One day, you'll learn the names of the trees.
You fork left under the ridge,
pick up the bridleway between two streams.
Here is Wool Clough. Here is Royd Edge.

The peak still lit by the sun. But
evening. Evening overtakes you up the slope.
Dusk walks its fingers up the knuckles of your spine.
Turn on your heel. Back home

your child sleeps in her bed, too big for a cot.
Your wife makes and mends under the light.
You're sorry. You thought
it was early. How did it get so late?

This poem provides a particularly suitable vehicle through which to explore the connections between time and space in our conceptualisations of contemporary poetic literature. A great deal of Armitage's work is considered in literary criticism as distinctively situated in the landscape of Northern England, from where the poet originates, and as having a special focus on place (see, for example, Coussens 2008; Cresswell, 2014; Habermann and Keller 2016; Kennedy 1996). Armitage's identity as a contemporary British poet – his situation in a specific temporal and cultural landscape – is also often a focus of critical appraisals of his work. This is perhaps driven by the fact that Armitage's writing navigates multiple generic boundaries between poetry, narrative and drama, as well as encompassing television, film, music and radio. Thain (2007), for example, focuses on the boundaries between physical and cultural spaces in Armitage's texts and argues that the places he explores in his work are often liminal or 'contested spaces', borderlands 'where urban and rural meet [. . .] charged with the potential for disaster' (Thain 2007: 65). Meanwhile, Habermann and Keller (2016) write about Armitage's *Stanza Stones* series of poems, which were carved into rocks across the Pennine watershed in West Yorkshire in 2013. They comment that this poetry

> achieves a perfect balance of flow and arrest, blurring the boundaries between human beings and the natural environment. Fusing materiality and meaning [. . .] the poems thus deny the categorical distinction, or ontological rift, which has for a long time riddled the relationship between the perception and consciousness of an observer and the natural world.
>
> (Habermann and Keller 2016: 4)

In a similar vein, 'Evening' can be seen as a poem which blurs a number of crucial borders and barriers: it constructs text-worlds which seem to muddy the lines between the observer and the observed landscape, as well as between conceptual spaces and perspectives. It is this spatial, temporal and psychological liminality which forms the focus of this chapter's coming discussion, and my aim here is to explore and understand the interconnections and interactions between each of these different dimensions of the poem.

## Deixis and poetic enactors

In Chapter 1, I showed how literary texts, and indeed all texts in general, are structured around a deictic zero-point or *origo*. This zero-point forms the perceiving centre from which the text's spatial, temporal and social relationships are all expressed and according to which our mental representations of language are created. We saw in the opening chapter how these relationships are established primarily through the use of deictic expressions, the meanings of which are crucially dependent on the context of their use. The occurrence of linguistic items such as demonstrative pronouns, verbs of motion, spatial adverbs, tense and aspect all enable readers not only to imagine a literary world in their minds, but a world which is constructed from a particular point of view and from within a particular context of perception and expression. In 'Evening', this point of view is created using a number of features, many of which, at first glance, appear to bear some resemblance to those we have already seen at work in Jo Bell's poem, 'Crates'. Specifically, Armitage's poem, like Bell's, contains a repeated use of the second-person pronoun 'you', which opens the text and remains consistent right through to its final stanza. The second person in 'Crates' was shown in Chapter 1 to refer across the ontological boundary between an imagined text-world and the reality of the discourse-world in a doubly deictic manner (Herman 1994). I pointed out there how the 'you' in Bell's text picks out a fictional entity in the world of the poem, while at the same time reaching into the real world to make a direct address to the actual reader situated there too. The first thing to note about 'Evening', then, is that the same pronoun here has a rather different texture, function and effect.

In Herman's (1994, 2002) terms, the second person which opens Armitage's poem in the first line, 'You're twelve. Thirteen at most', appears to refer to an entity who exists only within the frame of the fiction. Even if the reader of the poem were in fact to be twelve years old at the point of reading, the 'Thirteen at most' here signals that this is still not a statement of a discourse-world fact, but an estimation only. The textual 'you' in the opening of 'Evening' is thus being used to construct a possible version of a fictional person from the speaker's point of view. That speaker is the poetic persona in the text, who is a fictional enactor and another imagined being, who belongs at the text-world level of the discourse. The poetic persona is also the logical addresser responsible for the horizontal 'you' address. Unlike in 'Crates', the presence of this addresser-enactor in the text-world is not made explicit through the use of a first-person 'I' sitting alongside the second-person 'you', but is instead inferred by the reader in the discourse-world. Furthermore, the time and place from which the address is made is never described or fully developed in the poem. This is also the case in 'Crates' and is common in other kinds of literary and non-literary discourses too.

In Text World Theory terms, this phenomenon creates an 'empty text-world' (see Lahey 2005, and also Gavins 2007: 133–4 for a summary), a conceptual space which is most often text-initial and most often contains the enactor to whom the speaking voice of a fictional text belongs. However, the setting and contents of empty text-worlds remain under-defined, by the text at least. Most often, no further information is given about where the speaking voice is located, what surrounds them, or even what their motives and intentions might be. Empty text-worlds can potentially offer readers a space in which they might imagine all of those things and where they might project their own assumptions and beliefs about their imaginary interlocutor, based to a great extent on their discourse-world knowledge. Quite often, however, readers can forget that the empty text-world containing the speaking voice of a text even exists, as the text-worlds depicting the main action or information in the discourse become of central concern instead. The addresser-enactor in 'Evening', then, seems to be speaking to another text-world enactor from an unknown place and time. No further world-building elements for this situation, other than the presence of the voice itself, are provided over the course of the poem. Once again, we can see that the emphasis in Armitage's poem is, as it was in Bell's text, on the physical and emotional situation of the 'you' addressee, rather than on that of the poetic voice making the address. That emotional and physical situation is described in a text-world which is separate from the world containing its describer. From its very first line, 'Evening' creates a world which is in some way remote from the poetic persona responsible for its construction.

As with many other literary texts, the extent to which the reader of the poem will align the textual enactor of the poetic persona with their notion of the actual author in the discourse-world will vary from person to person and will depend on a range of textual and contextual factors, including their knowledge of that author, any of the author's previous works they may have encountered, as well as personal reading tendencies and preferences. As Semino (1995) explains:

> The perceived distance between poetic *personae* and authors is determined by a combination of textual evidence and extra-textual information. In the case of William Wordsworth's 'I Wandered Lonely as a Cloud', for example, a strong identification between poet and *persona* is encouraged by factors such as the evidence of Dorothy Wordsworth's diaries, the reader's generic expectations about Romantic poetry and the fact that the *persona* is referred to as a *poet* within the text itself. In Browning's dramatic monologues, on the other hand, a clear discontinuity is established between the author and various figures who act as first person speakers, which include the monk of 'Soliloquy of the Spanish Cloister' and the sixteenth century Italian duke of 'My Last Duchess'.
>
> (Semino 1995: 147)

Semino goes on to point out that perceived discontinuity between the author of a poem and its poetic persona will be even greater if that speaking voice takes the form of an entity which does not possess the power of speech in the real world, such as an animal, inanimate object or dead person. In 'Evening', the poetic persona appears to be a living human and, although the text does not include any first-person pronouns, a close alignment between the discourse-world poet and the text-world poetic persona can be seen to be encouraged by a number of stylistic features that suggest that the poem is depicting a personal memory of some kind. This memory seems to be the poetic persona's recollection of a younger enactor of himself. It is framed through the second-person address in the text, as the 'you' is positioned as the central enactor in the recollected and recounted worlds that unfold over the course of the poem.

Herman identifies this type of self-address as one of several types of textual 'you' at play in Edna O'Brien's novel, *A Pagan Place*, too, commenting that, in such cases, '*you* is a pro-nominal stand-in for an *I* who figures as the protagonist of the narrative that she addresses to herself and that we eavesdropping readers (quasi-voyeuristically) overhear' (Herman 1994: 384). Although no reporting clause, such as 'I remember', 'In my memory' or 'To my recollection', is included anywhere in Armitage's poem, there is a vagueness to its first lines that indicates something recalled, perhaps incompletely. For example, along with the lack of precision already noted in the sentence 'Thirteen at most', the title of the poem itself, 'Evening', is non-specific and indefinite and could refer to any given evening, or even all evenings, past, present and future. Further references to time and duration elsewhere in the first stanza are similarly under-specific, for example in the unmodified 'time' in the third line, as well as 'long' in the fourth line. This vagueness continues into the first line of the second stanza with the non-specific adverbial 'One day'.

This temporal marker creates a world-switch (see Gavins 2007: 48, and Chapter 1 of this volume), shifting the deictic parameters of the text-world to a future time-zone in which the addressee has learned the names of the trees. Interestingly, this switch is both indistinct and fleeting: the future text-world it takes us to lasts for just one line in the poem, and it remains ambiguous whether the learning of names has already taken place at the point where the addresser-enactor is narrating his recollection of his younger self, or whether this is yet to happen to him. Other world-building elements in the first few lines of 'Evening' echo this lack of clarity. In terms of the spatial deixis provided elsewhere in the first stanza, although 'the house' and 'the back door' are both specific and definite references, they also describe near-universal architectural features of any imaginable home. They are therefore highly dependent on discourse-world knowledge and so add little in the way of specific detail to our mental representation of a particular place being portrayed in these lines. What is more, the promise 'not to go far' in the final line of the first stanza reflects the same under-specific quality which characterises the temporal deixis in the opening lines of the text. The fact that the people to whom this promise is made are not named either, even though they must logically exist in the text-world, only adds to the overall sense the beginning of the poem creates of a memory of a past self, somewhat hazily and imprecisely brought to mind.

The world-building elements contained in the first few lines of 'Evening', then, support an interpretation of the poem as a self-addressed recollection. I would go further, however, and argue that this interpretation is strengthened by the fact that the poem's deictic under-specificity is reflective of stereotypi-cal adolescent language. The common tendency in teenagers to reply to their parents' questions about their activities and whereabouts with evasive, mini-malistic responses (e.g. 'Where are you going this evening?', 'Out.') have long featured as common examples of linguistic under-specificity in linguistics and pragmatics textbooks. In my own reading of the text, then (and perhaps as a result of my current discourse-world position as the parent of two teenaged daughters!), the first stanza of Armitage's poem creates a world which not only has spatial and temporal parameters which are ill-defined, but which also captures some of the elusory character of the adolescent enactor at its heart. It is also important to note that, since it represents a memory being recalled by the poetic voice, the world constructed in the first stanza of 'Evening' is not a text-world, but an epistemic modal-world. It is a version of reality filtered through a textual enactor's perspective and contains the potentially unreliable contents of the speaker's mind, which are positioned at a further ontological distance from the reader in the discourse-world (see Gavins 2007: 109–25, and Chapter 1 of this volume).

There is also a layering of multiple voices occurring in this world, with 'There's still time. You've promised / not to be long, not to go far' containing clear indications of the presence of speech. Specifically, the reporting verb in 'You've promised' brings indirect speech into the poem first of all, through which the twelve-/thirteen-year-old's words are summarised in language consistent with the poetic persona's point of view (see Leech and Short 2007 for a comprehensive account of the representation of speech and thought in fictional texts). Although the text does not shift out of the filtering perspec-tive of the addresser-enactor here, there is a movement in time, as the tense of the poem takes us from the present time-zone constructed through the simple present in 'You're twelve' and 'There's still time', as well as in the present continuous in 'You're leaving the house', to the past perfect 'You've promised'. This shift positions the world in which the boy speaks at an earlier point in time from the world representing his departure from the house, even though both of these events are described from the poetic persona's recalling perspective.

'There's still time' also carries qualities of the speech of the enactor of the boy, who could plausibly be either thinking this sentence or saying it aloud. This is an example of Free Indirect Discourse, where the speech or thoughts of a fictional enactor seem to merge to some extent with those of the narrat-ing or poetic voice in a text. Although the reader doesn't 'hear' the speech or see the thought directly, they do get a flavour of *how* it was said or thought. There are no inverted commas or other punctuation markers to show that someone is speaking or thinking in Free Indirect Discourse, and the tense and deixis remain in keeping with those of the surrounding text. However, some indication of voice quality may be given or, as in this example, the register of the person speaking or thinking might become reflected in the language of the text. 'There's still time' would seem to fit this description, being minimalistic in its detail and in keeping with the somewhat oblique adolescent voice that might also be identified in the indirect speech in the final line of the stanza, 'not to be long, not to go far'. In this case, the Free Indirect Discourse could be read either as the voice of the boy or as the speech of his parents, asking or telling him not to be long or to go far and, presumably, receiving some sort of agreement in response. In world-building terms, Free Indirect Discourse of all kinds creates another epistemic modal-world since it introduces at least one additional enactor-perspective into the text. Thus, in this line of 'Evening', the point of view of the boy, and possibly those of his parents too, become embedded within – or rather layered on top of – the initial world of the memory. By the end of the first stanza, at least three different voices can be identified as present in the poem: the voice of the poetic persona narrating the text; the voice of his earlier self; and the voice or voices of his parents.

As the poem continues into the second stanza, some of the indeterminacy and intangibility of the worlds constructed so far is counteracted by an increase in the specificity and definiteness of the text's spatial deixis. Once the boy leaves his house, more objects are introduced into the developing world of the poem through specific and definite references to 'the names', 'the trees', 'the ridge' and 'the bridleway'. Each of these helps to establish a picture of an unfolding landscape which is highly familiar to the boy as he travels through it, with even the lack of definiteness to 'two streams' suggesting that these bodies of water may simply be too small or insignificant to be locally named. In the final line of the second stanza, 'Here is Wool Clough. Here is Royd Edge', the spatial and temporal deixis is particularly proximal and definite. The present tense, the repeated demonstrative 'Here', and the use of proper names, all tether the perspective in the poem to a set of geographical features, known and closely manifest to the boy. The two enactors of the boy and the poetic voice become more tightly aligned here too, with the boy focalising the world-building elements of the poem, which are, of course, also familiar items to the later version of himself narrating the text. The immediacy of 'Here is', in particular, suggests that the landscape being described is seen both by the boy and by the poetic persona in the same place and at the same time. Another layering happens in this moment, then, as the empty text-world containing the narrating adult seems to merge with the text-world containing the younger enactor of himself. They appear for the duration of these lines to be co-located and experiencing the same environment simultaneously.

In my own reading of the poem, the mentions of 'Wool Clough' and 'Royd Edge' caused further connections to be made between the poetic voice and the actual author of the poem as well, as Semino (1995) suggests can be commonplace in poetic discourse. These are real places in West Yorkshire, known to me in my discourse-world both as features of a landscape close to where I grew up and close to what I know to be the poet's own home town. They therefore act as the sort of extra-textual information which Semino identifies as encouraging a close association between my conceptualisation of the poetic persona and the real-world poet. However, even my ability to use my discourse-world knowledge to represent these places clearly in my mind did not lead to me read the textual 'you' in 'Evening' as reaching beyond the text-world enactors. Although I recognise the proper names in 'Evening' as having counterparts in my real world, the proximal demonstrative 'Here' and present tense 'is' continue to keep the deixis of the text locked firmly within the fictional frame of the poem; I may know these places, but I am not 'Here' and now in relation to them as I read.

In the third stanza of the poem, the boy continues his movement through the landscape depicted in the worlds of the poem and the spatial deixis of the text remains highly specific and proximal to his perceiving zero-point. 'The peak' and 'the sun' are again both introduced through specific definite reference, while 'still' in the same line suggests a familiarity with these features over a prolonged period of time, perhaps even beyond the span of a single day. This particular temporal marker also has an additional meaning, of course, which is equally plausible as an interpretation in this instance: 'Still' can either be read as an adverbial description giving duration to the verb 'lit', or as an adjectival description giving post-modifying stasis to the noun phrase 'The peak'. The second of these possible readings, if pursued, leads the peak to take on a marked permanency and solidity as a geographical feature, providing a stationary world-building backdrop to the function-advancing verbs through which the boy's contrasting dynamic physical movement has been described up to this point: 'leaving', 'go', 'fork', 'pick up'. As the third stanza of the poem continues, however, two metaphors occur which shift the movement in the text from the physical and literal walking of the boy through his immediate environment to the figurative progress of time. These metaphors – 'Evening overtakes you up the slope. / Dusk walks its fingers up the knuckles of your spine' – not only personify the abstract concepts of 'evening' and 'dusk' but do so through metaphors that have a distinctly physical and proximal texture.

The conceptual processing of metaphor in language is a major area of research in cognitive linguistics and there are a range of different but broadly complementary approaches to its analysis. Across these approaches, there is common agreement that metaphorical language of all kinds operates through the interaction of discrete conceptual spaces in the minds of discourse participants to form a new, integrated understanding. Human beings deploy their existing knowledge of the world dynamically as they produce and encounter language in order to comprehend the often novel and creative ways in which metaphors frame our day-to-day experiences. Text World Theory borrows its approach to metaphor from the related cognitive framework of Conceptual Integration Theory (see Fauconnier and Turner 2002 for a full account). According to this theory, our cognition of metaphors depends on 'input spaces', which Fauconnier and Turner describe as 'small conceptual packets constructed as we think and talk, for purposes of local understanding and action' (2002: 40). These conceptual packets are activated by the language of the text and are created from our previous experiences, knowledge and physical interactions in and with our real-world environments. For example, the word 'evening' in Armitage's text will cue a packet of information in the minds of the participants which will vary in its detail and nature from person to person. It will, however, be structured around existing knowledge of this time of day and will contain the data needed to understand this concept in the unfolding discourse. Similarly, the conceptualisation of the word 'overtakes' depends upon the deployment of existing knowledge that this verb is a form of physical movement, that can be performed by humans, other animals, as well as vehicles, and so on.

In metaphorical language, however, individual conceptual spaces are not simply activated by the text but are brought together in the minds of the participants to interact in a unique way. This is achieved initially through a process of 'cross-space mapping', by which readers and listeners are able to identify connections between the input spaces cued by a particular metaphor (Fauconnier and Turner 2002: 41). In 'Evening overtakes you up the slope', for instance, correspondences can be found between the input spaces needed to conceptualise 'evening', 'overtakes', and the enactor depicted by the 'you' pronoun in the text. Specifically, the capacity for movement, which is part of our basic understanding of human beings and essential to our comprehension of the verb 'overtakes' too, can also be identified as a component of the 'evening' input space: the movement of the sun across the sky, for example; the way that the increasing darkness that results from this moves across a landscape; or the movement that can be perceived in evening shadows. According to Conceptual Integration Theory, these points of commonality feed into a conceptual space known as a 'generic space', which contains those elements of understanding that can be found in all the separate input spaces. These elements are projected into a final 'blended space', which crucially has what Fauconnier and Turner call an 'emergent structure' (2002: 42–4) all of its own. Through a process of 'elaboration' (Fauconnier and Turner 2002: 44), relations are made available in the blend that do not exist in the different input spaces; additional structure may be added, and the newly constructed integrated space is developed dynamically and imaginatively. In the case of the metaphor 'Evening overtakes you up the slope', the input spaces containing the reader's understanding of evening as a time of day, as well as the human actions of walking and overtaking, are combined to form a world that not only includes all of these factors, but in which time becomes a fellow walker, accompanying the boy in his movement up the slope, mirroring his movements across the countryside, but at a faster pace. Meanwhile, in the second metaphor in this stanza, the proximity to the boy of the now personified figure of time becomes even more tangible and tactile, as dusk is first described as the touch of a hand ('Dusk walks its

fingers'), before the boy's spine becomes similarly hand-like and his verte-
brae transform into 'knuckles'. This line constructs a more complex concep-
tual network, which involves input spaces not only relating to these various
body parts, but with the preceding blended space of 'Evening overtakes you
up the slope' also acting as an input into this newer, more elaborate blended
world.

The third stanza of 'Evening' ends with a further blurring of linguistic
and conceptual boundaries, as the line beginning 'Turn on your heel' invites
another pair of equally plausible interpretations. This sentence could be read
as containing an imperative verb, 'Turn', issuing a directive to the boy from
the poetic persona. In this case, 'Turn on your heel' would be modal-world-
forming in Text World Theory terms, since it contains deontic modality
expressing a degree of obligation or permission. As we have already seen in
Chapter 1, this sort of modality requires a separate conceptual space to be
fully understood, since the actions it describes may or may not be carried out
in the text-world of the poem and are instead imagined as a comparatively
remote possibility. A second reading of this sentence is that it is an abbrevi-
ated description of an action already undertaken by the boy. Since the tense
of the poem remains in the present here, it is easy to interpret 'Turn on your
heel' as simply having had the second-person 'you' ellipted from its beginning
(so, with 'You turn on your heel' as the possible fuller version). Similarly, the
second half of the line, 'Back home', can be read one of in two ways: either
as having had the imperative verb 'go' elipted at its start ('Go back home'),
creating another deontic modal-world; or as a description of a shift in place,
from the slope to the boy's home.

The running-on of this sentence into the poem's final stanza, however,
does little to resolve this ambiguity, as it introduces yet further indetermi-
nacy to the poem as it continues, 'your child sleeps in her bed, too big for
her cot'. Although the syntactic structure of this line would seem to confirm
that 'Back home' is a spatial adverbial causing a world-switch to a new loca-
tion, its semantic content causes a new, logical discontinuity in the poem.
Up until this point, of course, we have followed the progress of a young boy
across a landscape in a narration that has not only remained chronologically
consistent throughout, but that has also included a number of stylistic fea-
tures that act to reflect the boy's age. However, in this final stanza, it appears
that the same boy now has a wife and a child of around a couple of years
old, without any indication of such a significant shift in time having taken
place being given anywhere else in the language of the text. This slippage is
not only subtle, but disorienting, perhaps all the more so because the social
deixis of the poem remains proximal here in spite of the movement in time.
The final stanza of 'Evening' remains in the second-person, with 'your wife',
'your child' and 'her bed' marking out yet more world-building elements
that are not just familiar but familial to the addressee. They also further
confirm the horizontal nature of the textual 'you' in the poem, with the social

relationships between these enactors being clearly defined as exclusive and personal, adding to the disconcerting impossibility of these lines.


## Time in the mind

The discussion of 'Evening' so far has noted a number of places in the poem where time is constructed through temporally deictic expressions and features, such as the use of tense and aspect, temporal adverbials, and so on. However, the human understanding of time more broadly and our expression of that understanding through language is more complex than this simple identification of linguistic items might at first suggest. As Evans (2004) explains, time has structure for human beings and serves to distinguish our present from our past, as well as allowing us to anticipate our future:

> Time emerges from perceptual mechanisms which correlate with the dynamic nature of consciousness, undulating from focal state to focal state. It provides a means of segmenting and so analysing experience, processing raw perceptual data into events and states, into change and stasis, experiences which can be encoded in language. It has perceptual, conceptual and external sensory dimensions.
>
> (Evans 2004: 251)

In spite of its structured nature, however, Evans points out that time is nevertheless not something we are able to point to or observe in our everyday world, but instead forms an abstract part of our internal, cognitive architecture. This presents a considerable challenge to how we conceptualise time as a phenomenon and then go on to articulate that conceptualisation in discourse. To do this, we need to make use of a much wider range of linguistic resources than deictic expressions alone, with one of those most frequently drawn upon being the use of metaphors of space (see also Bender and Beller 2014; and Núñez and Cooperrider 2013 for an overview). As Evans goes on to explain:

> Paradoxically, time provides structure to our experience, and yet we relentlessly ascribe structure to it, formulating concepts and models of time as if it had none of its own. We think of it as a quantity, as valuable, as a person, as an indefinitely extending matrix, as duration, as a point, and so on [. . .] Time often appears to employ language (and hence conceptual structure) that derives from domains which are not purely temporal in nature, such as space. One solution to the metaphysical difficulties associated with time has been to view time as inhering in the physical world. On this 'physicalist' view, the reason language employs spatial 'metaphors' for time, e.g. *a long time*, is that

time is (in some sense) part of the fabric of existence and hence enters
into everything.

(Evans 2004: 251–2)

These are interesting observations when considered in terms of Armitage's
poem, which appears to work throughout to undermine any sense of the
segmentation and coherent structuring of time. Rather than organising and
expressing the experience of time in manageable and cognisable chunks,
'Evening' blurs and confuses the lines between our conceptualisations of dif-
ferent temporal zones and moments. This blurring effect is enacted not just
through the temporally deictic elements of the poem, but through the close
interaction of those elements with the spatial dimensions of the text too. To
understand how this works, it is useful to return at this point to some of the
key components which give the worlds created in 'Evening' their temporal
parameters, before examining how these are intertwined with the description
of space in the poem.

As I have already noted a few times in the discussion so far, one of the
defining aspects of 'Evening' is its retention of a consistent present tense
throughout the majority of the text, which not only serves to keep the chro-
nology of the narration steady up until the final stanza, but also adds to the
poem's highly proximal feel. 'Evening' is greatly focused on the inner experi-
ence of the enactor of the boy in the poem as he travels across a landscape,
and all of its world-building elements are presented as being close and famil-
iar to his deictic zero-point. As I have also pointed out earlier in this chapter,
in some places this proximity makes the exclusive and horizontal nature of
the second-person address in the poem clear too. Even if the reader has the
discourse-world knowledge to recognise some of the names and places in the
text as having counterparts in reality, we are still not in the here and now of
their perception by the boy, but only party to a potentially unreliable memory
of that experience, shared with us by the poetic persona. Furthermore, else-
where in the text, there are numerous references which foreground time as
a theme, as well as an essential aspect of the poem's world-construction.
The title of the poem is, of course, the most obvious of these and the most
prominent. However, the word 'evening' is also repeated twice more in the
text, along with several other temporal locative nouns, such as 'dusk' and
'one day'. Age is mentioned too, in 'twelve. Thirteen at most', and the poem
includes various temporal adjectives, such as 'long', 'early', 'late' and even
'still'. Finally, we have seen how the foregrounding of the concept of time
is further achieved through its personification in two metaphors across the
third stanza of the poem. Time and temporality, then, are not just part of the
basic deictic make-up of the worlds of 'Evening' but form an extended motif
that is conspicuous from the start of the poem to its close.

An abundance of research exists in cognitive psychology and cognitive lin-
guistics to suggest that not only are the understanding of temporal progress

and the understanding of physical space closely linked in the human cognitive system, but to suggest too that differing cultural, linguistic and physical contexts can affect how time is both perceived and described. For example, a range of studies have shown how various contextual factors, including social stress (Hedger et al. 2017), the perception of other people's emotions (Droit-Volet and Meck 2007), and even colour (Shi and Huang 2017) can affect how accurately people perceive time when asked for estimates of duration. What is more, as Bylund and Athanasopoulos (2017) point out, different languages use different kinds of spatial metaphors to articulate the understanding of time. Where English and Swedish speakers tend to talk about time in terms of spatial length (e.g. 'a long time' or 'a short break' in English), Spanish and Greek speakers tend to use spatial metaphors of volume for the same function (e.g. *un pequeño descanso*, 'a small break', or *mucho tiempo*, 'lots of time', in Spanish). In their study, Bylund and Athanasopoulos asked groups of Spanish and Swedish bilinguals to estimate the time taken firstly for a line to progress across a screen, and secondly for a container to become full. They found that when their participants were prompted by the Spanish word for duration (*duración*), they used volume-based metaphors to express their estimates, whereas when prompted by the Swedish word for duration (*tid*) they expressed their estimates using length-based metaphors. Interestingly, in the poem 'Evening', metaphors of both length and volume are used at different points in the text to conceptualise time, and these are often surrounded by other, non-metaphorical references to these concepts too. At the beginning of the poem, for instance, the temporal metaphor 'not to be long' is accompanied by numerous other descriptions of length and of lines in the landscape that remain solely spatial in nature: 'not to go far' comes straight afterwards, for example, as well as the descriptions of 'the ridge', 'the bridleway' and 'streams', all in the first two stanzas. Even 'leaving the house by the back door' represents a linear movement through a space, while both 'Wool Clough' ('clough' being an Old English word meaning a steep ravine or valley) and 'Royd Edge' also suggest linear forms in the countryside.

A shift happens in the middle of the poem, however, where the description of stasis in the third stanza seems to overwhelm those of spatial and temporal progress and movement that have occurred in the poem up until this point. In the line 'The peak still lit by the sun', we have already seen that 'still' can be read in two ways – either as a description of duration or as a one of the stillness of the peak. In either case, it suggests a degree of steadiness and motionlessness which has not been present in the text before this point. It is at this moment, too, where the boy himself slows enough, possibly to the point of standstill, for time to overtake him, walking past him, again in linear fashion, up the slope. In contrast with the preceding three stanzas of the text, the final lines of 'Evening' are full of such descriptions of stasis in both time and space. The child mentioned in the first line of the last stanza, for example, is asleep. Furthermore, 'Your wife', while she 'makes and mends', presumably does so seated in order to fit 'under the light' and therefore with minimal movement. Crucially, there is no report of any physical motion of the 'you' enactor in the poem at all in the final four lines of the poem; he suddenly becomes a stationary observer of a scene, rather than an active traveller through or across a spatial background. It is interesting to note in these closing lines, too, that a further example of the human synthesis of temporal conceptualisation with spatial understanding is captured in the clause 'too big for a cot', which represents the child's age through a description of her size. Indeed, on the whole, the final stanza of 'Evening' sees a shift from the lines, lengths and trajectories which have permeated the poem until now to a greater density of descriptions of volume and stillness. Following the brightness and fullness of the image of the peak lit by the sun in the third stanza, we then encounter the 'big' child, as well as a second image of fullness, with the light in the final stanza forming a sizeable bright canopy under which the woman sits. Each of these volumetric, rather than lineal, descriptions have a defamiliarising and disconcerting effect, since they are drawn from domains of physical understanding that are not normally deployed to represent the progress of time in British English. I would even go so far as to argue that the choice of phrase 'makes and mends' in the final stanza causes another seizure or even reversal of time by its conspicuously archaic nature. This colloquialism originates in the nineteenth-century British navy, where a 'make and mend day' was regularly set aside for repairing uniforms. After a peak of usage in the mid-twentieth-century war years, where reusing resources became of paramount importance and a matter of national duty in the UK, this expression has since fallen out of widespread use and is therefore also foregrounded in 'Evening' as an antiquated form.

A range of individual linguistic features, then, combine to create a palpable shift in the texture of time by the end of Armitage's poem, from something moving and progressing, most often through space, to something arrested and still. At the poem's close there also emerges a greater focus on the mental activity of the enactor of the boy, now a grown man, rather than on his physical activities. Along with the absence of verbs of motion that I have already noted, in the penultimate line two modal-worlds occur, both reflecting the focalising enactor's inner mental state. The first is a boulomaic modal-world, created by the adjectival phrase expressing regret, 'You're sorry'. The second follows immediately afterwards in the form of an epistemic modal-world, created by 'You thought'. The focus here, then, has turned from the external environment of peaks, edges, ridges, bridleways, and so on, to the internal landscape of the 'you' addressee's thoughts and feelings. This gradual change in focus has also, of course, accompanied the changing age of the boy to the point of adulthood. As readers, we have moved with him in his physical journey from home and across the countryside, but also in his psychological journey: we have witnessed the youthful action of the boy transform into a more reflective mode in maturity. It is worth noting, too, that the mental state of the adult addressee-enactor at the close of 'Evening' is one of bewilderment, and that his emotions here are represented as regret and confusion. This confusion reintroduces some of the vagueness of the first two stanzas of the poem, but it is a vagueness which has taken on a slightly different flavour by this point. Where the boy-enactor's indefiniteness seemed deliberate and evasive through the poem's representation of his adolescent speech, the adult-enactor's vagueness appears to be the result of genuine disorientation and bemusement. Something of the exuberance of youth has been lost here and replaced with a lack of certainty and confidence, specifically in the ability to estimate and predict the passage of time.

## Chronostasis in poetic space

What makes 'Evening' such a fascinating poem from a Text World Theory perspective is the challenge it presents to the fundamentally text-driven basis of the framework. According to the text-world approach to discourse, our conceptualisations of language are always tied to the words written on a page or spoken by participants. From the vast store of knowledge we have at our disposal in a discourse situation, the text itself will determine which areas of our cognitive architecture we need to access in order to make sense of the language we encounter (see Chapter 1 of this book and Gavins 2007: 33). The worlds we create in our minds of literary and non-literary discourses alike may be fleshed out and made immersive from our individual experiences, but they are built primarily and essentially from the words we read or hear as we communicate. In Armitage's text, there is no doubt that a significant movement in time takes place between the beginning and the end of the poem. Part of this movement is gradual and made explicit by the descriptions of the boy making his way through a changing landscape in the first three stanzas of the text. There is a second dimension to the progress of in time in the poem, however, which is much more dramatic and, perhaps paradoxically, much more difficult to locate linguistically. At some point in 'Evening', a temporal shift of a decade or more occurs and the boy who leaves home at the start of the poem becomes a fully grown man with a wife and child, located in a different 'home' from the one in which he began his journey. It is almost impossible, however, to identify a single textual feature which clearly indicates where in the poem this shift takes place. Although the noun phrase 'your child' in the first line of the fourth stanza clearly reveals that we are located in a different time-zone at this point in the text, when rereading the whole poem it is possible to interpret any one of the lines from 'You fork left under the ridge' as representing the viewpoint of an adult addressee-enactor. A temporal illusion occurs somewhere in the poem, a slippage in the normal progress of time that is unmarked linguistically and therefore goes unnoticed until the final stanza.

At first, time appears to pass normally in 'Evening' as the reader tracks the enactor of the adolescent boy through space, through time, and across the lines of the poem. The sequential nature of the poetic reading experience is important here, as we have already seen Phelan (1996) argue in Chapter 1 of this book, particularly in a text that seems to be playing with our perception of temporal and spatial change. The movement of the reader's eyes across the lines of the poem can be seen to mirror the movement described in the text itself; as the boy moves through space and through time, so too do we, both in the physical reality of our discourse-world reading situation and imaginatively in our text-world-building activities. Our conceptualisation of imagined movement is enabled by the deictic cues which construct the worlds of the text, which dictate their spatial and temporal parameters, and which signal any changes to those co-ordinates. Dussol (2011) points out that a density of temporal deixis, and of deictic terms in general, is not uncommon in nature-related poetry. Armitage's text can surely be considered to fall into this category, focusing as it does, in part at least, on the human interaction with rural space. Dussol argues that such poems are normally centrally concerned with capturing the 'here and now' of a particular physical encounter with nature and with creating a sense of a close connection with the poetic persona's reality. He presents a discussion of the poem *Scenes of Life at the Capital*, by Philip Whalen, in which one section describes a wasp moving from book to book along a shelf before flying out through a window and into a garden. Dussol shows how the sequential nature of reading poetry can mimic movement in time and space in the real world:

> After enumerating all the books ignored by the wasp, the speaker's gaze becomes one with the insect's, losing itself first in the window glass which, from the wasp's point of view, makes more entertaining reading, then beyond it, returning to the garden. Here deixis consists in listing the authors and titles in the order in which they were visited and neglected by the wasp. The linear order of the poem reproduces the wasp's movement in space so that the reference gap is bridged.
>
> (Dussol 2011: 106–7)

The first three stanzas of Armitage's poem, of course, enact sequential movement in the same way and bridge 'the reference gap', as Dussol puts it, between the reader and the perceiver of an imagined rural landscape in a similar manner too. The adolescent enactor in 'Evening' advances through his environment at the same time and in the same order as the reader advances their 'gaze' through the lines of the text. Armitage's poem deviates from this consecutive ordering and mirroring of experience, however, by enacting a slippage in the normal progress of time and of reading. He creates a hiccup in the temporal development of the poem and in our conceptualisation of it, breaking the fluidity of its movement and causing both disorientation and a sense of the sudden stalling of time.

The effect this creates can be seen as akin to a phenomenon of visual perception known as *saccadic suppression*. As Krekelberg (2010) explains in his succinct overview of this common characteristic of human vision and cognition,

> Even though we are usually unaware of it, we move our eyes about twice every second. These eye movements are highly targeted. For instance, when asked to judge the wealth of people in a picture, our eye movements target their clothes; when asked about their age, we look at their faces. As a consequence of these eye movements, the input to the visual system is much like an amateur video; short, relatively stable snapshots, alternated with rapid, jerky movements.
>
> (Krekelberg 2010: R228)

The 'fast, ballistic eye movements' (Bremner et al. 2009: 12374) we make more often than our hearts beat are known as *saccades* and they involve a large movement of the image of the environment on our retina. The brain, however, transforms this confusing input into stable perceptual experience by suppressing some of the stimulus it receives through our eyes. There are a number of possible ways in which such suppression may occur in order for the rapid movement of the eyes to become unnoticeable, as Krekelberg goes on to discuss:

> The simplest to envision is probably a reduction of the visual response of the relevant neurons. If most neurons respond less, then it is likely that the observer will see less. Another possible mechanism relies on the fact that, once the eye has moved to its new position, a clear image will be on the retina. The neural activity corresponding to this new (and important) image could 'wipe out' the information that entered the visual system during the eye movement.
>
> There are other possibilities: for instance, the eye movement could introduce so much noise in the visual system that it can no longer distinguish among different inputs. Or the eye movement could generate such strong neural activity that it saturates the visual system and new inputs would not lead to changes in the response.
>
> (Krekelberg 2010: R229)

Krekelberg points out that there is currently no academic agreement on which of these mechanisms might be in action in the brain, but that it is possible that a combination of all them may be involved (see also Ibbotson and Cloherty 2009; Watson and Krekelberg 2009). Interestingly, studies have also found that not all visual stimuli are suppressed equally by the brain: stimuli

processed by the subsystem that serves motion and space are strongly sup-
pressed, whereas stimuli processed by the object and colour vision subsystem
are not suppressed at all (see Ross et al. 1996).

One after-effect of saccadic suppression which is particularly interesting in
our consideration of 'Evening' is the phenomenon of *chronostasis*, a distor-
tion in the perception of time which occurs around each saccade in human
vision. Georg and Lappe (2007) explain:

> Although saccadic suppression occurs over a substantial time inter-
> val around the saccade, there is no 'perceptual gap' during saccades.
> The mechanisms underlying this temporal perceptual filling-in are
> unknown. When subjects are asked to perform temporal interval judge-
> ments of stimuli presented at the time of saccades, the time interval fol-
> lowing the termination of the saccade appears longer than subsequent
> intervals of identical length. This illusion is known as 'chronostasis',
> because a clock presented at the saccade target seemingly stops for a
> moment.
>
> (Georg and Lappe 2007: 535)

So, when subjects are asked to shift their focus to the arms on a clock, the
first second seems to them to last longer than subsequent seconds (see also
Knöll et al. 2013). Chronostasis-like or 'stopped clock' states have also been
observed in the perception of other actions, such as key-presses, voice com-
mands and voluntary arm movements. Armitage's poem seems to imitate this
kind of distortion in the perception of time in its final lines. The text shifts
our focus in the closing stanza to a new spatial and temporal environment so
quickly and abruptly that there appears to be a suspension of time as a conse-
quence. The adolescent enactor moves from one space and time to another so
rapidly that his perception of that movement seems to be suppressed and he
loses track of both where and when he is. The reader, of course, follows this
journey too, the movement of our eyes shifting from one line, one moment,
to the next so that we experience the same temporal slippage and the same
eventual disorienting chronostasis as the boy. At the end of 'Evening', we find
both ourselves and the adolescent enactor not just in a changed environment,
but in an environment which has taken on a completely different, suspended
temporal texture.

## Text-worlds as palimpsests

Text World Theory expects all alterations in the deictic parameters of a
text-world to be signalled in language. In Armitage's poem, however, this is
not the case. The key linguistic cues which would normally indicate a switch
between worlds, from one time or place to another, are not present, or at least

not immediately identifiable in the text. As a result, no switch is perceived until we, as readers, are located on the other side of a temporal and/or spatial boundary. A similar effect has been identified by McLoughlin (2019) as being at work in Philip Gross's poem, 'Tuonela' (Gross 2013). McLoughlin shows how Gross deflects attention away from the deictic shifts which take place across the poem, looking, in particular, at the following lines:

> But the swan's imperceptible
> way of having glided, though it seemed a pale-
> etched shape in glass with dark behind it …
> this is what unnerves.
>
> From the train now, rush-hour stasis:
> late October morning, light enough
> for a shuffling of greys, enough dark
> still for lights on: Tuonela

McLoughlin argues that the 'now' in 'From the train now' shows that a shift in time has taken place in the poem, from the point at which the swan was gliding across a lake to the point at which the poetic persona is on the train. However, he points out that, although the 'before state' and the 'after state' are both visible in the text, the movement between those two states remains invisible. McLoughlin goes on to argue:

> We may think of this in terms of the liminal [. . .] in the sense that the states either side of the limen are rendered visible to us, but the liminal processes which are involved in crossing the line between these states is being obscured.
>
> (McLoughlin 2019: 93)

The subtle slippages between worlds and between states in Armitage's poem can be seen to operate in much the same way (see also Thain 2007 on liminality in some of Armitage's other works). Even though 'Evening' contains multiple verbs of motion ('leaving', 'go', 'fork', 'pick up', 'overtakes', 'walks', 'turn'), for example, none of these work to make the movement from the world of the boy's adolescence to that of his adulthood explicit. Indeed, there is no verb at all in the clause 'Back home' which links the third stanza with the fourth, between which it becomes clear that a significant movement in time has taken place. As McLoughlin puts it, 'This feeling of being between worlds, and of being at the crossing point between these worlds, creates a strong sense of liminality. We find ourselves in transition' (2019: 95). Although we are aware of having moved to a new location by the end of Armitage's poem, and although we can see both sides of the limen which divides the boy's youth from his maturity, the means by which we arrived there are concealed from view.

Rather than presenting spatio-temporal shifts which are detectable in language, then, what 'Evening' creates is a layering of transitional text-worlds, one on top of the other, and with no clear distinction drawn between them. Another way of thinking about this is to see the worlds of 'Evening' as a kind of conceptual palimpsest, with the old, remembered world of youth still perceptible, still tangible beneath the newer world of adulthood. What is more, this layering effect happens throughout the text, as multiple moments of linguistic ambiguity blur the lines between one conceptual space and another. Right from the start, the line 'You're twelve. Thirteen at most', for example, presents a dual possibility, with each of these eventualities being equally plausible but never fully resolved one way or the other in the world of the poem. The same palimpsestic balancing of possibilities happens again in the layering of voices which occurs at the end of the first stanza, discussed earlier in this chapter. We have seen how the represented speech here could be read as belonging to any one of the number of enactors the poem creates: the poetic persona, his earlier self, his parents. As the text moves into the second stanza, the temporal adverbial in 'One day, you'll learn the names of the trees' creates further unresolved ambiguity. I have pointed out already that it is never made clear whether the learning of names ever actually takes place or is yet to come, even from the poetic persona's point of view in the empty text-world from which he makes his address to his younger self. We have seen, too, the similar dual interpretations possible in 'The peak still lit by sun', as well as 'Turn on your heel' and 'Back home'.

The whole text of 'Evening' is thus woven through with ambiguity from its start and at various points enables two possible readings of the same linguistic item at once. The last two lines of the poem continue this pattern and the text closes with the same indefiniteness, the same potential for double meaning that has characterised its world-building throughout. At the poem's end, there is a re-emergence of multiple voices in the text and a reoccurrence of Free Indirect Discourse in 'You're sorry. You thought / it was early. How did it get so late?' The first part of these lines, 'You're sorry. You thought / it was early', could be interpreted as a representation of inner thoughts only. However, the question mark which ends the poem in 'How did it get so late?' suggests that these internal thought processes may in fact be externalised in speech as well. The tense remains in the present to begin with too, and the pronoun 'you' keeps the deixis of this part of the text consistent with the rest of the narration, all typical features of this type of speech and thought representation. As with the instance of Free Indirect Discourse in the first stanza of the poem, and in keeping with the ambiguity we have seen across the whole text, it is not clear who is speaking or thinking here. 'You're sorry. You thought / it was early' clearly mixes the voice of the poetic persona with that of the earlier enactor of himself, speaking to his wife as she makes and mends. However, the closing question 'How did it get so late?' leaves further room for uncertainty. This sentence could be read either as continuing the same blend of the voices of the poetic persona and his earlier self, begun in the preceding line, or as a representation of the voice of his wife. Just as in the first example of Free Indirect Discourse in the poem, all three voices become present in this moment, all three equally possible and plausible, all three layered one on top of the other.

There is a further muddying of lines and boundaries to be found at the close of 'Evening', though, enabled mainly through the fundamentally indeterminacy of the pronoun 'it'. This dummy subject, which has no definite referent in idiomatic English, is repeated twice in the last line of the text: 'it was early. How did it get so late?' Its reach is so broad and abstract, in fact, that it opens sufficient space in the poem to include yet another possible voice – that of the real reader of the text. The third interpretative possibility here is that the closing question in 'Evening' is asked by the reader on experiencing the disorienting slippage in time and space that the poem has led them through, a possibility which becomes all the more conceivable if the text is read aloud. Pursuing this line also results in a shift in the referential reach of the second-person pronoun 'you' in this part of the poem. This address has already seen its boundaries pushed in the final stanza, as the boy addressee becomes an adult and the same pronoun is used to refer to both of his temporally separated enactors. The final transcendence executed in 'Evening', though, is one across the ontological boundary between text-world and discourse-world. If we read the repeated 'it' in the final line as potentially reflecting the voice of the reader, as well as those of the poetic persona, his earlier self and his wife, then the second-person pronoun extends beyond its horizontal address here too. The reach of 'you' suddenly becomes vertical and breaks out of the frame of the fiction which has constrained it until this point in a doubly deictic manner. Not only have all three of the fictionalised voices present in the poem at this moment lost track of time, but you, the reader, have too; you are also sorry, you thought it was early. How did it get so late?

# 3 Intertextuality

## Understanding intertextuality in the mind

Intertextuality has played an integral role in literary creativity and reading for centuries. The construction of cohesive connections between texts within texts has a history almost as long as writing itself, and the complex dialogues these connections generate have been traced back as far as the Old Testament and beyond (see, for example, Draisma 1989; Moyise 1995; Sweeney 2005). The prevalence of intertextual references, echoes, pastiches and parodies throughout literary history marks out these stylistic features as essential for inclusion in this book's exploration of the cognitive experience of reading poetry. The lengthy tradition and broad proliferation of intertextuality in literature inevitably mean that there exists a matching abundance of literary criticism on the topic (see Allen 2011 for a useful overview). Indeed, as Allen (2011: 2) notes, like many other popular critical concepts, 'intertextuality' has become a term greatly overused by literary and cultural theorists, leading to a muddying of its meaning over time. However, in her recent investigation of contemporary readers' encounters with intertextuality, Mason (2015, 2019) has shown that this is a phenomenon nevertheless which is widely recognised by readers both inside and outside academia and which forms an important part of our everyday interactions with literary discourse. Readers of all kinds frequently detect or formulate relationships between texts, authors, themes and styles, and integrate these unproblematically into their responses to literary works.

Situating texts within genres, comparing current reading experiences with previous textual encounters, and using literary knowledge to recognise connections between writers and their works are all commonplace readerly activities. This chapter seeks, therefore, to explain the conceptual mechanics of intertextuality as one of the most widespread and ubiquitous features of contemporary poetry. Jameson (1991) argues that intertextuality is not simply common in Western literature produced since the Second World War but is a defining feature of the whole of postmodern culture. He describes intertextuality – which he finds to be prolific in film, advertising, architecture and literature – as involving the interplay of 'multiple surfaces' (Jameson 1991: 12). He points out that during this interplay a single textual element can carry with it the memory of an entire earlier creative tradition. This is a core notion which underscores much existing research on intertextuality (see Genette [1979] 1992, [1981] 1997a, [1987] 1997b and Kristeva 1980, for key accounts): despite their differing points of focus, differing analytical approaches and differing motivations for examining textual interconnections, the majority of academics agree that the meaning of each individual text is, in part at least, dependent on its relationship with other texts.

As I have already explained in Chapter 1, it is not my interest in this book to add to the plentiful field of literary-critical debate on different aspects of poetic discourse. The same applies here in my investigation of intertextuality, a concept which I am not seeking to define in a novel way. I continue to be much more interested in *how* intertextuality operates at a linguistic level in poetry and in the effects it has in the minds of readers. For the purposes of this book, then, I am particularly concerned with examining how the stylistic *form* of one text can make itself *felt* in that of another; how readers are able to identify this as a linguistic phenomenon; and how the different surfaces of language involved in such intertextuality interact with one another. In the discussion which follows, I draw primarily on Mason's (2015, 2019) research on readers' experiences of intertextuality in narrative, but I extend this work for the first time towards an account of the cognition of intertextual connections in poetic discourse. I also explore how research methods and instruments from the field of corpus linguistics may help to enhance further our understanding of poetic intertextuality in the mind. Furthermore, since I am interested in how intertextuality operates as a general discourse feature and in minds beyond my own, I include in this chapter a discussion of some responses made to poetic text by a group of 15–16-year-old students of English from a secondary school in the north of England. Their reactions to and interpretations of intertextual references in poetry shed interesting light on how contemporary audiences identify and conceptualise relationships between texts.

### Poetry reading in the flesh and in the mind

My investigation of the cognitive underpinnings of intertextuality is here once again framed around a single poetic case study. Sinéad Morrissey's poem, '1801', is typical in its linguistic and cognitive architecture as a contemporary intertextual poem and is reproduced in full below, by kind permission of the author.

## 1801

A beautiful cloudless morning. My toothache better.
William at work on The Pedlar. Miss Gell
left a basket of excellent lettuces; I shelled
our scarlet beans. Walked out after dinner for letters—
met a man who had once been a Captain begging for alms.

*

The afternoon airy & warm. No letters. Came home
via the lake, which was near-turquoise
& startled by summer geese.
The soles on this year's boots are getting worn.
Heard a tiny wounded yellow bird, sounding its alarm.

*

William as pale as a basin, exhausted with altering …
I boiled up pears with cloves.
Such visited evenings are sharp with love
I almost said, *dear, look*. Either moonlight on Grasmere
                                   —like herrings!—
or the new moon holding the old moon in its arms.

'1801' is a pastiche of Dorothy Wordsworth's journals, the bulk of which were written in the homes she shared with her brother, William, in Alfoxden in Somerset and Grasmere in the Lake District between 1798 and 1803. The textual interrelationship between the poem and the journals is one which is often explicitly stated by Morrissey at the start of her public readings of her text. This includes that to be found on the open-access website of *The Poetry Archive* (Morrissey 2015), at the beginning of which Morrissey states that, 'This poem, '1801', is inspired by Dorothy Wordsworth's journal.' From a linguistic point of view, poetry readings such as this one, particularly when performed before a live audience, share a good deal of their pragmatic structure with other traditions of oral performance, such as folk music and storytelling, as well as occupying a similarly precarious position in today's increasingly electronic world of entertainment and culture. My own experiences running the Lyric poetry festival at the University of Sheffield from 2011–14 confirmed to me that the audience for the majority of live poetry in twenty-first-century Britain is a relatively small and specialised one. This makes most contemporary poetry readings intimate but also attentive affairs: the Lyric audience, for example, numbered around 500 people for the most popular poets on the programme, but a smaller section of this audience, highly loyal and passionate about poetry, would return again and again to see less well-known authors too. These were sophisticated consumers of poetry in the main, familiar with a wide range of writers and texts, and committed to spending considerable amounts of their leisure time attending readings, often by relatively unknown writers.

The first thing to note about the live reading of a poem by its author in front of an audience is that this reading takes place in a shared discourse-world. Unlike the rest of the poetry looked at so far in this book, the participants in the discourse occupy the same spatio-temporal environment. In these cases, the poet performs a dual role of both writer and speaker, with the audience as their listeners and co-participants in a face-to-face language event, rather than as readers interacting with the text in private. As in all other shared discourse-worlds, all the participants have access to a range of additional information and situational cues upon which they may draw in their construction of a text-world. These may include facial expressions, gestures and intonation, as well as elements of the immediate physical environment, which may be referred to at any moment as the discourse unfolds.

It is common, but by no means mandatory, in the discourse situation of a live poetry reading for the poet to preface the performance of a poem with an explanation of its origins, the process of its composition or a summary of its meaning from the poet's point of view. Again, this practice bears many resemblances to the situating of songs and narratives in a historical context and in a wider cultural tradition that commonly takes place in storytelling and folk music performances. Many poets will draw attention to a particular line or phrase in their poem, foregrounding this for their audience even before the text as a whole has been shared. The information provided to the audience at this point exists outside the poetic text itself, as 'paratext' in Genette's ([1987] 1997b) terms. The most useful explanation of the function of such paratext is succinctly given by Genette in his introductory commentary:

> [The] text is rarely presented in an unadorned state, unreinforced and unaccompanied by a certain number of verbal or other productions, such as an author's name, a title, a preface, illustrations. And although we do not know whether these productions are to be regarded as belonging to the text, in any case they surround it and extend it, precisely in order to *present* it, in the usual sense of this verb but also in the stronger sense: to *make present*, to ensure the text's presence in the world, its 'reception' and consumption.
>
> (Genette [1987] 1997b: 1)

Although Genette is talking in this paragraph specifically about the paratext surrounding printed books, his argument still holds in the case of live poetry readings. Just like a written prologue, a poet's preamble leading up to a reading plays a powerful influencing role in the audience's conceptualisation of a poem. It exists, in Genette's terms again, as 'a privileged place of a pragmatics and a strategy [. . .] at the service of a better reception for the text and a more pertinent reading of it' (Genette [1987] 1997: 2). Genette goes on to explain that by the notion of a 'more pertinent reading' he means that which is constructed from the author's point of view. We can therefore see any introductory discourse around the live reading of a poem as an attempt by the poet to exert some degree of authority and control over its reception, however successful or unsuccessful this attempt may ultimately turn out to be. This discourse is linked to the poem itself not only by its occurrence in the same physical space – the same discourse-world as the poetic text (see Gavins 2007: 18–34, and Chapter 1 of this book) – but also through any exophoric references the poet makes into that text. In much the same way as a folk musician may detail the long history of a traditional song about to be performed, its passage through time from one musician to another, its key themes, features and possible meanings, poets frequently contextualise and mediate their poetry for the listeners participating with them in the discourse-world of the poetry reading.

If a poet makes an explicit link to another text, writer or genre in a paratextual introduction to a poem, whether written or spoken, this can also be seen as an attempt to establish a particular attitude in the reader or audience, to cue the background knowledge needed to recognise and process intertextual connections. Panagiotidou (2012: 50) has argued that intertextuality is greatly dependent on readers adopting a receptive 'literary stance' in their encounters with texts, or 'a readiness to accept things, to deal with . . . processes, events, people', as Wagner (1983: 102) puts it. Furthermore, in her study of live poetry in performance, Novak (2011) has suggested that an audience at a poetry reading may be in possession of a unique predisposition to poetic language, a special awareness of its complexity, and a willingness to find meaning within this. Following Müller-Zettelmann (2000), she argues that

> in the case of poetry concepts of genre would entail a heightened focus on form in expectation of a certain density and enhanced artificiality which demand a high level of attention. Thus, while live literature generally focuses on the orally delivered text more than theatre, live *poetry* demands an even higher degree of concentration on the performer's words [. . .].
>
> (Novak 2011: 61)

From this perspective, paratextual information provided by a poet about connected texts acts to prompt an already especially alert group of readers or listeners to the need to seek out and resolve intertextual references in the poem to come.

This prompt, of course, is no guarantee that such resolutions will in fact be made, or that the cueing of knowledge about another piece of literature or another author will necessarily by met with a positive response from the audience. Thus, when Morrissey signals that '1801' is inspired by the journals of

Dorothy Wordsworth in her prologues to the poem, her audience may react with either delight or despondency or something in between, and they may or may not hold the knowledge needed to identify the points of connection between the texts concerned. Although a wide literary knowledge is more likely in an audience for a live poetry reading, such as the loyal followers who regularly attended the Lyric poetry festival, even these specialist readers cannot be entirely relied upon to share the poet's specific familiarity with Dorothy Wordsworth's writing style.

Despite the obvious possibility that a writer's knowledge and a reader's or audience's knowledge may not match up in the discourse-world of an intertextual text, Mason (2015, 2019) notes that literary criticism on intertextuality abounds with elitist assumptions based on idealistic notions of readership. Discussing the influential work of Riffaterre (1990), in particular, she points out:

> This conceptualisation of intertextuality as both directed by an author and necessary for accessing a text's 'true meaning' is not only a dictatorial and highly privileged vision of reading but is also ill-equipped, on a purely practical level, to account for readers who do not identify the prescribed references or who make other interrelations which fall outside the scope of 'what the author intended'[. . .] This approach to intertextuality can only delineate idealised, highly-informed, readings of a narrative which seek to identify the 'appropriate' links to be made by investigating and hypothesising authorial intention. Intertextual links are presented as finite, objectively valid and objectively present in the narrative.
>
> (Mason 2015: 47–8)

Mason argues instead for the importance of a reader-centred approach to intertextuality, one which recognises the essential role played by the reader and by reader knowledge in the conceptualisation of literature.

## Intertextual reading

In her examination of connection-making between narrative texts specifically, Mason reframes intertextuality as operating through two distinct components: 'narrative interrelation', and 'intertextual reference'. Mason explains:

- A *narrative interrelation* is the cognitive act of making a link between a narrative and at least one other. Narrative interrelations are mental processes; they cannot be accessed or examined directly. They may occur spontaneously to readers when they read or think about a nar-

rative, or they may be prompted by their exposure to an intertextual reference.
- An *intertextual reference* is any articulated, examinable product of narrative interrelation. Readers produce intertextual references but also encounter them embedded in narratives, as the textual trace of an interrelation made by the author, or in the discourse, written and spoken, of other readers.

(Mason 2019: 21)

For the purposes of understanding intertextuality in poetry, or indeed in any other non-narrative text, I would argue that the notion of a 'narrative interrelation' which Mason outlines here should be broadened out and reconceptualised as a 'textual interrelation'. This is easily done, and without any negative impact on the usefulness of this idea as a means of illuminating how intertextual connections operate both on the page and in readers' minds. Indeed, Mason herself suggest that such a broadening of her terminology would be advantageous and that 'It would be perfectly possible to scale the parameters for defining what counts as intertextuality from the level of "narrative" to the level of "text"' (Mason 2019: 25). From this point of view, then, the formulation of a conceptual link between texts is one which can be made by either authors or readers, sometimes as the result of a linguistic item in a text, and sometimes spontaneously. This internal, cognitive process is quite separate from the sorts of articulated, explicit references to related texts that can be found in literary works themselves, but that are also frequently made by readers in their discussions of literary experiences with others, by authors in the discourse they produce around their writing, as well in literary marketing and publicity.

Mason's research is invaluable for a number of reasons. Firstly, it challenges the elitist view of intertextual writing and reading put forward in the majority of other criticism, and provides an alternative, replicable and retrievable means of analysing textual interconnection. Secondly, and perhaps even more importantly, the framework Mason proposes is based on substantial empirical evidence drawn from readers' responses to intertextuality in online and face-to-face reading groups, as well as in classroom environments. Within this wide-ranging data, Mason finds that intertextual references can serve several purposes for readers: from creating synecdochic or metaphorical relationships, to enabling the expression of disanalogy between particular objects and experiences. All of these common activities around literary reading are dependent on the structures of background knowledge, discussed in Chapter 1 of this book, which the participants bring with them to a discourse-world: in order to identify a link between one text and another, to recognise a familiar literary style, or even to be able to say that one literary text is completely different from another, readers must access pre-existing conceptualisations arising from previous experiences.

These literary knowledge schemas are what enable readers to formulate a range of different connections across texts and beyond. As Hartman (1995, 2004) points out, some of these connections, which he classifies as 'primary endogenous links', are made within a single text, for example if a reader identifies repeated themes or events occurring in separate sections of the same narrative. Readers may also make 'secondary endogenous links', connecting one literary experience with another across potentially multiple different literary works, as well as 'exogenous links' between a literary text and their personal experiences in the real world.

In her own account, Mason argues that intertextual references exist along a cline of visibility. She explains that all intertextual connections are dependent on at least one 'point of contact' (2019: 75–7) between texts or between experiences being recognised or perceived by a reader; these points act as a catalyst for the interrelations readers conceptualise as they read. According to Mason, at one end of the spectrum these textual features can be highly visible or 'marked' in a literary work. In such cases, she explains, 'two narratives are not simply being juxtaposed but the grounds on which they are being linked are explicitly presented to other readers' (Mason 2015: 125). Marked intertextual references are at their most obvious when explicit mention is made of the title of a connected text (for example '*Wuthering Heights*'). However, readers can also be encouraged to recognise literary interrelationships through the 'unmarked' use of other themes, objects, characters and locations from that text (such as 'Heathcliffe', 'Cathy', 'Thrushcross Grange', and so on). Furthermore, Mason argues that intertextual references can be 'specific', where a marked or unmarked link is made to a single literary work, or 'generic', where a connection is made to a broader range of texts or even a whole genre.

Where an intertextual reference occurs in a way that is unmarked, Mason is keen to point out that this will not necessarily be more difficult for readers to recognise or use as the basis for the formation of a conceptual interrelation. She explains:

> In particular, it is useful to identify that some specific unmarked references can utilise highly recognisable features. That is, we can reasonably (though not categorically) assume that, for people who do have an archived narrative schema for *The Wizard of Oz*, that schema is likely to include 'Toto' and perhaps 'Kansas', or even the highly popularised quote 'Toto, I don't think we're in Kansas anymore'. Other examples might include 'ruby slippers' or 'yellow brick road', for example. In this sense, highly recognisable features arguably 'mark' out the presence of a specific unmarked reference, and are therefore much more likely to prompt an interrelation.
>
> (Mason 2015: 135–6)

Thus, readers with an existing knowledge of other texts being referred to in an intertextual literary work may identify both marked and unmarked references to those texts. Without this pre-existing schematic knowledge, however, even marked specific references will not result in the formulation of a corresponding textual interrelation in a reader's mind.

## Identifying points of contact

On encountering the poem '1801', readers may or may not be primed to participate in intertextual reading, depending on whether or not they have been made aware of the text's connection to Dorothy Wordsworth's journals through paratextual information. Within the text itself, however, there are numerous stylistic features which nevertheless work to generate conceptual links between these works. It is here that corpus-linguistic methods can be very helpful in beginning to uncover where such interrelations are formed in the language of the text itself. Corpus linguistics is one of the most rapidly developing methods of analysing naturally occurring discourse, in which samples of language are collected and computerised to form electronic corpora which can then be searched and analysed using various different kinds of software. This enables linguists not only to examine very large amounts of linguistic data at once, if need be, but to do so systematically. Due to the very recent histories of both disciplines, the benefits of using corpus-linguistic technologies in combination with cognitive analysis of literary texts are only just beginning to be explored. As Stockwell and Mahlberg (2015: 131) have already argued, though, these benefits are potentially bi-directional: where corpus-linguistic evidence can enable the theoretical hypotheses of cognitive theories of reading to be tested, verified and refined, cognitive analyses of literature can in turn add a reader-focused, experiential dimension to what might otherwise be generalistic studies of language. They go on to point out that, used in an integrated manner, corpus linguistics and cognitive poetics can 'uncover patterns across a text that can make claims for the generation of subtle *textural* effects in a reader's mind' (Stockwell and Mahlberg 2015: 144).

In the present exploration of the intertextuality of '1801', corpus-linguistic methods can be used to reveal atypical features of Dorothy Wordsworth's writing style which might be recognised as points of contact with her work by contemporary readers of Morrissey's poem. The replication or echoing of such features in a contemporary text would most likely act to cue conceptual interrelationships or, at the very least, be foregrounded in contemporary discourse as a result of their peculiarity. To investigate this possibility further, I created an electronic corpus from Dorothy's diaries (specifically, the 2002 edition of *The Grasmere and Alfoxden Journals* published by Oxford World Classics) and compared this to a much larger reference corpus in the form of the *British National Corpus* (BNC) (2015). The BNC is a 100-million-word collection of written and spoken English collected at the end of the twentieth century. It provides a sample of normative contemporary English language use, against which Wordsworth's writing style of 200 years earlier can be analysed. Corpus linguistics of this sort can help to reveal, for example, which of the lexical choices made by a writer are unusual or remarkable when compared with contemporary everyday discourse. When such a comparison is made (in this case using AntConc corpus analysis software) between the written component of the BNC and Wordsworth's journals, the words listed in Figure 3.1 score most highly for their 'keyness', or atypical nature.

At the top of this list is 'wm', the abbreviated form Dorothy uses 177 times throughout her diaries to refer to her brother. Added to the 258 instances of the unabbreviated form, 'William', it is clear that he forms the core focus of a substantial portion of her writing. 'Coleridge' is another unsurprising keyword in Dorothy's journals, scoring highly for keyness here as a name which is unusual in the BNC reference corpus, but which refers to a pivotal figure in Dorothy's and William's lives. Perhaps more remarkable, however,

| Types Before Cut: | 4616 | | Types After Cut: | 3569 |
| --- | --- | --- | --- | --- |
| Rank | Freq | Keyness | Keyword | |
| 1 | 177 | 2358.924 | wm | |
| 2 | 221 | 2263.977 | coleridge | |
| 3 | 916 | 1989.208 | we | |
| 4 | 302 | 1948.384 | walked | |
| 5 | 131 | 1876.468 | sate | |
| 6 | 258 | 1579.922 | william | |
| 7 | 278 | 1401.222 | morning | |
| 8 | 92 | 1368.083 | rydale | |
| 9 | 306 | 1101.685 | went | |
| 10 | 949 | 837.862 | i | |
| 11 | 116 | 632.519 | clock | |
| 12 | 103 | 623.305 | till | |
| 13 | 175 | 605.510 | upon | |
| 14 | 141 | 593.748 | evening | |
| 15 | 308 | 588.862 | very | |
| 16 | 123 | 549.551 | wrote | |
| 17 | 132 | 528.931 | o | |
| 18 | 101 | 523.820 | dinner | |
| 19 | 108 | 517.669 | tea | |
| 20 | 106 | 516.146 | mary | |
| 21 | 109 | 498.847 | beautiful | |
| 22 | 90 | 498.680 | lake | |
| 23 | 57 | 489.149 | orchard | |
| 24 | 104 | 467.334 | trees | |
| 25 | 185 | 465.378 | came | |
| 26 | 60 | 411.675 | sara | |
| 27 | 40 | 405.651 | keswick | |
| 28 | 87 | 374.959 | wood | |
| 29 | 62 | 339.713 | moon | |
| 30 | 32 | 333.040 | ambleside | |

**Figure 3.1** Dorothy Wordsworth's journals keyword list

is that Dorothy's use of the first-person plural pronoun, 'we', is atypically frequent too in comparison with contemporary English usage. In terms of its keyness in her writing style, it scores much more highly than the first-person singular 'I' (which is also a keyword at tenth in the list in Figure 3.1), suggesting that Dorothy's journals are concerned more with shared activity, specifically between Dorothy, William and Coleridge, than with her own singular perspective in a way that is distinct from written English today.

The keyword list also reveals a similarly distinctive emphasis on time and place in Dorothy's journals in comparison with contemporary discourse. The verbs carrying the greatest keyness scores in the diaries are notably 'sate' (again unsurprising, given its archaic spelling), 'walked', 'went' and 'wrote'. Indeed, 'went' and 'walked' in particular are also the top two verbs Dorothy uses most frequently across her journals (shown in the frequency list in Figure 3.2) after the simple past form of the copular verb 'to be'. The prevalence of these verbs in Dorothy's writing reflects both the fact that she, William and Coleridge spent much of their daytimes walking and visiting friends and neighbours in the Lake District, as was common at that time,

| Word Types: 4616 | | Word Tokens: 47753 |
|---|---|---|
| Rank | Freq | Word |
| 1 | 3477 | the |
| 2 | 1820 | and |
| 3 | 1371 | a |
| 4 | 1212 | to |
| 5 | 997 | of |
| 6 | 949 | i |
| 7 | 916 | we |
| 8 | 902 | in |
| 9 | 635 | was |
| 10 | 528 | with |
| 11 | 505 | at |
| 12 | 453 | it |
| 13 | 359 | he |
| 14 | 320 | had |
| 15 | 308 | very |
| 16 | 306 | went |
| 17 | 302 | walked |
| 18 | 301 | on |
| 19 | 299 | s |
| 20 | 280 | but |
| 21 | 278 | morning |
| 22 | 258 | william |
| 23 | 256 | were |
| 24 | 245 | as |
| 25 | 242 | from |
| 26 | 235 | that |
| 27 | 231 | not |
| 28 | 230 | by |
| 29 | 221 | coleridge |
| 30 | 211 | for |

**Figure 3.2** Dorothy Wordsworth's journals frequency list

but also that Dorothy chooses to give this activity prominence in her diaries. Most of the sitting Dorothy reports takes place either in the evening or along the way on her many walks. A concordance analysis, looking at the words which occur alongside 'sate', shows that this occurs mainly under trees, in the orchard, or beside walls during the day, and beside the fire in the evenings, and is most often accompanied with a report of pleasant conversation with William and Coleridge.

The temporal framing Dorothy provides around such activities can be seen to be reflected not only in the keyness ratings for the temporal adverbials 'morning' and 'evening', but also in the keyness of 'clock', which is eleventh in the list in Figure 3.1. An examination of the co-text surrounding 'clock' in Dorothy's journal reveals that all but two of the 116 instances of this word are references to precise times in the day, such as 'one o'clock', 'two o'clock', and so on (the exceptions being one reference to a 'clock ticking' and one to a 'church clock'). These occurrences also account for the vast majority of uses of 'o', which appears in seventeenth position in Figure 3.1. It is worth pointing out, however, that half a dozen of these 132 items are exclamations and occur in sentences such as 'O the Darling!' (Wordsworth 2002: 74) and 'O the unutterable darkness of the sky and the earth below the Moon!' (Wordsworth 2002: 81) – a point to which I will return later in this chapter.

On the whole, then, Dorothy is careful to give highly specific deictic detail throughout her writing, according to which the temporal parameters of the text-worlds she describes can be clearly established. 'Dinner' and 'tea' are also interesting items when considered in terms of their temporal signification. The three words which most commonly occur alongside 'dinner', for example, are 'before', 'after' and 'till', all of which again add temporal specificity to Dorothy's descriptions of events and activities. 'Tea' has a similar deictic function, being most frequently preceded by the temporal adverbial 'after' (39 times), with the verb 'drank' (33 times) being the next most frequent collocate with this item. This would seem to suggest that Dorothy views 'tea' as an important temporal marker in her day at least as much as, if not slightly more than, an activity in which she frequently participates. Temporal deixis is also not the only unusually frequently occurring linguistic feature in Dorothy's journals: she is equally focused on providing spatial markers around which a text-world representation of her life can be constructed. A number of key locations in the Lake District, such as 'Rydale', 'Keswick' and 'Ambleside', score unsurprisingly highly for their keyness when Dorothy's text is compared with the reference corpus. However, other features of the local landscape and of the countryside more generally also stand out as key nouns. Her frequent mentions of such geographical details as 'lake' (used 90 times), 'orchard' (used 57 times), 'trees' (used 104 times), 'wood' (used 87 times) and the 'moon' (used 62 times) all emerge as prominent textual elements that make Dorothy's writing distinctive from contemporary written English.

All in all, a corpus-linguistic analysis would seem to suggest that the singularity of Dorothy Wordsworth's writing style emanates to some degree from her descriptions of time spent mainly with William and Coleridge, of the surrounding natural landscape, and from the situation of both of these components of her life within a clearly defined temporal frame in her journals. The aspects of the journals which distinguish them most from contemporary discourse are thus an emphasis on the description of time spent sitting, writing or walking through the beautiful Lake District countryside, and on the normally shared nature of all these activities. It is possible to argue on the basis of this that, in any pastiche of Dorothy Wordsworth's style, such atypical themes and features might form obvious points of contact with her texts when used in a contemporary discourse situation.

## Reading textual interrelationships in '1801'

If we return at this point to Morrissey's poem, it can be seen that many such stylistic motifs, defining of Wordsworth's style, are indeed functioning in '1801' as what Mason (2015, 2019) would term unmarked, specific intertextual references to Dorothy's diaries. First of all, the poem shares the same focus on time identified in Dorothy's journals and makes this evident from its title (a date two years after the Wordsworths moved from Dorset to Dove Cottage) onwards. This date, of course, also acts as a linguistic cue for readers' broader schematic, historical knowledge; whether they have any existing experience of Dorothy Wordsworth's life and writing or not, '1801' will bring with it a range of preconceived assumptions based on more general knowledge about the early nineteenth century, the precise nature and scope of which will vary from reader to reader.

As we have already seen Mason (2015, 2019) point out, a reader-centred approach is needed in order to understand more fully the potential impact of this varying knowledge on the conceptualisation of the intertextual dimensions of literary texts. It is therefore essential to engage with responses to '1801' beyond my own experience if a properly context-sensitive understanding of the cognition of the textual interrelations in the poem is to be achieved. So, as part of a wider, ongoing project to bring the text-world approach to discourse into secondary school classrooms in the UK, in spring 2018 I collaborated with a teacher of English at a large comprehensive school in Sheffield to design and undertake a small-scale empirical reader-response experiment with a group of twenty-nine students aged between fifteen and sixteen years old. The students were of mixed academic ability and the experiment took place during one of their regular English lessons and in their usual learning environment with only their teacher present. As a group of respondents, these young people represent a non-specialist audience of readers located in the same geographical area of the UK as I am, but who might be argued to be more in tune with contemporary, informal English usage, as well as with poetic deviations from that usage, than a forty-six-year-old professor of English language and literature might hope to be. Their responses to the language of Morrissey's poem therefore provide both a useful point of comparison with my own subjective response. In the same vein as Mason's research on the reception of narrative intertextuality in classroom settings, the students' reactions to '1801' also give an insight into how textual interrelations in poetry are received by students in a secondary school learning environment.

In a lesson which followed a structure very similar to their usual English classes, the students were all given a copy of Morrissey's poem printed in the middle of a sheet of A3-sized paper. Students of this age group in the UK are required to analyse and discuss unseen literary texts as part of their GCSE examinations, and at this particular school they regularly undertake practice analyses of this sort in their English lessons. '1801' was presented to them in this learning context. They were given a short introduction to the objectives of the class by their teacher at the beginning of the session and clear instructions to respond to the poem in the same way they would any other unseen text. The students' responses were initially formulated and written down individually, directly onto the printed poem sheet, before the whole class discussed the text further together. Firstly, the class were asked to write down anything which the title of the poem brought to mind for them. In addition to this, they were asked to focus specifically on words or phrases in the poem which they felt were unusual, which stood out to them for whatever reason, or which they felt they would be unlikely to use in their own everyday language. The students annotated '1801' with these thoughts and ideas and were then encouraged to complete a longer discursive piece of writing about the text to close the lesson.

Among the students' initial annotated responses to the poem's title were one-word notes and short phrases commonly including 'pre-Victorian', 'revolution', 'poverty', 'Georgian England', 'factories', 'simplicity' and 'new era'. Some students appeared to have a more detailed historical knowledge of the period and included comments such as 'start of the Industrial Revolution', 'mass poverty in England', 'changing society' and – particularly interesting in intertextual terms – 'similar time period to The Prelude, Jane Eyre', and 'This period is just before the writers of classics such as Jane Eyre, Charles Dickens' novels and others such as Pride and Prejudice'. It is clear from these notes and comments, then, that the date in the poem's title activated a range of different background knowledge for the students, which for some led to the formulation of textual interrelationships with other literary works. It is worth noting here that all the other texts mentioned by the students on their poem sheets had been studied in one form or another at other points during their GCSE English course, although only three students actually articulated these specific, marked interrelations in their written work. However, the repetition of the other keywords listed above multiple times across the annotations the students produced over the course of their lesson also indicates that some broader elements of discourse-world knowledge – to do with English history, widespread social injustice in the nineteenth century, and a sense of coming change – were shared by the majority of the class. I will return to the students' responses to specific parts of the rest of the poem, through which the impact of their discourse-world knowledge might be identifiable, at various points throughout the discussion of the style of '1801' to come.

To focus back on the text itself for now, however, in terms of the construction of a mental representation of the poem, a number of temporal world-builders help to outline the deictic configuration of this specific text-world, echoing the style of Dorothy's writing in the process. For instance, several of the temporal adverbials which feature as key terms in Figure 3.1 also appear in Morrissey's poem. The first line, for example, begins 'A beautiful cloudless morning', including both 'morning' and the pre-modifier 'beautiful', listed twenty-first in terms of its keyness in Figure 3.1. Later in the same stanza, the progress of time is marked in much the same way as frequently occurs in Dorothy's journals with the key item 'dinner' pre-modified with the temporal adverbial 'after'. Added to this, 'afternoon' appears in the first line of the second stanza, while 'evenings' occurs towards the end of the poem. Here, Morrissey's choice to use a plural form and thus produce a generalised statement about all 'such visited evenings' brings with it a certain timeless quality.

'Visited' is also an interesting choice of pre-modifying adjective, since its meaning is ambiguous in this particular context – it is unclear in this line whether evenings are the subject of a visit or visits, or whether 'visited' is being used in its alternative, archaic sense to mean 'afflicted' or 'attacked', normally by illness. Given that no visitor is mentioned anywhere else in the poem, but a description of William 'as pale as a basin, exhausted with altering' is, I would lean towards the latter interpretation. From this perspective, it is not only the evenings which are perpetually affected but also William himself. Furthermore, the implication of an archaic meaning for 'visited' (the latest occurrence of which is recorded as 1665 in the *Oxford English Dictionary*) is another generalised signal towards readers' broad historical knowledge: it is a usage which is likely to *feel* old to contemporary readers, even if 1801 is actually a little late for it to be common in the everyday discourse of that time.

Indeed, this likelihood was very clearly born out in the secondary school students' reactions to the poem. Of the twenty-nine students in the class, twenty of them underlined or annotated the line 'Such visited evenings are sharp with love' as one containing phrases or words they found unusual or would not normally use in their own day-to-day discourse. Many of them, although not explicitly commenting on the archaic nature of the verb 'visited', made comparable notes such as 'not a phrase you would hear now', with one student suggesting 'formal language suggests their relationship is strained or burdened'. Connected with this, the metaphor at the heart of the line, 'sharp with love', was interpreted universally by those students who chose to comment upon it as expressing some sort of turmoil or tension between William and the 'I' enactor in the poem. One student, for example, noted that this line was 'oxymoronic . . . something which pains the narra- tor', while another questioned 'the love is painful?', and another suggested the metaphor 'could be trying to reveal an underlying tension or jealousy in the relationship'.

In many of their annotations, the students also drew connections between this line and other metaphors and phrases in the text in order to construct an extended interpretation of the whole poem that framed the relationship described within it as burdened or difficult in some way. Among the lines they identified as supporting this reading were the 'tiny wounded yellow bird, sounding its alarm' in the second stanza, and the 'Captain begging for alms' at the end of the first stanza. Both of these were described by the students multiple times as 'sinister' or 'dark', with the Captain, in particular, being commonly connected to a suggestion of a backdrop of wider political upheaval or war. Furthermore, the first line of the third stanza, 'William as pale as a basin, exhausted with altering', was underlined as unusual language by twenty-one of the twenty-nine students in the group (e.g. 'don't call them basins – olden days'). Once again, this line was universally interpreted by those who provided more detailed commentary on it as further indicating underlying pain or difficulty in the poem. Interestingly, there are no occur- rences of the string 'as a basin' anywhere in the 100 million words of the BNC, and only one string in the comparable simile form 'like a basin'. In Dorothy Wordsworth's diaries, however, the following simile occurs in a description of a view over Stowey in Somerset: 'the distant prospect on the land side, islanded with sunshine; the sea, like a basin full to the margin' (Wordsworth 2002: 147).

Throughout the poem, a sense of timelessness or stasis is achieved through other means which also help to capture the abbreviated nature of journal writing as a discourse genre. Specifically, the copula verb 'to be' is ellipted in numerous places across the stanzas of '1801'. For example, in the first line of the poem 'it was' or 'it is', or even some other first-person form, such as 'we had', is absent from the opening sentence, 'A beautiful cloudless morning'. Similarly, the copula is ellipted from the next sentence, 'My toothache better', and from the next line, 'William at work on The Pedlar', and so on. Across the whole text, the copula is deleted from a total of seven sentences, leaving these constructions without clear, tense-based temporal parameters. This is typical of the journal genre, where the time and space for writing are often limited and abbreviation is common, and all of the students responding to the '1801' in their English class without exception commented that it bore resemblance in some way to a diary. In other places in the poem, the same condensed style is maintained through a lack of first-person pronouns (note, too, the use of an ampersand in place of 'and' in the middle line of the second stanza). For example, 'Walked out after dinner for letters' is not tied to a specific agent in the poem, nor is 'met a man who had once been a Captain', nor 'Came home / via the lake', and so on. In these cases, ambiguity arises around who, precisely, is completing the actions described and a depersonalised tone is constructed across the text as a result.

The syntactic structures contained in '1801' thus not only form an intertextual connection with the genre of journal writing as a whole, but they can also be seen to make more subtle links with wider knowledge about Dorothy and William Wordsworth's relationship and their lives together for those readers in possession of this background information. In choosing to limit the use of personal pronouns in her text, Morrissey blurs the lines between two characters: the narrating voice of Dorothy, and her brother, William. Even for readers with no existing knowledge of this couple's notoriously intimate relationship, a slippage persists throughout the poem between brother and sister, as Morrissey resists explicitly attaching numerous actions to one or the other of them. Not only could any one of the five verbs in '1801' ('walked', 'met', 'came', 'heard' and 'exhausted') equally plausibly have either Dorothy or William or both as agent, but Morrissey also includes a further ambiguous sentence in the second stanza with 'The soles on this year's boots are getting worn'. Here, the choice of 'this year's' over a possessive pronoun or noun means that the boots could belong to either sibling, or the sentence could be read as referring to their possessions collectively. It is worth noting at this point, too, the temporal quality of 'this year's' as a pre-modifier, again placing emphasis on time and the consequences of its passing (the wearing down of boots), rather than on individuality and proprietorship. The level of closeness between William and Dorothy that these features suggest was not lost on the secondary school readers, with twenty-two of the twenty-nine students noting in their work that they assumed the couple to be husband and wife on their initial reading of '1801'.

The spatially deictic elements of Morrissey's poem also act to echo Dorothy Wordsworth's life and writing style as unmarked, intertextual references to a specific set of base texts. William's presence as a world-building element in the poem is the most obvious example of this. Other spatial world-builders – objects and locations – with high keyness ratings in Dorothy's journals also appear in Morrissey's text: specifically 'lake' and 'moon' (repeated twice) from the top thirty items listed in Figure 3.1, along with other nouns with similarly high keyness ratings, such as 'letters' (keyness rating 193.778 and also repeated twice in the poem), 'moonlight' (keyness rating 206.424) and 'Grasmere' (keyness rating 256.952). Other nouns in the poem, while they may not score highly in terms of their peculiarity compared with contemporary discourse, nevertheless maintain the emphasis throughout '1801' on the natural environment ('geese', 'bird' and 'herrings', for example), or add to the overall nineteenth-century feel of the text ('boots', 'alms', 'pears with

```
down the  winter cherry tree. I sowed French   beans and weeded.  A coronetted landau went by, wh
  . They brought in two pikes.  I sowed kidney  beans and spinnach.  A cold evening.  Molly stuck t
      . Rain in the night. I tied up scarlet    beans, nailed the honeysuckles, etc, etc. John was
evented by the excessive heat. Nailed up scarlet beans in the morning. . . . Walked over the mount
posing all the morning. I shelled peas, gathered beans, and worked in the garden till half past 12.
       went into the garden, and sowed the scarlet beans about  the house. It was a clear sky.   1
Saturday Morning, 5th May. We sowed the scarlet  beans in the orchard, and read Henry V. there.
have lilies, and many other flowers. The scarlet beans  are up in crowds. It is now between
nailed up the honeysuckles, and hoed  the scarlet beans   Monday . . . We sat out all the day. . . .
  . In the morning we observed  that the scarlet beans were drooping- in the leaves in  great numbe
```

**Figure 3.3** Concordance for 'scarlet beans'

cloves', and so on). Among those nouns which are foregrounded as a result of their scarcity in the context of contemporary language use, the 'scarlet beans' stood out particularly strongly to me in my own reading of the poem. The uncommonness of this particular noun phrase for today's readers of Morrissey's text is indicated by the fact that there are no mentions of 'scarlet beans' anywhere in the BNC. Notably, in the secondary school students' responses to Morrissey's poem, eighteen of the twenty-nine respondents underlined this phrase as unusual or uncommon usage.

In Dorothy's journal, by comparison, eight out of her eleven mentions of 'beans' are pre-modified with 'scarlet'. Furthermore, as can be seen in the concordance in Figure 3.3, in the majority of these instances the beans are the objects of Dorothy's activities (sowing, nailing, tying, hoeing. and so on) presented in the same syntactic structure as 'I shelled our scarlet beans'.

What this concordance analysis makes clear is that '1801' not only successfully utilises some of the most unusual lexical features of Dorothy Wordsworth's written language, but does so within similar syntactic structures, many of which also mimic the genre of journal writing more broadly. The poem describes everyday scenes of William's writing, Dorothy's work in the garden, walks in the countryside, the preparation of food, and sitting together in the evening, all of which are likely to form intertextual connections for any reader of Morrissey's poem who is also familiar with Dorothy Wordsworth's texts. Furthermore, the entire lexis of '1801' is predominantly Germanic in origin, which fits with the habitual, domestic text-world the poem sketches out. As Verdonk (2013: 169–70) explains, Germanic lexis is normally associated with 'things which are fundamental, familiar, concrete or emotional in our lives' (2013: 169), and so is perfectly in keeping with the scenes of the Wordsworth's day-to-day home life in Grasmere which Morrissey chooses to recreate here. The data gathered from my reader-response study with school students would also suggest that this focus on domestic matters in the poem stood out as unusually strong for an audience of young readers in urban Northern England. One of the most frequently commented-upon phrases in '1801' for them was 'excellent lettuces', which twenty-two of the twenty-nine students involved in the experiment underlined as a remarkable description, variously suggesting this noun phrase represented 'a fantasy world', 'childhood', 'simple times' and 'happiness', and a day-to-day existence which, to them, was 'too picturesque, too perfect'.

## Layered voices, connected texts

Despite all the linguistic points of contact identified between '1801' and Dorothy Wordsworth's journals so far, it is important to understand that Morrissey's poem is not a direct replication of Wordsworth's diaries; it is a pastiche in poetic form, an intertextual homage to another writer, and an artwork in its own right, not a facsimile copy of another work or another's writing style. Not only is Morrissey careful to embed Wordsworth's voice at the heart of her text through the stylistic echoes examined in the preceding sections of this chapter, but she also ensures that her own voice and her own identity as a poet resonate throughout the poem. Indeed, Morrissey weaves several other texts and voices through the poem alongside those that are identifiably hers and Dorothy's. The resulting textual and conceptual structure is a highly complex one and one which would appear to be typical of postmodern intertextuality, as described by Jameson:

> depth is replaced by surface, or by multiple surfaces [. . .] objects that were formerly 'works' can now be reread as immense ensembles or systems of texts of various kinds, superimposed on each other by way of the various intertextualities, successions of fragments, or, yet again, sheer process.
>
> (Jameson 1991: 77)

The superimpositions achieved by Morrissey in '1801' include not only the layering of the style of Dorothy Wordsworth's journals with the text of her own poem, but also further fragmentary references to the work of Dorothy's brother, William, as well as to other poets and other texts.

For example, although Morrissey's references to Dorothy and her writing remain unmarked throughout the poem, she chooses to make a marked, specific reference to William's poem 'The Pedlar' in the opening stanza. Furthermore, the later description in the final stanza of 'William as pale as a basin, exhausted with altering' echoes Dorothy's twenty-three mentions across her journals of her brother's extensive work on this poem, frequently accompanied by commentary on its negative effects on his health and mental well-being. Whether or not the reader of Morrissey's poem holds existing knowledge of the complex and lengthy production history of 'The Pedlar' from 1798 to 1804 (the chronology of which is meticulously documented by Butler (1977)), there can be little doubt from its appearance in '1801' of this text's troublesome nature in William's and Dorothy's lives. The presentation of 'The Pedlar' in this way also acts as an interesting foregrounding device for the process of writing itself, adding a self-conscious layer of reflection by one writer (Dorothy) on the fraught rewritings of another (William) within the poetic text of yet another (Morrissey).

A number of other stylistic choices in '1801' also work to emphasise this self-consciousness and bring Morrissey's voice – as the ultimately controlling author – to the forefront of the poem. For instance, it is interesting to note that no marked mention is made in the poem of Coleridge, despite his position as a dominant figure in Dorothy's journals and in her and William's life together. His omission from Morrissey's text ensures that the focus of '1801' remains solely on the Wordsworths and that their relationship is presented, in this text at least, in an exclusive state. The only other two people to feature in the poem – Miss Gell and the former Captain encountered on a walk – appear fleetingly in the text, with Miss Gell in particular described only through her departure and parting gift of lettuces. Furthermore, the sense of timelessness created in '1801', through the ellipted copula verbs and the scarcity of tense identified earlier in this discussion, can be seen to present William and Dorothy's life together in a kind of snapshot form: this is a representative picture of their relationship as a whole, rather than a replication of a single, time-anchored diary entry. Again, Morrissey's authorial choices can be seen more clearly here when the style of her poem is compared directly with Dorothy's own language: Dorothy does not ellipt the copula from her discourse as a recurrent pattern, nor does she avoid the use of finite verbs in general. Where Dorothy's journal entries describe discrete events, located at specific temporal points and marked accordingly with tense, the text-world described in Morrissey's poem contains no greater temporal specificity than the year 1801 and achieves a more universal, emblematic feel through the amorphous deictic parameters set by the poet. '1801' thus reaches beyond the temporal boundaries of the individual events it contains and gestures towards a broader, perpetual state of existence for the couple.

The poeticism of Morrissey's text is key to an understanding of the careful layering of voices and styles in '1801'. At no point is this more strongly apparent than when the sound patterning crafted throughout the poem is considered. Morrissey uses a regular rhyme scheme in '1801', albeit one which mixes slant rhyme (for example, 'better'/'letters', 'Gell'/'shelled', 'home'/'worn', 'turquoise'/'geese', 'altering'/'herrings') with eye rhyme ('cloves'/'love'). The final lines of each stanza also end with a slant rhyme ('alms', 'alarm' and 'arms') and Morrissey even goes so far as to line-up 'herrings' with 'altering' in the layout of the poem on the page to make her pattern work. The punctuation of 'like herrings!', it is worth noting here, is reminiscent of Dorothy's frequent use of exclamation marks – forty-two times throughout her diaries – which have already been pointed out earlier in this chapter in their repeated appearance in proximity to 'O!' In fact, the penultimate line of '1801' is a direct quotation from the journals, where Dorothy describes 'a very fine moonlight night – The moonshine *like herrings* in the water' (Wordsworth 2002: 30, my emphasis).

The final line of the poem is another unmarked intertextual reference to Dorothy's journals, in which she refers on Tuesday, 4 May 1802 to 'the crescent moon with the "auld moon in her arms"' and says on the following day that 'the moon had the old moon in her arms, but not so plain to be seen as the night before' (Wordsworth 2002: 96). As the quotation marks used by Dorothy indicate, however, this phrase is not her own, but originally comes from the traditional Scottish ballad 'Sir Patrick Spens'. The ballad exists in many different forms, one of which, to make matters even more complex, was used the same year by Coleridge to open his poem 'Dejection: An Ode':

Late, late yestreen I saw the new Moon,
With the old Moon in her arms;
And I fear, I fear, my Master dear!
We shall have a deadly storm.
(Ballad of Sir Patrick Spence)

The lunar phenomenon being described here is that of 'earthshine', where the unlit part of a crescent moon can be seen to glow faintly alongside the bright shine of the crescent itself. This glow is caused by light from the nearly full earth, illuminated by the sun, shining onto the moon's surface. In the ballad 'Sir Patrick Spens', and in folklore more broadly, this phenomenon was seen as a forewarning of maritime disaster. Dorothy chooses a more archaic spelling of 'auld' in her diary entry, suggesting that she is quoting one of the many versions of the original ballad, rather than its appearance in Coleridge's text. However, the inclusion of the image in Morrissey's poem makes this an intertextual reference embedded three times over: Morrissey forms an intertextual connection to Dorothy's intertextual reference to both the ballad and Coleridge's own intertextual use of it in his poem. Coleridge is thus given his place in the text-world of '1801' after all, albeit in an indirect, unmarked form. It is perhaps worth noting, too, that this is achieved through a metaphor in which the crescent moon is presented as both nurturing ('holding the old moon in its arms') and outshining a fainter presence.

Once again, the nature of the reader's own schematic knowledge will dictate to a great extent how this metaphor is interpreted, if indeed its intertextual dimensions are detected at all. In my own reading of '1801', my knowledge of Sinéad Morrissey and Dorothy Wordsworth as writers, rather than of Coleridge or the ballad 'Sir Patrick Spens', was pivotal to my understanding of these lines. This is not just the result of my greater depth of knowledge of these two authors than of Coleridge, but is due in part at least, I would argue, to other stylistic choices made by Morrissey that again make her own presence in the poem more strongly felt. For example, in the final stanza of '1801' both the unmarked intertextual reference 'like herrings!' and the unmarked intertextual reference to Coleridge and the ballad 'Sir Patrick Spens' are preceded by a direct representation of Dorothy's speech to William in the line 'I almost said, *dear, look*'. Here, the italicisation strongly suggests that these are words actually spoken by Dorothy to her brother, such that the 'almost' included in the reporting clause could be easily overlooked. This is not direct speech, then, but direct almost-speech, or perhaps unvoiced direct thought. Either way, Dorothy's own writing style is not being reflected here, since her diaries contain no direct report of her speech to William, although she does report the speech of others in direct form on numerous occasions, as well as her own speech to people other than her brother. Morrissey almost corrects this in '1801' – almost allows Dorothy to voice the unspoken to William – but ultimately chooses to keep Dorothy silent in the situation of an evening 'sharp with love'.

The students in my reader-response experiment may have brought a very different set of discourse-world knowledge with them to their reading of '1801'. However, this did not prevent them from experiencing strong reactions to the closing lines of the poem. Indeed, the final metaphor of the text was the most annotated part of the poem, with twenty-four of the twenty-nine students underlining it as a noteworthy or unusual use of language. Furthermore, in their longer discursive writing and in the notes they made directly onto the poem, a consensus was identifiable across their readings of this part of the text. While none of them made any mention of Coleridge, the ballad 'Sir Patrick Spens', or Dorothy Wordsworth's writing anywhere in their annotations, the students who chose to make further comment on the line 'the new moon holding the old moon in its arms' were in close agreement about its meaning. A total of six students made extended notes here and their remarks all centre around the presence of Morrissey's poetic voice which they felt clearly in this phrase. As one student put it, 'the ending metaphor brings Morrissey into the poem. It suggests that the modern writers are holding onto and building on the old writers.' Another respondent commented that the line 'subtly honours Dorothy', while elsewhere noting that the poem as a whole 'honours her wish, keeping her unnamed', while another student suggested the metaphor 'may be Morrissey talking of her care of unknown past poets'.

Morrissey's strong authorial presence in the text can also be felt in the instability she adds to the closing two lines of the poem. If we look again at the two metaphors introduced here – 'moonlight on Grasmere / –like herrings!–' and 'the new moon holding the old moon in its arms' – what is most intriguing in their presentation is the odd use of an 'either ... or' syntactic set-up. Not only does Morrissey bring Dorothy just to the brink of speech in this final stanza, but she also suggests here that if Dorothy had spoken she could equally possibly have said one of two things. Looked at another way, these alternative metaphors, which remain ultimately unexpressed by Dorothy in the text-world of the poem, can be seen as another means through which Morrissey renders '1801' as a generalised, typical snapshot of the Wordsworths' lives and of Dorothy's writing, rather than a replication of a single day. By indicating that Dorothy has a choice over two potential expressions, she at the same time points to her own choices as the poet voicing another writer. There is a suggestion at this point not only of the two possible things Dorothy could have said to her brother but did not, but also of an array of other typical 'Dorothy-like' language Morrissey could have chosen to represent in the poem. Even in settling upon 'moonlight on Grasmere / –like herrings!–/' or 'the new moon holding the old moon in its arms', Morrissey presents these two metaphors as evenly balanced, equally plausible, and somehow equivalent in meaning, despite the fact that they depict two distinct images of the moon. In so doing, she foregrounds her own controlling influence and creates a clear layering of textual worlds. Morrissey simultaneously describes the Wordsworths' world, using a style greatly similar to Dorothy's own writing, *and* points to the situation of writing the poem and exercising her own choices over its content and form.

This layering of conceptual spaces results in an even more interesting set of textual interrelationships once the poem is read aloud. In a live reading situation, Morrissey's textual voicing of Wordsworth becomes a physical voicing too, in a discourse context in which our notions and understanding of authorship are already greatly pertinent. As Novak explains, while discussing the key differences between the performance of poetry and other forms of theatre,

> unlike in live theatre, live poetry audiences cannot usually draw on a conventionalised distinction between a real-life actor and an easily identifiable character whose name can be listed in the programme [. . .] in live poetry the poet-performer presents him- or herself rather than *re*presenting a fictitious character [. . .] Rather than 'standing for' a fictive character as a person, the poet presents his/her own text and thus '*performs* authorship' in live poetry.
>
> (Novak 2011: 186)

Thus, even though Morrissey's text centres around characters distinct from herself in space, time and being, she is nevertheless reading words written by her, not acted or performed by someone else, and in front of an audience, the presence of which is almost always directly acknowledged by a poet in a live poetry reading. Morrissey's own authorship is therefore highly foregrounded, as Novak describes. Even in the recorded version of '1801' available on *The Poetry Archive* website, in which the poet is not face to face with her audience, Morrissey achieves a foregrounding of her own authorial presence by other, textual means. In her paratextual introduction to the poem in this recording, she states that '1801' is 'inspired by Dorothy Wordsworth's journal', once again pointing explicitly to her own writing process.

Through techniques such as this, and through Morrissey's inclusion of the sustained, self-conscious poeticism identified throughout the text over the course of this chapter, a complexity of intertextual layering is created. This reaches far beyond the simple replication of a writing style or the marked reference to other texts and other authors. It bears a much closer resemblance to the palimpsestic layering of worlds and voices which Armitage creates in 'Evening' and which I discussed in Chapter 2. In Morrissey's text, the world of William and Dorothy forms the foreground in our conceptualisation of the poem, and it is their environment, their activities, their relationship and the language Dorothy uses to describe them that shape our text-worlds of '1801' most perceptibly. However, beneath this and also tangible and linguistically distinguishable in the poem is the craft and the style of the younger poet who is re-voicing and revivifying Dorothy, along with even more subtle traces of other texts and other poetic voices. In this case, then, the palimpsest is not a layering of worlds which are all contained within the same fictional frame, as we saw in 'Evening'. Rather, Morrissey's intertextual technique extends outside the world of '1801' and interweaves textual characteristics drawn from multiple poets and multiple discourses. '1801' thus achieves a co-presence of poetic voices which was as pertinent and affecting to the non-specialist student readers of the poem as it was in my own experience of the discourse. As we have seen one of these students so astutely point out, this co-presence brings with it a consequent co-creativity through which Morrissey reveals herself as the new poet holding the old poet in her arms.

# 4 Absence

## The affirmative and the negative in language

The main focus of this book so far has been on how readers construct mental representations of poetic discourse based on what is either contained in or evoked by a text. The preceding chapters have explored how poetic worlds are built in the mind primarily from the deictic cues provided by the language of a poem. We have seen how poetic discourse can establish the spatial and temporal dimensions of a text-world and how that world can become populated with objects and enactors, also nominated by the linguistic items in a text. However, these world-building elements are only the most basic foundations of the mental representations readers create from literary language. The poetic worlds we produce in our minds become elaborated and enhanced by the additional information we bring to them, as we flesh out their linguistic skeletons with our own inferences and imagination, drawing on our personal and cultural experiences to develop uniquely detailed conceptualisations of poetry. In the last chapter, I examined how some poems make connections with other worlds built from other texts too. I extended work by Mason (2015, 2019) for the first time to account for poetic discourse and showed how textual interrelations can be made either as marked intertextual references by a poet, or through the internal connections made between texts by readers. In one form or another, though, each of the poetic analyses undertaken to this point has been interested in linguistic and conceptual *presence*. My preoccupation so far has been with how the words on the page are transformed into an imaginative architecture – how the affirmative in literary language becomes affirmative in the reading mind. There are a great many contemporary British poems, however, which operate around what is *not* made present in a text, what is lost, or what cannot be communicated through language. This chapter investigates this literary phenomenon and seeks to understand how poems that are centrally concerned with the expression of *absence* function linguistically and conceptually.

Negative constructions in language generally have been subject to a vast amount of academic attention over many decades and from a range of different disciplinary perspectives, including not only in linguistics, but in philosophy and psychology as well (see Hidalgo Downing 2000a for a particularly clear and useful overview of some of this work). Out of all of this research, Givón's (1993) function-based grammar of English has had perhaps the greatest influence on how the majority of contemporary cognitive theorists view linguistic negation. It provides the most helpful approach to understanding this feature of language for the purposes of the present book too, since it takes both a discourse-level approach to the topic and recognises the significant communicative impact negation can have during a language event.

Givón explains that negation involves a form of strong assertion in much the same way as *realis*, or indicative mood does (in sentences such as 'Ada sings and plays her guitar at the weekend', or 'Edith draws comic books in her spare time', for example). He goes on to add:

> [Negation and *realis*] thus contrast with both *presupposition* (where a proposition is not asserted but rather taken for granted) and *irrealis*, where a proposition is only weakly asserted. This is important to remember when the discussion turns to the social, interactional or affective correlates of negation [. . .] negation is a confrontational, challenging speech act. Being both a confrontational speech act and a strong assertion, it often yields problematic social consequences.
>
> (Givón 1993: 188, original emphasis)

In other words, Givón argues that a full appreciation of the potential communicative power of negation is dependent on extending our consideration of how it operates far beyond its various possible syntactic forms or its logical mechanics. Most preceding work in linguistics on the subject before Givón had taken this kind of limited formalist focus (again, see Hidalgo Downing 2000a: 23–49 for a detailed overview of this research). From Givón's broader perspective as a discourse linguist, however, the use of negation in discourse can have appreciable pragmatic and emotional effects in the discourse-world, and understanding these is essential to a comprehensive understanding of negation as a whole. This is all the more important given the often provocative or disruptive nature of the effects of negation in a social context.

Givón goes on to point out that, in cognitive terms, negation acts as a foregrounding device too. This is because it reverses the normative means through which human beings understand stasis as a conceptual background, against which descriptions of events or change stand out in our minds. This understanding stems from our visual perception: the human eye is able to focus on only one object at once, which becomes sharpened and defined against a less distinct backdrop. Furthermore, cognitive linguistics recognises that this normative, embodied perception becomes expressed through language as a contrast between a profiled linguistic *figure* and a non-profiled *ground* (see Langacker 1987, 1991 and Giovanelli and Harrison 2018: 33–59 for a useful overview). For example, in the sentence 'The little boy ran across the field', the little boy forms the centre of our conceptual attention as the subject of the sentence and is a strongly profiled figure moving against the stationary background of the field. Givón explains that there is a predominance of language in everyday communication which fits this standard conceptual structure, and that this predominance also affects how we perceive departures from it made through negation:

> The frequency skewing of events vs. non-events in our construed experience thus guarantees that events, the salient figure, are more **informative** than non-events [. . .] Negation may be viewed as a pun, a play upon the norm. It is used when – more rarely in communication – one establishes the event rather than inertia as the ground. On such a background, the non-event becomes – temporarily, locally – more salient, thus more informative.
>
> (Givón 1993: 190, original emphasis)

When negation does occur in language, therefore, it is discoursally and conceptually deviant, drawing attention both to itself as a linguistic form and to the non-events it describes.

Givón identifies three main types of linguistic negation in English (1993: 202–3). The first of these, 'syntactic negation', he claims is the most widespread and involves syntactic patterns using 'not', 'no' and 'never' (for example, in sentences such as 'John didn't catch the bus', or 'There are no teachers in the classroom'). In the second type of negation, 'morphological negation', affixes such as 'un-', 'dis-' and 'anti-' (for example, in 'un-American behaviour' or 'I disbelieve her story') are used to reverse the affirmative. Finally, Givón argues that there are words which, although they may be presented in an affirmative syntactic form, are 'inherently negative' by their semantic nature, among which he lists adjectives such as 'sad' and 'absent'. This final category is a particularly interesting one, since it would seem to be subjective to a considerable extent and sometimes involve conflicting dimensions of negativity. McLoughlin (2013: 220) notes, for instance, that the word 'bald' is inherently negative, since it describes a lack of something – in this case, hair. However, he goes on to argue that this lack, although essential to the meaning of the word 'bald', may only carry negative social connotations for some speakers, whereas others might attach more positive evaluation and emotion to baldness.

Negation has received a considerable amount of attention from a Text World Theory perspective to date, too, with theorists in this field being in broad agreement with Givón over the essentially foregrounding effects of negative constructions of all types (see Hidalgo Downing 2002 and 2000a for a comprehensive account). Negation is seen from a text-world point of view as calling to mind the world-building and function-advancing components of a mental representation in order for them to then be negated (for a wider discussion, see Giora et al. 2004; Hasson and Glucksberg 2006; Tottie 1982; Werth 1999). It also acts to defeat discourse-world expectations and generate implicature as a result. Echoing Givón's arguments along a similar line, Nahajec (2009) insists that a full consideration of the communicative scope of negation is essential to understanding its broad-ranging pragmatic effects:

> in order to deny a prior proposition, implicit or explicit, we have to conceptualize or create a mental representation of what is being denied. Negation then is essentially context dependent; in order to understand a negated proposition, a reader or hearer must cognitively process both the semantic content of the proposition, and also its context of use; both the local context of the preceding text and the larger context of the text's production including the social and cultural knowledge shared by writer and reader [. . .] As such, negated propositions can be viewed as bearing an asymmetrical relationship with positive propositions; prior expectations, both explicit and implicit, trigger more meaning than is available in the semantic content alone.
>
> (Nahajec 2009: 110)

So, when conceptualising a negated sentence such as 'The little boy did not run across the field', the reader or hearer must first mentally represent an affirmative situation in which the little boy *did* run across the field, in order then to understand the reverse of that state of affairs, in which he did not. Furthermore, the sentence carries a wider set of presuppositions and implicatures which may add to its overall meaning and pragmatic impact, including, in this example, that there was some assumption in the context of the utterance that the boy either would or should run across the field. This view of negation as a complex, conceptually foregrounded, and challenging linguistic form is particularly compelling in the exploration of poetic texts and their communicative potentiality. Indeed, negation in poetic discourse especially has been of great interest to text-world theorists who have chosen to focus on this aspect of language (see, for example, Hidalgo Downing 2000a, 2000b, 2002; Gavins 2013, 2014; Gavins and Stockwell 2012; Giovanelli 2013; McLoughlin 2013; Nahajec 2009). As McLoughlin argues, the ability of negation to construct conflicting text-worlds in the minds of readers and to signify beyond the semantic confines of the text 'allows it significant power as a poetic trope' (2013: 220).

## Poetic negation in the mind

As I have previously discussed elsewhere (Gavins 2016), in literary criticism and theology, poetic texts which centre around absence and negativity have long been recognised as belonging to a tradition of 'apophasis' (see, for example, Franke 2005; Gibbons 2007, 2008; Katz 2013; Pritchett 2014; Van Winckel 2008). Gibbons (2007) explains that this term originates from the Greek words *apo*, meaning 'away from' or 'in opposition to', and *phanai*, meaning 'to say'. It is used in literary-critical and theological scholarship to describe texts which attend to concepts that are present through their absence, or for which no adequate language exists. In a spiritual context, the indescribable nature of God is typical of the kinds of topics apophatic texts tend to focus upon. For instance, the thirteenth-century theological philosopher, Saint Thomas Aquinas, states at the beginning of his *Summa Theologiae*: 'Now, because we cannot know what God is, but rather what He is not, we have no means for considering how God is, but rather how He is not.' Gibbons goes on to point out, however, that apophasis is more complex than the simple use of negation in a given text, but is an 'impulse to proceed by indirection, evoking the impossible or not quite conceivable' (Gibbons 2007: 19). Furthermore, Gibbons argues, 'apophatic poeticism is an imagining by means of the negative, an entry into negative or empty or hidden or invisible space or paradoxically opposite points of thought and feeling' (2008: 39). Apophasis, then, in poetry and in theology, sets out to articulate that which is inarticulable, or 'that aspect of reality that is an absence', as Gibbons puts it (2007: 22). This broader notion of negativity in poetry, its aims and its functions, fits neatly with the text-world view summarised in the preceding section of this chapter, which was originally put forward by the framework's originator, Paul Werth.

In his monograph, *Text Worlds: Representing Conceptual Space in Discourse* (1999), Werth argues that a wide range of linguistic components can contribute to an overall conceptual negativity that can extend across an entire discourse. For instance, in his analysis of an extract from E. M. Forster's novel *A Passage To India*, Werth (1999: 320) includes stylistic features such as negative modification, words with negative meaning, and concessives (such as 'although', 'except for', and so on) in a list of items which he argues contribute to an overarching 'megametaphor' of negativity in the text (see also Werth 1994; as well as Giovanelli 2013 for a related discussion of nightmare worlds as negation in the poetry of Keats). In order to explore further this notion of the accumulative power of different forms of negativity in poetic discourse, this chapter will examine the poem below: 'Hearsay', by John Burnside. The text is reproduced here in full, with the kind permission of the poet:

**Hearsay**

At the back of my mind, there is always
the freight-line that no longer runs
in a powder of snow

and footprints
from that story we would tell
of the girl from the next house but one

who should have been tucked up in bed
when she went astray,
a huddle of wool in the grass, or a silver bracelet

falling for days
through an inch and a half
of ice.

Nothing I know matters more
than what never happened:
the white at the back of my mind and the legends we make

of passing cars, or switchyards in the rain,
or someone we saw by the wire
on an acre of ragweed,

*acting suspicious*, or lost, where the arc-lights decayed
and the souls of the dead went to dust
in a burrow of clinker.

My reasons for selecting this text as a case study for this chapter should be immediately apparent, since there are multiple instances of syntactic and inherent negation easily identifiable in the poem. I will also argue shortly, however, that a more subtle and nebulous undercurrent of negativity runs persistently throughout the text through other stylistic means too.

'Hearsay', as well as several of Burnside's other poems, has received previous treatment from a cognitive point of view by Mort (2014) in her study of the connections between neuroscience and poetic creativity. Mort notes other critics' tendencies to focus on the prevalence of themes of liminality in Burnside's work (e.g. Brown 2011; Richardson 2002) and on his navigation of an apparent border between absence and presence. She points out that Burnside's poems frequently concern themselves with 'lost futures', often at the expense of descriptions or explorations of the current moment. She notes that,

> the reader often gets the sense that he is more fascinated by what did not happen than what did [. . .] A John Burnside poem will often ask the reader to imagine something impossible, then extend that image through descriptions of an invented place that is in itself something of an impossibility.

(Mort 2014: 182–3)

Mort argues that the poet's focus on the liminal and the lost results in a proliferation of parallel, ghost-like worlds to be found across his poetry. She further argues that this may be connected to the mental condition of apophenia. Burnside has written extensively in his memoirs about experiencing apophenia, which causes the spontaneous perception of connections and meaningfulness between unrelated phenomena. According to Mort, the negative tropes to be found in Burnside's work are one of the means which enable him to forge multitudinous links between normally distinct worlds and images.

On the whole, Mort's concerns throughout her research lie with the poet's mind and with the possible motivations and cognitive forces behind its creative expression. My own focus, by contrast, is on the effects of such expression on readers' conceptualisations of poetic texts. With the poem 'Hearsay', I am particularly interested in the sense of unease the negation in the text generates, which I would argue bears a close resemblance to similarly unnerving uses of negativity I have identified at work in other contemporary poetry (Gavins 2013, 2016). This is a poem which defeats readerly expectations of reliable world-building multiple times over and which, I would argue, accesses an especially deep sensation of foreboding and fear as a consequence. The stylistic techniques through which this disquieting feeling is achieved will be the focus of the coming sections of this chapter.

## Compressions and negative imprints

Broken down into its component morphological parts, the title of Burnside's poem captures the entirety of human language in a single word: what is heard ('hear'), and what is said ('say'). It therefore foregrounds a theme of communication from the outset of the text. However, the everyday meaning of the word 'hearsay' is of something heard and then passed on or repeated by someone else. It is something *not* heard first-hand, something *not quite* said; a word suggesting distance between speakers and hearers, as well as the distortions, misrepresentations and untruths which become possible as a result. The title of the poem, then, may bring the concept of human communication to the forefront of the reader's mind, but it at the same time also suggests that this communication may not be wholly reliable and establishes a sense of uncertainty that goes on to run throughout the discourse. Taking a much broader perspective across the text as a whole, it is also possible to identify two main lexical fields in operation in the poem, with a clear distinction drawn between them. The first of these fields concerns the industrial and the urban and is cued by such words as 'freight-line', 'cars', 'switchyards', 'wire', 'arc-lights', 'dust' and 'clinker'. The second lexical field is that surrounding the more natural and rural elements in the poem, made present through such words as 'snow', 'grass', 'wool', 'ice', 'rain' and 'ragweed'. Notably, these are polarised and oppositional areas of human experience and their co-presence in the text fosters a tension between two realms of understanding from the very beginning.

The poem can be seen to bear some similarities with 'Evening', by Simon Armitage, which I examined in Chapter 2. Like that text, 'Hearsay' is framed as a memory from its opening line: 'At the back of my mind, there is always'. In this case, however, the poem is positioned as the remembrance of a first-person poetic persona, in contrast with the second-person, shifting and sometimes doubly-deictic address of 'Evening'. The focalising enactor of Burnside's poem thus initially appears to present a more stable perspective than in Armitage's text, with the temporal adverbial, 'always', here giving an additional persistence to the memory it describes. Even though this poetic persona remains consistent throughout the poem, however, it is important to remember that it still represents a filter between the reader and the text-worlds of 'Hearsay'. The opening line, 'At the back of my mind', positions everything else which follows in the poem within an epistemically remote modal-world, which may or may not prove to be a reliable source of world-building information. The reader is given no information with which they can anchor the voice of the poetic persona in time and space, and yet this first-person point of view forms their only access point to the text.

Furthermore, time, just as in 'Evening', has a slippery nature in 'Hearsay' too. For example, although we are told as the poem begins that there is 'always' (continuously and persistently) a freight-line, we are also immediately informed in the following line that it 'no longer runs'. The continuous aspect of this sub-clause mirrors the sense of an ongoing phenomenon established in the first line, while at the same time destabilising that main clause through the negation it contains. This negation requires the reader to re-conceptualise the world-building element of the freight-line with further information provided subsequent to its introduction in the text-world. As with all negation, an inference is triggered here which extends beyond the semantic content of the proposition: in this case, a presupposition that the freight-line used to run at some point in the past. This earlier state of affairs must be imagined first before the more recent, defunct state of the railway can be understood. What makes this line in 'Hearsay' even more interesting is that it is an example of fictive motion. These types of sentences depict a stationary situation, even though they contain a verb of movement. In 'the freight-line that no longer runs', the verb 'runs' is not actually referring to a change in state at all but is a metaphorical description in which movement is attributed to a motionless railway line. In a series of psychological experiments, Matlock (2004) showed that fictive motion is processed in the mind the same way as literal motion, with respondents taking longer to comprehend sentences that described slow movement compared with sentences that described fast movement in both fictive and literal contexts. In some ways, therefore, the line 'the freight-line that no longer runs' can be seen to enact a kind of double-negation. On top of the syntactic negation it contains, it additionally removes the object which one would normally expect to be moving in a literal description of this situation – a train – and figuratively displaces its motion onto the stationary track instead.

There are a number of other places elsewhere in the poem where the syntactic structure of the text makes it difficult to pin down the precise temporal parameters of its text-worlds and where this leads to a sense of indeterminacy and uncertainty. For instance, in 'that story we would tell' in the second line of the second stanza, the past tense of the text is given a habitual aspect, with the world-switch this creates representing not a single telling of a story at a single moment, but many tellings over an extended time and by multiple unspecified people. This is a typical example of what Fauconnier and Turner (2002) term 'compression', a cognitive phenomenon which sometimes occurs as a part of conceptual blending, which I introduced in Chapter 2. In that discussion, we saw how literary metaphors, and metaphors generally, require us to merge a series of individual input spaces into a new, integrated mental representation, which Fauconnier and Turner call a 'blended space'. Many of the vital aspects which connect the different input spaces feeding into a blend can be compressed or made more conceptually manageable as part of this process. As Turner explains:

> Compression, as a term in cognitive science, refers not specifically to shrinking something along a gradient of space or time, but instead to transforming diffuse and distended conceptual structures that are less congenial to human understanding so that they become more congenial to human understanding, better suited to our human-scale ways of thinking.
>
> (Turner 2006: 18)

Compression is not limited to figurative language alone and can form an essential component of our conceptualisation of a range of different features of everyday discourse, including the use of continuous and habitual forms of tense and aspect. For instance, if I were to say, 'I go to contemporary dance class on Mondays', this sentence can only be understood through the compression of multiple different mental representations of multiple different occurrences into a unified and human-scale conceptualisation. Similarly, in the line 'that story we would tell', it would be too complex and unwieldy for the reader to mentally represent all the diffuse instances of the telling of a story this phrase describes. Instead, this string of occurrences is compressed into a more simple and unified conceptual space which blends together all of its intrinsic parts into a workable mental representation.

While the resulting blend may be human-scale and more congenial to our understanding, as Turner puts it, it nevertheless loses its temporal specificity in the process: in blending together so many separate moments, the compressed mental space becomes temporally indistinct. Furthermore, there is in this example a strong hint of childish fictionalisation, since a story is being told multiple times over by an unspecified group of people in the past. This would seem to be an activity more likely to be undertaken by children, and the fact that the story is about 'the girl from the next house but one', too, would seem to fit with this interpretation. The suggestion of children telling tales thus underscores this repeated event with a further element of unreliability. Elsewhere in the text, the description of a silver bracelet 'falling for days', which spans the end of the third and beginning of the fourth stanzas, operates in a similar way to the compressed blend of the storytelling, since the temporal extent of this event is extended too and must be compressed in order to be comprehended. Finally, the line 'the legends we make' at the end of the fifth stanza also takes a habitual aspect, again describing many discrete instances of legend-making, which become compressed and then lose their temporal distinctness.

The opening lines of the poem achieve a particular density of negation and absence, both through the syntactic negation which occurs in 'no longer runs', and through a range of more subtle images of lost or disappearing text-world elements which start to accumulate as the poem progresses. Not only is there an obsolete freight-line in the opening stanza, but these static rails and the non-event they represent are also being covered, and presumably obscured from view, by 'a powder of snow'. We are presented at the start of the text, therefore, with a railway line which was once active, definite and visible, only to be forced to adjust our conceptualisation of this to one which is not only disused, but is also just a faintly discernible outline underneath a layer of snow. In the next line of the poem, there are 'footprints' too, adding to the memory world in which we are situated as readers another detail which is not, strictly speaking, a solid text-world presence either. Footprints in snow are not objects or entities in themselves but rather a residual marker of the feet that made them and are now gone. They are an empty outline, a physical and conceptual imprint, or an indicator of what was present and moving in the world and now is not. Furthermore, in the second line of the second stanza, we realise that these footprints are not actually part of the world of the disused freight-line at all and may not in fact be made in the snow covering its rails. They are 'from that story we would tell', and therefore a component of a different world entirely, a world which we have seen is temporally compressed and depicts a recurrent childhood act of storytelling. The deixis through which the story itself is positioned here is also worth noting, since the demonstrative in 'that story' seems to suggest not only a narrative that is habitually and repeatedly told, but one that is also known and familiar to the reader as well as the poetic persona. Of course, the reader is not actually party to the story at all, nor are its contents revealed at any later point in the poem. There is an additional sense in this line, then, of something which, if it is not being deliberately withheld, is at least not being fully shared. The defeat of discourse-world expectations which the use of negation brings with it, in Nahajec's (2009) terms, is thus echoed in a similarly defeated expectation of shared knowledge here.

Images of loss and absence and the negative conceptual imprints they leave behind them continue to proliferate in 'Hearsay' through the third stanza. In these lines, we are given more details of the story which was repeatedly told at indistinct points in the past. This creates a world, as I have noted, which is embedded in the memory world that opened the poem, as we are told that the story was 'of the girl from the next house but one / who should have been tucked up in bed / when she went astray'. Here, an interesting image of something missing, or at least not fully present in the text-world, is once again created with the image of 'the next house but one'. This phrase constructs a representation of three buildings. The house in which the narrator was located at the time the story was told and the house in which 'the girl' lived are the two most obvious and easily conceptualised of these. There is a third building nominated by the phrase, however – the house which existed between them and which is suggested here only as a minimally detailed space between two more concrete objects ('but one'). It is also worth noting that this description places the girl herself at an exaggerated physical remove from the deictic centre from which the poem is being narrated: she is not from the same environment as the poetic persona, nor from the house next door, but from the house next door to that one.

This stanza also contains a deontic modal-world, which becomes embedded again in the world of the childhood story. We are told that the girl from the next house but one 'should have been tucked up in bed', a description which positions the situation in which that was the case as expected or desired, and which carries a strong moralistic overtone. Ultimately, however, it is a situation which is remote and remains unrealised. Interestingly, three further absences occur as a result of this modal-world-building. First of all, the modal auxiliary 'should' reflects, as does all modalised language, the perspective or attitude of a particular speaker. However, this speaker is not explicitly named in the poem. It is not made clear whose opinion is being expressed here and a number of possibilities are equally imaginable and plausible: the first-person poetic persona, for example; the girls' parents; the other children telling the story; the police investigating the girl's disappearance; or the press reporting it could all have expressed this sentiment potentially. Since none of these sources is specified, however, they exist only as a ghostly set of possible voices, inferred and almost present in the text-world, but never fully realised and assigned responsibility for this use of modality. The second absence which results from the use of the deontic modal auxiliary 'should' is the girl herself, who exists as an enactor only in the remote world this line of the poem builds and only temporarily: she 'should have been tucked up in bed', but is not. The inherent negation in the word 'astray' in the next line reverses the state of affairs depicted in the deontic modal-world, removing the girl from her bed and from all the other worlds of the poem entirely. Once again, the negativity in this part of the poem acts to defeat expectations that have been established elsewhere in the discourse: a world is initially constructed containing an enactor of the girl in a specific spatial location, but this world is then immediately negated and its enactor becomes permanently lost, since where she 'went astray' to is never confirmed. Finally, the people who should have been responsible for the action of tucking the girl up in bed are also obscured or removed. This is a passive construction in which these agents – her parents presumably – have been deleted. Thus, the girl and her parents become ghostly presences, further imprints in the worlds of the poem, in much the same way as the indistinguishable multiple voices elsewhere in the text who may or may not have been responsible for commenting on her whereabouts.

The two images which close the third stanza and move into the fourth are also worth examining as further examples of the almost undetectable in 'Hearsay'. Both of the world-building elements – 'a huddle of wool' and 'a silver bracelet' – here replicate the texture and appearance of their surroundings, the first being located 'in the grass' and the second 'falling for days / through an inch and a half / of ice'. Their presence in the poem is therefore also as lost things, as figures which are practically impossible to spot against their conceptual backgrounds – the strands of wool matching the tangle of the grass and the silver of the bracelet echoing the translucence of the ice. The second of these two images is impossible to conceptualise at all under a literal interpretation too. These lines makes sense only as a metaphor for the melting of ice, causing an imperceptible downward movement of the bracelet over an extended period of time. This metaphor also echoes other images of melting which form a coherent and cohering strand across the text, with the snow covering the freight-line, the footprints, the ice, and later 'the white at the back of my mind' all emphasising a feeling of transience and impermanence that permeates the poem.

Perhaps the most syntactically complex use of negation which exists in 'Hearsay', however, occurs at the start of the fifth stanza in the two lines, 'Nothing I know matters more / than what never happened'. The first part of this construction, 'Nothing I know', creates a negated epistemic modal-world, in which it impossible for the reader to conceptualise what *is* known by the poetic persona. This nothingness is nevertheless foregrounded in this sentence, though, since it takes subject position in the construction and remains the focus of the rest of these lines, in spite of its intangible and undefinable nature. It is then compared with 'what never happened', which doubly defeats any attempt at concrete world-building and carries with it a weight of pragmatic significance in the process. The past tense here creates a world-switch to an earlier time-zone. However, this world is another negated one in which an undefined 'what' is not happening. In this way, two consecutive worlds are produced in the poem which contain nothing and cannot be mentally represented.

Even though, as I noted at the start of this analysis, the focaliser of 'Hearsay' is a consistent first-person poetic persona, this does not mean that the world-building process is any more straightforward for the reader of this text than it is in the slippage that occurs between addressees that we saw in 'Evening' in Chapter 2. The text-world enactor who forms the reader's only access to the worlds of 'Hearsay' appears to be withholding information in various places, failing to provide the affirmative deictic detail needed for us to build a stable world of what is known to them, what may have happened in the past, and thus what matters to them now. Even knowledge and understanding, therefore, become obscured and unattainable items in Burnside's text.

## Estranging unreliability, occlusion and neglect

The reliability of the poetic persona as a source of world-building information is brought further into doubt in the final line of the fifth stanza. The phrase 'the white at the back of my mind' echoes closely the first line of the poem, 'At the back of my mind', which established the world of the text as recalled memory in the first place. By this point in the poem, however, that memory appears to have become further obscured or hazy. I have already noted above that the imagery of this line is reminiscent of the images of snow and ice that appear elsewhere in the text and there is a suggestion, perhaps, of a memory becoming clouded or being concealed here in much the same way as the disued freight-line becomes covered by snow in the opening stanza. Indeed, 'the white at the back of my mind' could be interpreted as an anaphoric reference back to the same image which opens the poem, but this time with most of its finer details removed and only the whiteness of the snow remaining. Furthermore, in this stanza the stories from earlier in the poem are also echoed again, but they have shifted now to 'the legends we make'. This shift is a significant one, since 'legends' carry a greater suggestion of implausibility than a 'story', adding to the overall drift of unreliability that takes places across the entirety of the poem.

As 'Hearsay' progresses, then, there is a growing sense of the potential instability and untrustworthiness of the worlds the poem is building, worlds which are constructed as fading memories, or embedded stories and legends. Alongside this, many of the text-world elements in the discourse are transient or difficult to conceptualise. They either go missing entirely, like the girl from the next house but one, or they are in the process of melting, like the snow and ice, or they exist as barely detectable imprints against their conceptual ground, like the wool, the bracelet, the footprints and the ghostly voices expressing opinion on the whereabouts of the girl. We have also seen suggestions that the first-person poetic persona is withholding information from the reader which might help them to create a more stable mental representation of the text – some confirmation of who thinks the girl 'should have been tucked up in bed', for example, or a more detailed explanation of 'that story' which is presented as known and familiar to an audience that has had no prior encounter with it.

In Chapter 1 of this book, I discussed how some poems which contain elements of unreliability such as these can nevertheless establish and maintain a close bond with their readers. In that chapter, I adapted Phelan's (2007) notion of 'bonding unreliability' in narrative fiction to explain how Jo Bell's poem, 'Crates', positions its audience in such a way as to encourage them to participate willingly in the poem's meta-textual games. In 'Hearsay', by contrast, no such encouragement is given. Instead, a series of accumulating signs indicate that the poetic persona may be under-reporting or misreporting facts, without this being mitigated by other techniques, such as the inclusive direct address contained in 'Crates'. This sort of unreliability would appear to fit more closely with Phelan's notion of 'estranging unreliability' which, we may recall, he describes as follows:

> in estranging unreliability, the authorial audience recognizes that adopting the narrator's perspective would mean moving far away from the implied author's, and in that sense, the adoption would be a net loss for the author–audience relationship.
>
> (Phelan 2007: 225)

In Burnside's poem, then, the distance between the narrator and the authorial audience is increased rather than reduced, as it becomes increasingly challenging for the reader to anchor the text-worlds of 'Hearsay' to stable objects, enactors, times and locations.

The estrangement of the reader from the poetic persona is made even more acute by a repeated syntactic and conceptual pattern which occurs at various points in the poem and through which individual images replace one another in turn. This pattern begins in the final line of the third stanza with the two images I have already discussed above of 'a huddle of wool' and 'a silver bracelet'. The important thing to note here, though, is that these world-builders are not linked through the additive conjunction 'and' when they appear in the poem, but through 'or'. This has the effect of presenting these two phrases as equivalent and potentially interchangeable alternatives, rather than as discrete and autonomous objects. Stockwell (2009) notes that the worlds created by a literary work can be richly detailed and ever-shifting conceptual spaces. He explains:

> [the literary text-world] consists of a number of colours, edges, forms and surface textures that are available for processing into recognis-

able and attended objects: more objects vying for attention than can be assimilated in totality, so that one interpretative configuration or another must be imposed to make sense of what is being experienced. The configuration that is actually chosen will be the product of a moment-by-moment adjustment in which certain elements in the space distract the attention of the reader and others are relatively neglected.

(Stockwell 2009: 20)

Stockwell argues that those elements in a literary text which take our attention and become our core focus can be seen as textual 'attractors', while elements which were either never prominent in the first place or have faded into the background of our perception are subject to 'neglect' (2009: 20–1). He goes on:

Neglect can be a matter primarily of readerly disengagement, and this can take the form of a reader consciously *lifting* the element out of the focused domain of awareness: there is a sense that the element is still 'there' but is on its way out of focus. Alternatively, the readerly disengagement can be more a matter of attentional *drag*, with a sense that the element is now part of the background but there is still a whiff of it in the air. Lastly, the neglect can seem to be more a matter of textual patterning, such that another focused element comes to *occlude* the previously focused figure. This occlusion can be instant for an element that is linguistically removed from the scene (for example, by negation or a verb of disappearance, death or removal), or it can be gradual, where the element simply fades away by not being mentioned for a duration of several clauses.

(Stockwell 2009: 21–2)

This dynamic process of shifting attention and neglect can be seen to be at work at various points in Burnside's poem. In the third stanza, for instance, the first image of wool in grass is occluded by the next image of the bracelet. As a consequence, the original focus of our attention (the wool) falls into perceptual neglect and eventually becomes lost to our 'domain of awareness' as Stockwell puts it, other than as a memory or vague conceptual imprint.

Crucially, as I have already pointed out earlier in this discussion, the images which are being switched between here are objects which would be difficult to see in reality and are therefore difficult to conceptualise too; one form of near imperceptibility is simply replaced by another. Furthermore, there is some ambiguity over what 'a huddle of wool in the grass' might refer to, making this even more challenging as a world-building element. I would argue that the proximity of this phrase to the mention of the girl going astray in the previous line makes an interpretation that this is a reference to the girl herself highly persuasive. From this perspective, the wool may be part of her clothing and the word 'huddle' suggests that she may be hiding in the grass. However, I would go even further to suggest that 'Hearsay' contains a number of features which sit alongside its repeated uses of negation and foregrounded themes of loss and absence to encourage a much darker reading of this part of the text. These features build up gradually and cumulatively, with each new instance impacting on how we read and respond to the next.

The specific choice of 'huddle' as the opening noun in a noun phrase describing a physical shape, for example, is an important and impactful one. If this line is indeed read as referring to the girl, then she is crouched or hunched up in a foetal-type position. There are many aspects of our discourse-world knowledge which feed into a representation such as this one, including the kinds of situations where such a position might be typical – in sleep, for example, in infancy, or in self-defence. How readers conceptualise and respond to the complete description of 'a huddle of wool' is affected by this initial lexical choice. Compare, for instance, how differently alternative descriptions of the same shape might read: 'a bunch of wool', 'a pile of wool', 'a ball of wool', and so on. As readers, we project our own experiences into this part of the text, just as we do in all others, and this particular image emphasises the youth and innocence of the girl, while at the same time inviting us to assume that she may be unconscious and in a physical position which is typically associated with a primordial response to attack. Read in this way, 'a huddle of wool' becomes another one of a series of images of fragility which populate the poem: of snow underfoot, of a young girl curled up in an attempt to protect herself, of the delicacy of a silver bracelet, of melting ice.

In the preceding lines of the poem, 'astray' as a description of the girl's whereabouts is another example of how specific micro-level lexical choices can have much wider effects on our overall macro-level interpretations of texts. This word carries additional connotations over and above its core meaning of something going missing. The *Oxford English Dictionary* gives two meanings for 'astray': '1. Out of the right way, away from the proper path, wandering'; and '2. Away from the right; in or into error or evil'. A suggestion is being made here, then, not just of someone geographically lost, but morally lost too. The application of this adverb to a young girl in Burnside's text brings a sub-text of sex and possible child abuse to the poem. Furthermore, not only has the girl gone astray from her bed, but we also have the presence of footprints in the first stanza, suggesting someone else was involved in her disappearance. The *British National Corpus* (2015) provides evidence that our typical understanding and use of 'astray' in everyday discourse is in collocation with the verb 'to lead': there are 18,703 occurrences of 'astray' in the corpus, fifty-seven of which appear in conjunction with 'led', 'lead', 'leading' or 'leads', more than twice as many as the second most frequent collocate 'gone'. On top of this, the fact that the girl features in a story which is told multiple times by those who live in her community could quite logically lead to a conclusion by this point in the text that the huddle of wool in the grass is the girl's dead body. With all of this considered, there is a much more sinister dimension to the fact that 'a huddle of wool in the grass' is an image of something difficult to spot: the possibility that this concealment may have been done deliberately by someone other than the girl. Following this interpretative line has a knock-on effect on the image of the silver bracelet too, which could also plausibly be one of the girl's possessions, either lost by her or discarded by whoever may be responsible for her death. The equivalence given to these two items through the use of the 'or' conjunction supports a view of them as two examples of the same thing too. What they would seem to be, all these features considered, is potential evidence of what happened to the girl which might be of crucial importance in a criminal investigation. However, they are items of evidence that seem to have been missed, or are likely to be missed, one of them occluding the other and then itself melting slowly away.

The same structure of occlusion and neglect is repeated in the final two stanzas of 'Hearsay' too, as 'or' is used again to link a series of otherwise disparate world-building items. In this part of the text, 'the legends we make' are fleshed out further to contain 'passing cars, or switchyards in the rain, / or someone we saw by the wire / on an acre of ragweed, / *acting suspicious*, or lost, where the arc-lights decayed'. Each of the core world-building elements which make up the individual noun phrases here – cars, switchyards, someone seen acting suspicious, or someone lost – are once again introduced into the poem as equally possible, with none of them being given greater stability or a more privileged ontological status than any other. Note, too, how the phrase 'where the arc-lights decayed' initially sets up a concept of bright and voluminous lights, only to switch these off and render them dilapidated and defunct. Furthermore, the shared and equal ontological status of each of these descriptions is one of 'legends', implausible stories, exaggerated and untrustworthy. There is also a current of movement present in the final two stanzas of the poem, which adds to the transience of these particular world-builders. Like the bracelet moving slowly through ice, the cars, for example, are 'passing'. The 'switchyards in the rain' bring with them a suggestion of travel too, being specifically a mechanism to enable choice in a railway journey between one rail and another equal possibility. What this stanza creates, then, is a series of epistemic modal-worlds – one thing, or possibly another, or possibly another – without the poetic persona responsible for their construction confirming the actual existence of any of them.

What is more, the enactor who is nominated as part of the list of serially occluding images in the final stanza – described as being 'by the wire / on an acre of ragweed, / *acting suspicious*, or lost' – is positioned within another embedded epistemic modal-world, since this person is only 'someone we saw'. It is not made wholly clear who is doing the seeing here either – whether it is the poetic persona, or whether the experiences of one of the other more ghostly figures which populate the text are being represented. The italics which mark out '*acting suspicious*' from the rest of the poem would seem to suggest that this is an instance of direct speech (Leech and Short 2007), but no speaker is given explicit responsibility for the words themselves. This phrase, of course, picks up and confirms the sinister theme introduced in the third stanza, as does the fact that the person being described here remains an unnamed and indefinite 'someone'. That 'someone', it should also be noted, seems to have been seen standing in a field ('an acre of ragweed' being the additional detail given here), which would fit with the reading I suggested a moment ago of the 'huddle of wool' referring to the girl's body abandoned in grass. It is possible too that '*acting suspicious*' could be the speech of an adult, since the phrase is one which is frequently characterised in British culture as typically used by police officers, barristers, judges, and so on. However, it is also possible that the speech belongs to a child, perhaps one among the group telling stories and legends elsewhere in the text. I would also argue that the way in which the typography here foregrounds the phrase, and separates it so clearly from the rest of the poem, gives a suggestion that the speaker is not believed. The italics not only set these words apart from the main narrating voice of the poem in terms of their appearance but, because they indicate the reported speech of a different enactor, they are also marked out in terms of their accuracy and dependability.

From a Text World Theory perspective, direct speech in literary fiction creates a world-switch (see Gavins 2007: 50 for a full explanation), most typically through a change in tense, which allows the content of someone's speech to be conceptualised separately from the main narrative. Although no change in tense occurs in this example, another enactor's words are nevertheless being represented, reflecting their deictic centre, not that of the poetic persona, and indicating their perspective and opinions. This not only shifts the spatial and temporal focus of the poem to a new text-world, but this text-world is also filtered through a new point of view. If the speaker is, in fact, a child, the style of representation in this instance can be interpreted as additionally suggesting that this child does not understand what the phrase being used means, or does not quite comprehend the significance of what they have seen. Not only that, but the assessment of the shadowy someone's behaviour the speech expresses is immediately destabilised through its occlusion in the next clause by a completely different evaluation: 'or lost'. This reading of the witnessed situation is presented as equally conceivable, equally believable, since neither of these parallel, conflicting worlds is ultimately confirmed as either true or false.

## Gestalts, fear and death

Throughout 'Hearsay', gaps and absences, both in the text-worlds of the poem and in our interpretations of them, are left by the use of various types of negation. These gaps are also left, however, through more a subtly imbued sense of something missed or missing, such as in the example of the *'acting suspicious'* direct speech I have just been examining. If we do read this moment in the poem as a child speaking, although that child may not appear to understand the importance of their words, the reader may nevertheless make inferences and suppositions to fill that void for themselves. Indeed, at each point in the poem where something is withheld, not fully formed, or not fully comprehended, an invitation is given for an interpretation or an inference to be made. The mind by its very nature finds absences of information and perception difficult to tolerate, as decades of research in Gestalt psychology has shown (see Köhler 1970 for a definitive overview of this area). Where insufficient detail is provided, human beings will instinctively complete partial representations, both visual and linguistic, with knowledge drawn from their previous physical experiences in interaction with the everyday world. For example, in his seminal work at the beginning of the twentieth century, Frederic Bartlett (1932) gave a group of North American respondents a Native American folk tale to read and remember. Asking his respondents to recall the story at longer and longer intervals of time, he found that they were most likely to remember those parts of the tale which corresponded closely to their own cultural and personal life experiences for the longest duration. Where elements of the story were forgotten, Bartlett's subjects would fill these gaps with details from more familiar stories or from their own lives. Whenever we are confronted with a void of knowledge or information, human beings will strive to fill this, most commonly completing our understanding with reference to our existing experience and knowledge.

As we have seen over the course of this chapter, 'Hearsay' is a poem which is littered with absences and which creates multiple negative spaces for the reader to fill. This is a text about a missing child, after all, which not only accesses our basic need to resolve gaps in our comprehension, but also taps into our essential nature as empathetic and curious beings to wonder where she has disappeared to, and how, and to what end. Elsewhere in the poem there are other voids and absences too, left not only by the missing girl, but by obscured objects, departed feet, melted ice, hidden evidence, fading memories, fading lights, possible interpretations discarded and replaced. Each of these is an example of a Gestalt, a partial representation which our minds instinctively seek to complete. Most importantly, the negation and overall negativity in Burnside's poem is cumulatively developed and extended across the whole text. Negation in 'Hearsay' is fundamentally apophatic in its nature, occurring not as an isolated incident or singular poetic motif, but as a coherent and repeated structure which underpins the entire discourse. I have argued elsewhere (Gavins 2016) that this kind of whole-text apophasis both causes and depends upon the interanimation of stylistic features in a literary work. Not only does apophasis build by degrees over the course of a poem,

but it draws its potency from the impact that the presence of one manifesta-
tion of negativity will have on another, and then on another, and so on.

In Burnside's text, the density of negation and of negative tropes gener-
ally is such that we are led as readers to fill in the absences contained in the
poem in particular ways. It is useful at this point to return to Givón's view of
negation, discussed at the beginning of this chapter, as a fundamentally chal-
lenging and disruptive feature of language, as something which is marked out
by its deviation from normative expression and perception and which con-
sequently foregrounds both itself and the non-events and non-occurrences
it describes. Each time negativity of some kind appears in 'Hearsay', then,
our attention is drawn to it, it defies our expectations, and it provokes us to
furnish the gaps and absences it creates using our own experiences and back-
ground knowledge. In a twenty-first-century reading context, and in interac-
tion with an unreliable and estranging poetic persona, I would argue that
those gaps and absences in Burnside's text are filled with a range of different
forms of fear: fear of the unknown, fear of something unrealised or withheld,
fear of sex and fear of death. These fears are introduced and nurtured in the
poem both through the recurrent presence of syntactic and inherent negation,
but also through the themes the text develops concurrently alongside these
features. The poem builds a tension between realms of experience, between
the urban and the rural, the past and the present. It plays on the unreli-
ability of memory and of language, and on the loss of the both the innocent
and of innocence more broadly. It is a poem narrated by an adult, looking
back on experiences in childhood which were only partially explained and
understood. It captures the 'legends' so often told to children with the aim of
keeping them safe – of missing girls and suspicious strangers –but which more
often than not only serve to spark misconception and terror.

'Hearsay', then, operates around what is known and what is unknown,
what is real and what is not, and around the gaps which exist between those
absolutes and which the human psyche instinctively seeks to bridge. It is
interesting to note, too, that as the poem moves through its exploration of
these boundaries and spaces, a shift takes place in its style of reference. In the
opening stanzas of the poem, the items which are introduced into the various
worlds of the poem predominantly take a definite article or are otherwise
specific and definite by their nature: 'my mind', 'the freight-line', 'that story',
'the girl', 'the next house but one'. The determiners which accompany these
items all assume a degree of prior knowledge on the part of the reader – they
are introduced as familiar objects and people. In the third stanza of the
poem, however, the world-builders start to lose some of this definiteness and
familiarity, as a movement takes place towards indefinite and non-specific
reference instead: 'a huddle of wool', 'a bracelet', 'days', 'an inch and a half
of ice', and eventually the more extreme intangibility of 'nothing' and 'what
never happened'. In the final two stanzas of the text, however, a further shift
back to mainly definite, specific reference occurs, with 'the white at the back

of my mind', 'the legends', 'the rain', 'the wire', 'the arc-lights' and 'the souls of the dead'. In this way, then, the poem travels from the known, through the unknown, and back to the known again. The known realm where it ends up, however, is particularly significant since 'Hearsay' closes with a focus on the greatest inevitability of all and the ultimate form of loss and absence: death.

It could be argued that death is present throughout Burnside's poem, at least in an unnamed, suggested, backgrounded form. I have discussed already how the text leads the reader towards making dark assumptions about the whereabouts and fate of the missing girl, for example, and how a sinister theme of the murder of a child is created and sustained in the text through her disappearance, the suggestion of an abandoned body, lost evidence, a suspicious figure, the inclusion of embedded legal register, and so on. By the final lines of the poem, however, the presence of death becomes more than just a vague undercurrent or a possible interpretation. In this stanza, 'the souls of the dead' are mentioned explicitly, as we are told that they 'went to dust / in a burrow of clinker'. An odd reversal seems to be taking place here in the normal human perception of the process of death and decay and the imagining of an afterlife beyond it. Instead of a physical being or remnants of a being becoming ethereal and ghostly over time, the opposite occurs in 'Hearsay': the souls of the dead become dust, rather than the other way around. Furthermore, in the closing line of the poem, that dust is located in 'a burrow of clinker'. 'Clinker' is an interesting and significant choice here, since it is itself a waste product and refers to the substances left over from industrial processes, such as the burning of coal. It is a dark and often glassy material, which is also used in sewage systems to filter human excrement. The image produced Burnside's text from this line, then, is one of discarded debris and decomposition. It is also, once again, a depiction of something almost undetectable: human dust on top of another dust-like residue, indistinguishable in the dark surrounds of a burrow. The souls of the dead thus become lost in the poem too, imperceptible and unseen against the decaying background that frames them in this line.

The whole-text apophasis of 'Hearsay' enacts a creeping, progressive loss of solidity and dependability. It takes the reader on a journey in which the foundations of communication – the 'hear/say' – are exposed as mere stories, potential distortions and untruths, as residue, human clinker. The text does not simply accumulate acts of negation and expressions of negativity either. It uses these features of language to extend its reach towards a reflection of the human condition. It presents only memories, legends and imprints, images which replace one another in turn, each one as transient and unstable as the last. As I have found in other examples of twenty-first-century apophatic poetry (Gavins 2013, 2016), what is key in Burnside's text is that individual elements of the linguistic style of the poem function interanimatively and across the entire discourse. The inclusion of syntactic negation in one line, for example, echoes the inherent negation in another, which reflects an image of decay in another, a faded memory in another, and so on and so on. Most importantly, it is the interaction of these features, not just their individual manifestations, which structures our conceptualisations of the text and our emotional responses to it. The apophatic poetics which underpin this poem, as well as many other similar contemporary texts exploring loss, absence and death, cannot be fully understood without proper consideration of the interrelationships between the individual textual features that accumulate to produce such resonantly disconcerting effects.

Furthermore, Text World Theory offers an analytical framework which is ideally suited to such a textually driven approach to understanding the inter-connectedness of the images that populate the discourse and their overall, summative conceptual effects. From a text-world perspective, it can be seen how each of the worlds which become embedded in the recounted memory of the poetic persona in 'Hearsay' are interdependent on one another and how the specific, individual forms of negation that characterise many of these worlds have a contagious effect across the whole text. 'Hearsay', then, is not a poem which simply contains multiple examples of negation and negativity, or even one which explores absence and loss as wider themes. It is a text which gives a sense of things missing, but which also embodies a much deeper sensibility of *missingness* as a tangible experience. It gives the reader, as we saw Gibbons describe it earlier in this chapter, 'entry into the negative or empty or hidden or invisible space' (Gibbons 2008: 39). Gibbons is not talking about the construction of a single, discrete mental representation here either. He is describing the phenomenon by which apophasis enables readers' access to a much broader, universal prospect on the human condition through an incremental poetic technique. In Burnside's poem specifically, not one but a multiplex of interwoven and echoic negative spaces are constructed as a sustained discoursal feature. As we inhabit these spaces as readers, as we are faced with their omissions, their insufficiencies and their obscurities, we are encouraged by other, darker dimensions of the text to fill these absences with our own experiences, our deepest vulnerabilities, our fear.

# 5 Performance

## Poetry in performance

The preceding chapters of this book have focused primarily on poetry as written text. My key purpose up to this point has been to further our understanding of the reading of poetic discourse as a solitary and internal activity. However, I acknowledged in Chapter 3 that poetry is often encountered in situations other than that of solitary reading. I made mention there of the shared experience of poetry, briefly examining the context of a live reading by a poet in front of an audience of listeners. I specifically talked about how a poet's preamble to a poem at such readings can act as a form of paratext, in Genette's (1987) terms, framing the text in a particular way and influencing its reception. I also discussed Panagiotidou's (2012) notion of 'literary stance'. Following her lead (as well as Müller-Zettelmann (2000), Novak (2011) and Wagner (1983)), I argued that the peculiarly specialist audience at a poetry reading might be exceptionally predisposed to processing complex text and to seeking out and resolving typical features of poetic discourse, such as intertextual reference. In this chapter, I will be returning to the shared experience of poetry in order to explore further how we conceptualise poetic discourse which is performed in some way.

There are a number of reasons why this is an important thing to do in a book on the cognition of contemporary poetic style. Firstly and most importantly, the performance of poetry is becoming increasingly common and increasingly popular as an art form in the twenty-first century. Live poetry is thriving in a variety of modes, most notably on the poetry slam scene, where poets normally compete with one another before a panel of judges to be chosen as the best performer. These poetic events, and many others like them, are frequently recorded and shared widely on digital platforms. The technological advancements of the last twenty years or so have, as a result, brought poetry to an audience that is much more socially and geographically diverse than it has ever been in the past. Secondly, and perhaps in part as a further consequence of the widening audience it has found over recent decades, performed poetry is becoming increasingly perceived and discussed as an important cultural phenomenon. Many of the British poets who create it – such as Caleb Femi, Kate Tempest, George the Poet and Solomon O.B – are finding growing recognition through mainstream literary awards, literary criticism and newspaper media, as well as through the numerous national and international prizes and publications dedicated to spoken word poetry. Finally, the discourse situation surrounding the performance of a poetic text is highly complex and presents significant challenges both to theories of cognition and theories of literary style; live poetry events of all kinds involve multiple participants in a dynamic and interactive setting, sharing a text which can be similarly shifting and evolving in response to its context. For all of these reasons, then, an account of contemporary poetry which does not pay attention to such a pervasive, multi-faceted and global literary phenomenon could be argued to be an incomplete one.

This is certainly not to say, however, that live poetry is an entirely new form of communication. The performance of poetic text has a long history, stretching back at least as far as the Anglo-Saxon period in the UK. Cultures all over the world have similarly strong and lengthy traditions of sharing literary discourse orally, not just in the form of poetry, but as storytelling and song as well. Nevertheless, in more recent decades, crossovers and collaborations between performance poets and musicians in various corners of the world have had a marked influence on the development and sustenance of a live poetry scene that is currently flourishing in Britain. This influence can be traced back along a number of key routes and creative movements. Perhaps most significantly for the present discussion, in the middle part of the twentieth century in the US, Beat poets such as Allen Ginsberg, Jack Kerouac and Lawrence Ferlinghetti forged close connections with many of the jazz musicians who were also composing and performing their work in 1940s and 1950s San Francisco, New York and Los Angeles. They often read their work with a jazz accompaniment, recorded with jazz musicians, and talked frequently about the influence of jazz compositional structures and rhythms on their work (see Campbell 1999; Hemmer 2006; Theado 2002). This led to the emergence of a considerable body of poetic work which was not just read with music, but which was written specifically to be performed. The impact of the Beat movement was felt strongly in the UK and the tradition of performed poetry, as a form distinct from more formal readings of poetic texts, continued to develop here through the latter half of the twentieth century. For instance, the Liverpool poets who emerged in the 1960s – Adrian Henri, Roger McGough and Brian Patten – established strong allegiances with jazz, rock and pop musicians and ultimately made way for later British spoken word artists, such as punk poet John Cooper Clarke, and dub poet Linton Kwesi Johnson.

At around the same time back in the US, a group of black poets and musicians known as The Last Poets were becoming renowned for their political poetry and rapping, and were having considerable influence on other crossover artists like Gil Scott-Heron. Scott-Heron began performing his critically acclaimed spoken word poetry, raps and melismatic soul and jazz music in the 1970s. He is now widely considered to be the father of the contemporary hip hop genre, within which the majority of contemporary rap performances are still situated, and which initially emerged from the poor, black neighbourhoods of New York. Interestingly, in a recent newspaper interview, looking back over fifty years since The Last Poets first performed together in Harlem, founding member of the group Abiodun Oyewole commented that, 'People say we started rap and hip-hop, but what we really got going is poetry. We put poetry on blast' (Bengal 2018). Bradley (2009) charts the evolution of hip hop from these earliest days and notes that, by the mid-1970s, many DJs had begun to add chant-like raps between and eventually over the top of the music they were playing. The style and delivery of these raps became increasingly complex over the years that followed. What is more, as Reeves (2008) explains, the DJs performing them again had clear links with jazz music; its often improvised, organic and syncopated style seeming once more to form a pertinent point of connection for rap artists in much the same way as it did for the Beat poets who preceded them. Hip hop DJs were also making use of a great many poetic techniques in their rapping:

> during their golden era, MCs were elevating the art of rhyme, utilizing the layered intricacy of sampled rhythms to enhance the meter of their poetry, approaching the delivery of their words like musicians and poets. With labyrinthine flows and off-rhyming techniques, this new breed of MC laced his/her lyrics with complex wordplay, titillating the ear and imagination of listeners much the way bebop pioneers intensified the riffs, solos, and chord changes of their swinging forefathers.
>
> (Reeves 2008: 67)

Rap music in the twenty-first century has a global reach. It has offered, in particular, as Reeves puts it, 'a voice to the power and pain of youth in the new sociopolitical fun house of black America' (Reeves 2008: 19) and is often recognised as a form of performed poetry in its own right. Bradley (2009: xi) argues that 'Every rap song is a poem waiting to be performed', and points out that rap artists employ many of the same rhythmic and expressive techniques as poets do in their use of metre, their manipulation of line breaks, their use of metaphor, and so on. Bradley also notes that where once poetry held a prized place in our public and private lives – commonly recited in the home, at weddings, funerals, births and festivals – it has more recently fallen into decline and comparative cultural absence. He argues that this may in part be due to contemporary poetry's increasing moves towards abstraction, which have alienated many readers and listeners. He draws the following comparison with rap music:

Rap never ignores its listeners. Quite the contrary, it aggressively asserts itself, often without invitation, upon our consciousness. Whether boomed out of a passing car, played at a sports stadium, or piped into a mall while we shop, rap is all around us. Most often, it expresses its meaning quite plainly. No expertise is required to listen. You don't need to take an introductory course or read a handbook; you don't need to watch an instructional video or follow an online tutorial. But, as with most things in life, the pleasure to be gained from rap increases exponentially with just a little studied attention.

Rap is public art, and rappers are perhaps our greatest public poets, extending a tradition of lyricism that spans continents and stretches back thousands of years. Thanks to the engines of global commerce, rap is now the most widely disseminated poetry in the history of the world. Of course, not all rap is great poetry, but collectively it has revolutionized the way our culture relates to the spoken word. Rappers at their best make the familiar unfamiliar through rhythm, rhyme, and wordplay. They refresh the language by fashioning patterned and heightened variations of everyday speech. They expand our understanding of human experience by telling stories we might not otherwise hear. The best MCs – like Rakim, Jay-Z, Tupac, and many others – deserve consideration alongside the giants of American poetry. We ignore them at our own expense.

(Bradley 2009: xiii)

Rap is thus an important creative, cultural and commercial phenomenon which makes deliberate efforts to connect with wide audiences. This is a view echoed by Pate (2010), who refuses to draw a distinction between rap and poetry at all and comments that,

Rap/poetry has become the form of expression of choice for those who stand in opposition to dominant powers throughout the world. In many ways, it works the same way poetic expression has always worked. While we think of poetry as an art form used by the elite, it is actually much more immediate and functional to the common folk.

(Pate 2010: 16)

The boundaries between rap music and a great deal of contemporary performance poetry are indeed often difficult to identify and this may be one of the main reasons why spoken word is prospering in the twenty-first century in comparison with written poetry. An ever-increasing number of poets who are part of the spoken word scenes in both the US and the UK are seeking to collaborate and associate themselves with the rap movement and its stylistic techniques. In doing so, they are both creating work which the general public finds more accessible and relevant to their everyday lives and redefining the parameters of poetic and musical expression. They are also identifying themselves with an art form which is, by its very essence, political, oppositional and highly emotionally expressive.

This chapter examines a piece of performed poetry by one of the most celebrated spoken word artists in the UK today, Kate Tempest. Tempest is a particularly interesting figure because she has been recognised equally for her poetry and her rap music. She won the Ted Hughes Award in 2013 for her work *Brand New Ancients*, which was both performed live with musical accompaniment in 2012 and published in written form the following year (Tempest 2013), while her albums *Everybody Down* and *Let Them Eat Chaos* were also both nominated for the prestigious Mercury Music Prize in 2014 and 2016 respectively. In both the style of her work and in where and how she chooses to share it, Tempest often plays with the boundaries between rap and poetry: she is equally likely to showcase her work at a music festival or on digital platforms as she is to publish a collection of written poems. She also occupies an interesting position as a British, white, gay woman who has made a considerable success of her rap music career in an environment which is still dominated by American, straight, black men and by an overarching discourse which is often hyper-masculine and hyper-heterosexual. To some extent, Tempest, like many other white rappers, could be seen to be appropriating the expressive style of a culture other than her own. In what follows, however, I hope to show how her creative output is much more complex than this and how she reshapes and redefines the cultural and stylistic boundaries of both rap and spoken word poetry through her writing and her performance. The poem I will analyse throughout the rest of this discussion is called 'End Times' and has previously only been available as a film of a live performance, which was published on YouTube in 2009 (Tempest 2009). In 2019, however, Tempest gave me her permission to transcribe the text of that performance for the purposes of this analysis, and this transcription is below.

### End Times

I can smell the thunder coming.
I can smell the rain.
Look, you're the only one I ever knew
Whose eyes could hold the flame
Without burning like the others burned.
She told me hell's to blame
And I told her, hell's a choice we make
And Blake would tell the same.

If all deities reside within,
How come I feel that presence above?
The love that unplugs the heart
And starts the floods again within me,

Drowning out the badness that I harbour
While my goodness battens down the hatches
And holds on to her partner.

She's saying 'Storm's coming'.
'Course it is.
It always is on nights like this,
'Cause the tower blocks are murmuring
And I can sense a turning wind
And I glimpse this man who isn't there
And I know that glitch for all it's worth,
Because I pass out full of madness
And I wake up drenched in thirst.
Like, give me whisky, give me beers to glug,
Just let me lose this fear
And I'll love anyone who's near
Enough to looking slightly like you.

All I'm trying to say:
Today's like all them other days.
And all I'm trying to do
Is mark it down and make it true,
To make it count for something,
'Cause I know nothing is eternal
And nothing means a thing
And nobody believes nothing,
That's why we live in all this sin,
And we mistake it for normality,
For something to attain.

My dissent sets me apart,
But today I smell that rain
Come to wash away these masks,
The marks imbedded on our weary hearts.
And this is merely metaphor,
But metaphor is flexing jaw
And getting ready for the fight.
It's come to fight with the surface world.

But we have lost our purpose,
Hurled into a furnace
Where the burn is near celestial,
Detestable outside, and yes, my chest is full
Of cider, gin and lightning
And my eyes will dim,
But the rhymes will sing in times to come.

Since I begun,
My head's been filled with end,
'Cause these people wear too many faces,
But I swear the truth will strike again.

You see, I wake up in the end times,
Curled up in the wreckage,
Thinking life will happen
Whether you dismiss it or expect it.
So look into my eyes,
You'll see your own eyes reflected.
I'm crying oceans into paragraphs
While behind our backs our shadows laugh.

We wake up in the end times,
Curled up in the wreckage,
Saying life's going to happen
Whether you dismiss it or expect it.
So let me look into your eyes
And see my own eyes reflected.
I'm crying oceans into paragraphs,
'Cause behind our backs our shadows laugh.

But look, when I'm telling rhymes I shut my eyes,
'Cause it helps me see stuff.
These words, they're like the leaves
In the bottom of the gypsy's teacup:
If you look at them right,
You might see the future in them.

See, I always knew that we were here for more
Than wash the dishes, do the cooking.
See, I'm here to speak for everyone
That never got a look in.
You know, all the ones who ain't good-looking,
The ones who hate the crooked wicked nature of the system,
For everyone who knows, fucking
Just 'cause we can't see the bars
Don't mean we aren't in prison.

I believe every soul is born blessed with true wisdom
And that life is about getting back
What was given before life.
How come we are all in these disguises hidden?
How come we sleep through life and live in dreams?
Is it 'cause we can't tell the difference?

Now, all my life people looked at me with real suspicion.
I'm like, I've got to be what I've got to be,
I'm the victim of my own condition.
And the meaning is the same
No matter which language speaks it:
The new paradigm begins
As soon as you're ready to perceive it.

And that's the real talk.
These are whirlpool words you can drown in,
But I'm so desperate for beauty
I'll turn scaffolding to mountains,
I'll turn traffic into breakers
While this illusion overtakes us.
I'm saying we need to learn to bite the hand
That bullies and berates us.
'Cause we're gonna wake up in the end times.
We're gonna be curled up in the wreckage,
Thinking, yeah, life's going to happen
Whether we dismiss it or expect it.
So let me look into your eyes
And see my own eyes reflected.
I'm crying oceans into paragraphs,
'Cause behind our backs our shadows laugh.

My aim in this chapter is to explore how the text of 'End Times' and its performance interact with and depend upon one another, producing what I believe to be a very particular type of cognitive experience. In order to follow the coming discussion, I would suggest that readers not only read the transcription of the poem above, but also watch the film of Tempest's performance of it, which is, at the time of writing, freely available here: <https://www.youtube.com/watch?v=jYMtmQ_H570>.

## The discourse-world of 'End Times'

I will not claim to provide an explanation of the cognition of *all* spoken word poetry in this chapter, nor even that of *all* Tempest's performed work. However, I will argue that the combination of the particular poetic text of 'End Times' and its performance result in an emotional experience that is heightened when compared with a solitary reading of the poem. I explained in Chapter 3 that the audiences attending live readings of poetry tend to be highly specialised and dedicated. I reflected in that chapter on my own experience of running a poetry festival for several years, where the majority of the audience were loyal returners, attending not just more than one reading within each festival, but multiple festivals year after year. The members of that audience were also predominantly white and predominantly middle class (being made up mainly of students and staff at the university, librarians, teachers and similarly professionally employed people). However, I would suggest that this audience profile pertains much more to traditional, formal 'readings' than to the live performances typical of spoken word poetry today. Audience members at readings by established poets who are known mostly for their written work fit the description well. Increasingly, however, the audiences for other kinds of live poetry are greatly diversifying.

Spoken word performances in the twenty-first century happen in a wide range of different contexts, regularly taking place not just in theatres and auditoriums, but as part of music gigs, at festivals, at political demonstrations, and more. As a result, spoken word artists are reaching an increasingly broad range of people, who are encountering their work from a variety of backgrounds and with a variety of different expectations. Furthermore, although the notion that the audience at a spoken word performance might adopt a 'literary stance' may still be accurate to an extent, it is also likely that the same audience will include many people who have little interest in written poetry, and have never attended a formal reading or indeed a poetry performance of any kind before. Their 'stance' may therefore be quite different from that, for example, of an audience listening to Sinéad Morrissey read her work at a university-based poetry event.

The audience attending a Kate Tempest poetry performance, in particular, is likely to be bringing with them a different set of expectations and assumptions from those brought by the audience at a formal reading. At least some of the people at a live performance of Tempest's poems may be viewing that situation mainly through the lens of their previous experiences of her music, rather than her poetry. The knowledge schemas they deploy in the discourse situation in order to understand both the text and its context may be drawn as much from preceding encounters with music as from their familiarity with literature. In my own admittedly limited experience of seeing Tempest perform – twice at spoken word events and once as a rapper – the audiences in both of these situations were more varied than I would normally expect to see in similar contexts. At Tempest's poetry performances, the audiences were on the whole much younger and more ethnically diverse than I have seen at the many dozens of traditional poetry readings I have attended or organised over several decades as a literary researcher. At her rap performance, there were a greater number of white people over the age of forty than I have witnessed at any other gigs over a similarly extensive history of attending rap and hip hop events. It would appear from even this narrow sample, then, that Tempest's appeal broadens the reach of both her rap and her poetry in conversely divergent ways.

In the staging and overall set-up of the video of 'End Times', there are a number of elements which play on this crossover and encourage connections to be made between Tempest's spoken word performance and a musical event of some sort. Specifically, the poem is not performed in a formal or traditionally literary environment, such as a lecture theatre or library. It takes place in what appears to be a recording studio, a location which is likely to activate the audience's musical knowledge schemas primarily – both for those viewing the film online and for those present at the time of the recording. The recording studio seems to be a relatively small space, dimly lit, and comparatively intimate and informal on the whole. From both the visual representation of the performance and from the applause at the end of it, it is possible to discern only a couple of dozen people present during the recording at most. There does not appear to be any kind of formal seating in the studio, with most audience members sitting on the floor and some perched on stairs. Tempest is also casually dressed and she is positioned, perhaps most obviously and crucially, in front of an old-fashioned radio microphone. All of these aspects of the discourse-world – which, it is worth noting, will have been deliberately chosen either by the director of the film or by Tempest herself – access areas of the audience's previous experiences which are more closely related to music than they are to literature. The video of 'End Times' is set up so that, from the very outset, the boundaries between poetry and musical performance are manipulated and blurred.

The physical setting of the film departs greatly from the sort of environment in which we would normally expect a more traditional reading to take place. Such readings tend to be much more formally arranged, with the audience kept at a significant distance from the poet who is reading. The reading itself typically also takes place behind a lectern or a stand of some kind, and often with a book or papers in hand. Tempest, by contrast, is known in her spoken word performances for memorising her work and for moving around her stage as she speaks. In the film of 'End Times', it is also worth noting that the viewer is positioned even more closely to Tempest than her live audience in the studio space. The camera angle is so close up that we seem to be 'on stage' next to the poet, seeing her only her face and shoulders from her left-hand side as she looks out to the crowd, rather than Tempest being captured in a wider, whole-body shot, representing something closer to her live audience's perspective. The video is also a one-shot with no edits and has a hand-held feel that moves slightly during the performance, all of which adds to the feeling of informality it generates.

Both in the 'End Times' video and more generally, Tempest frequently sways and pulls at her clothes or touches her body as she performs her poems. She is well known for gesturing with her hands, occasionally dancing or running across the stage, and even periodically falling to her knees. On the whole, Tempest's poetry performances tend to be dramatic and highly physical, where traditional poetry readings tend to be much more static and restrained. Furthermore, having both observed her rapping first-hand and in multiple recordings online, I would argue that Tempest tends to be less dynamic and physical in her music than in her spoken-word performances. Although she still moves around her stage and uses hand gestures when she raps, most often to mimic the beat of the music, these gestures and movements are on the whole less pronounced and exaggerated. When we compare Tempest's poetry performances with more formal poetry readings the contrast is even more stark. Where traditional readings normally include multiple material barriers between the poet and the audience – which might take the form of a lectern, a book, a raised stage, and so on – Tempest's more energetic and informal performances would seem to seek to break down these barriers and close the distance between the performer and her listeners. Having said all of this, the staging of 'End Times' in the film still bears enough of a resemblance to a poetry reading to make it recognisably a poetry performance and not a musical one. Crucially, there is not any music playing before, during or after the poem. Although they applaud and cheer at the end, the audience is silent as Tempest performs and no one appears to be moving around in the background. This means that audience members approaching this particular discourse situation with mainly their musical knowledge schemas activated are equally likely to have their expectations challenged as those approaching it with a purely literary set of assumptions in mind.

The discourse-worlds of spoken word poetry in general, then, tend to include a mixing of elements normally associated with both music and poetry, rather than a reliance on one over the other. In broad terms, spoken word performances tend to be comparatively informal language situations, so the overall set-up of 'End Times' is not out of keeping with this style. They tend to require the audience to access frames of knowledge from a mixture of genres and settings, and they also tend to break down both physical and social barriers between that audience and the performing poet. Gräbner (2011) further points out that the discourse-worlds of performance poetry are heavily embodied in nature and rely on all their participants making use of multiple different senses at once. She explains:

> the poetry performance [. . .] involves the listener and the poet on several levels of perception. In the poetry performance, rhythms simultaneously interact with body language, sound, music, tone of voice, tempo, pace, visual elements of the performance, the sound of words, and semantic meaning. I call this technique 'polysensual layering'.
>
> (Gräbner 2011: 72)

Poetry performances are thus complex and multi-sensory discourse events. When we watch Tempest perform 'End Times', for example, we are not just processing the words she speaks, but we are interpreting her body movements, her intonation and the timbre of her voice, as well as the emphasis she places on certain words and phonemes. The audience present with her at the time of the recording is also sensing the smells in the room, and the heat, movement and responses of other audience members, and so on. All of this embodied experience, which both the poet and the audience engage in simultaneously, has the potential to influence how the participants respond to the poetry being performed, and each individual layer of the polysensual situation interacts with those which surround it.

Many of the critical responses to Tempest's poetry suggest that the poly-sensual nature of her performances have a direct effect on the emotional impact of her words. In a review of Tempest's extended poem *Brand New Ancients*, for example, Isherwood states:

> While she moves casually across the stage, she often seems to be rever-berating like a tuning fork with the urgency of her telling, her arms sawing at the air in time with the propulsive rhythms of her speech, which also reflects hip hop and rap influences.
>
> (Isherwood 2014)

There are also suggestions elsewhere that, as a consequence, Tempest's poetic texts alone might lack some of the emotional power of her live delivery. McConnell, for example, says,

> While I have nothing but praise for *Brand New Ancients* as a perfor-mance piece, the published version is certainly energized by a recollec-tion of Tempest's performance. As a stand-alone poem, separated from its performative context, it easily withstands scrutiny, but is more like a libretto without its score and does not soar in the way the performance does. The rhymes can seem simplistic, the rhythms hard to capture.
>
> (McConnell 2014: 204)

Research in cognitive science would support this opinion that the affective dimension of Tempest's poems is diminished when they are encountered without her accompanying performance. Human beings depend greatly on gesture, intonation, facial expression and other contextual factors in order to determine the emotions of others and respond accordingly. The ability to attribute consciousness, wilfulness and personhood to other human beings is known in cognitive psychology as 'Theory of Mind' (see Baron-Cohen 1995; Baron-Cohen et al. 1985). It is a skill which develops gradually over time, with children under the age of five years, as well as children and adults with developmental conditions such as autism, having limited or no ability to do so.

There are two main theories in cognitive psychology about how human beings come to conclude that other people have a mind which works much the same way as their own and learn to read, understand and predict the behav-iour of others (see Carruthers and Smith 1996). The so-called 'Theory Theory of Mind' argues that individuals possess a basic theory of psychology which they use to infer other people's thoughts and feelings. Under this theory, it is suggested that human beings conduct their perspective-taking activities from a third-person perspective, developing and refining their theories of human behaviour through experience, in much the same way as a scientist would. By contrast, the more recent 'Simulation Theory of Mind' proposes that individuals anticipate and make sense of the behaviour of others by activating mental processes which, if carried into action, would produce similar responses in themselves. This theory holds that this cognitive activity is done in the first person and that we project our own mental states and responses onto other people in order to predict what they might be feeling or what they might do next. In either case, our successful reading of other human beings' minds is greatly dependent on our perceptions of their bodies and physical demeanour. Although understanding the emotions of others is not impossible without such contextual cues as movement and intonation, our capacity to do so is made far easier when we have access to these as an evidence base from which to draw our assumptions and make predictions.

In a live performance of poetry, then, the audience has much more perceptual knowledge available to them in the discourse-world than they would if they were separated from their co-participant in time and space. In solitary reading, by comparison, we must rely solely on the text itself in order to construct a mental representation of the discourse and we make inferences and assumptions based mainly on our own previous experiences, rather than based on someone else's physical appearance or behaviour. Tempest's ability to communicate her own emotions in 'End Times' and to have impact on those of her audience is evident in the comments beneath her video on the YouTube website. Among the 112 responses (at the time of writing) given by viewers of the film, comments such as, 'jesus christ, left me speechless', 'Complete Truth – Intensely beautiful, lost for words', 'Her passion – and her memory! – blow me away. What a poet! Powerful stuff', are all typical remarks. Again, in my own experiences of Tempest's performances, both as a rapper and a spoken word artist, I also have witnessed dozens of audience members being visibly moved at the end of these events. At both her poetry and rap gigs, I have seen first-hand significant numbers of people moved to tears, shaking their heads and making exclamations about the power of her work, as well as embracing fellow listeners. There is no doubt, then, that Tempest is capable of inducing strong emotional responses in her audience. However, I would argue that these responses are not solely dependent on Tempest's performance of her texts. Throughout the rest of this discussion, I aim to show that the power of 'End Times' is equally located in its stylistic techniques as it is in its live delivery and that, in fact, these two components of the discourse event are entirely co-dependent on each other.

## Conceptualising poetic text in context

In an examination of its linguistic style, the first thing to note about 'End Times' is the manner in which Tempest addresses her audience and at the same time establishes a poetic persona for herself in the poem. The text is narrated in the first person throughout and, in order to understand the significance of this, I would like to return briefly to a quotation from Novak (2011), that I first discussed in Chapter 3:

> unlike in live theatre, live poetry audiences cannot usually draw on a conventionalised distinction between a real-life actor and an easily identifiable character whose name can be listed in the programme [. . .] in live poetry the poet-performer presents him- or herself rather than representing a fictitious character [. . .] Rather than 'standing for' a fictive character as a person, the poet presents his/her own text and thus 'performs authorship' in live poetry.

> (Novak 2011: 186)

In all live poetry, then, poets present both their words and themselves. Although it is possible, of course, for someone else to read or perform a poem other than the poet who wrote it, we are especially interested in this chapter in a live event where the poet is performing their own authorship, as Novak describes above. In these situations, the audience is put in the position of perceiving both the text and a version of the poet responsible for writing that text as co-occurring representations. A strong claim to authenticity is being made in such discourse-worlds and these situations immediately establish a more intimate physical, social and emotional relationship between writer and audience than would occur in the split discourse-world of a solitary reading.

Interestingly, the first-person address Tempest's employs in her text is a typical feature of rap style too. As well as often presenting a subjective perspective, rap music also tends to be heavily narrative based, as Bradley explains:

> Rap shares most of the rest of its basic storytelling conventions with other narrative forms, poetic and otherwise. In a rap narrative, chronology usually moves from beginning to middle to end. It most often presents an initial situation followed by a sequence of events that leads to a change or reversal, culminating in a revelation of insight enabled by that reversal. It puts characters in relation to one another; for rap this usually means the first-person narrator in relation to others who sometimes are given voice as well – either through indirect quotation or through the introduction of another (or several other) MCs. Finally, it involves patterning of formal and thematic elements that support and extend the narrative action.

> (Bradley 2009: 162)

Rap often takes the form of a kind of dramatic monologue. Most importantly for the present examination of the boundaries between rap music and poetry, rappers' uses of a first-person perspective as a means of framing their narratives can be seen to enable the performance of authorship and authenticity in much the same way as occurs in live poetry. Bradley goes on to point out that the establishment of an authentic voice through the first person is one of the most central features of rap style:

> Voice in storytelling is the governing authorial intelligence of a narrative. Voice would seem to be a given in rap: the MC and speaker's voice are one and the same. We assume that MCs are rapping to us in their own voices and, as such, that what they say is true to their own experience.
>
> (Bradley 2009: 162)

Authenticity itself also commonly becomes a theme in many rap lyrics, with rappers frequently seeking to convey a 'street-conscious identity' or 'linguistic realness', as Werner (2019) puts it (see, as typical examples, 'The Real Slim Shady', by Eminem; 'I Gotcha', by Lupe Fiasco; 'What More Can I Say', by Jay-Z; 'I Am ...', by Nas; and 'DNA.', by Kendrick Lamar). Bradley notes, however, that lots of rap music is a blend of fact and fantasy, narrative and drama. Its dramatic monologue form not only allows the construction and performance of a version of self, but it also enables artists to create voices for other characters and perspectives alongside their own. As Bradley puts it, the style adopted by many contemporary rappers is frequently 'freeing them to say things they might not say in their own voice and explore territories of experience they might not otherwise visit were it not for the liberation of imaginative distance' (Bradley 2009: 165). However, even when rappers are representing other consciousnesses and narrating personae in their music, the moments at which they employ a first-person direct address to the audience nevertheless often creates an added sense of validity and credibility in their texts.

In 'End Times', we can see a very similar attempt to create authenticity and to establish the faithfulness of the poem at work both in Tempest's words and in the physical dimension of her performance. First of all, alongside the overarching first-person perspective, Tempest makes repeated reference to subjective sensual perception in the text, for example in her use of verbs such as 'smell', 'feel', 'hear', 'glimpse' and 'sense'. These representations of sensory phenomena are particularly dominant in the opening stanzas of 'End Times', so that the poem begins with a persistent foregrounding of Tempest's own embodied experience in the discourse-world. At the same time, in the video performance, Tempest's hand gestures are pronounced and eye-catching: she frequently touches her eyes and head, she holds her chest, and she closes her eyes too, as if to suggest deep immersion in the text she is reciting. Her gestures to her head are particularly repeated when she makes reference to her own senses. This is interesting when we look more closely at *how* Tempest is making use of sensory descriptions, since she does so frequently not just to communicate a physical sensation, but also to express knowledge or some degree of certainty or lack of certainty. As we saw in the opening chapter of this book, human beings often articulate their epistemic commitment to a proposition by referring to their physical perceptions in this way. As I explained in Chapter 1, the epistemic modal system in English enables the expression of all forms of knowledge, belief and opinion. It also contains a subsystem of linguistic items known as perception modality, where a speaker's epistemic commitment is communicated through reference to one of the senses, most often sight (e.g. 'I can see what you mean', or 'it's clearly working') (see Simpson 1993 for a full overview). I explained in the opening chapter too that, in all cases, such modalised items in a sentence have the effect of constructing a conceptual space that is separate from its originating world. The content of these modal-worlds, the situations they describe, are often unrealised at the time of their creation and have to be conceptualised by the hearer or reader as existing at some level of remoteness from their creator's reality (see Gavins 2007: 91–125). Many of Tempest's descriptions of her sensory experience function in this way and can be seen to have a dual purpose, where they both represent her physical sensations in the discourse-world and also express some form of epistemic attitude.

Let us examine the first example of this sort of expression in the poem in order to understand more fully how it might be conceptualised by the audience. Tempest begins 'End Times' with the lines, 'I can smell the thunder coming. / I can smell the rain'. In these two sentences, she is not just describing a perceived sensation in her immediate environment, but she is expressing her feelings of certainty that thunder and rain are approaching at the same time. Her use of the present participle 'coming' allows the audience to understand that it is not yet thundering or raining in Tempest's spatio-temporal location, but that these are imagined future situations, which may or may not eventually come into being. Alongside this, the lexical verb 'smell' is being used as a form of perception modality. This is not unusual in everyday discourse and 'smell' is most often used in idiomatic metaphorical expressions to express varying levels of epistemic commitment, for example in 'I smell a rat', or 'she smelled something fishy going on'. In this particular example, 'smell' is being used to communicate a large degree of confidence. However, it is nevertheless an expression of subjective opinion. It therefore has to be mentally represented in an epistemic modal-world which is separate from reality – a possibility only, albeit one that is framed by the speaker as highly likely to become actualised. Having said all this, the fact the verb 'smell' is uttered as part of the live performance of 'End Times', in which both the poet and her audience are co-present in the same location and at the same time, shifts the meaning of the verb considerably. For the audience in the recording studio with Tempest at the time of the filming of the poem, the lines beginning 'I can smell ...' not only represent the inner workings of the poet's mind and her confidence in what she is saying, but they also refer directly into the discourse-world they share with her. Tempest is thus grounding what is in fact merely her own opinion about a future event in a physical, actualised and communal environment. Even if the audience in the recording studio with the poet at the time of her performance cannot, in fact, smell what Tempest claims to smell, they are nevertheless likely have the experience of seeking out that sensation in their immediate situation in order to verify what she says. This has the effect of locating Tempest's text firmly within the shared reality of the performance. It not only expresses the poet's high levels of assurance in her predictions of coming thunder and rain, but it anchors them in the discourse-world level of the language event, rather than them remaining as solely imaginary text-world elements.

Overall, Tempest's epistemic commitment to the propositions which make up 'End Times' is highly positive throughout the poem and she makes frequent use of decisive or affirmative modality across the text. She says, for example, 'I know that glitch for all it's worth', in the third stanza; 'I know nothing is eternal', in the fourth; 'I swear the truth will strike again', in the sixth; 'I always knew we were here for more / Than wash the dishes, do the cooking', in the tenth; and 'I believe every soul is born blessed with true wisdom', in the eleventh. She also refers to the knowledge of other people in the tenth stanza in, 'For everyone who knows, fucking / Just 'cause we can't see the bars / Don't mean we aren't in prison', adding collective support to her own opinion in the process. It is worth noting here, too, the repeated refrain, 'look into my eyes, / you'll see your own eyes reflected', which appears first at the end of the seventh stanza, again in the modified form of, 'let me look into your eyes / And see my own eyes reflected', at the end of the eighth, and finally in its original form at the end of the entire poem. These lines are a further reference or appeal to a shared experience, suggesting a close affinity between Tempest and her audience. Interestingly, Tempest's only two uses of deontic modality in the poem, which occur in the middle of the eleventh stanza, function to strengthen her expressions of the certainty of her feelings too. She says, 'I'm like, I've got to be what I've got be, / I'm the victim of my own condition'. The repeated modal auxiliary 'got to' in this line, although deontic in nature, is actually used to communicate epistemic certainty once again – that Tempest's own sense of her state of being is so assured that it is an absolute necessity controlling her behaviour.

Tempest's use of tense in 'End Times' adds to the sense of immediacy and certainty created elsewhere in the poem. The present tense and present participles dominate the text, not just in the sensory verbs I have already mentioned, like 'smell', 'feel', 'glimpse', 'see', and so on, but also in other statements about the poet's state of mind and emotions, such as 'I'm trying to say', in the fourth stanza; 'my chest is full', in the sixth; 'I'm the victim of my own condition', in the eleventh stanza, discussed above; 'I'm crying oceans into paragraphs', in the seventh, eighth and thirteenth stanzas; and 'I'm so desperate for beauty', also in the thirteenth stanza. A picture of the wider environment surrounding the poetic persona is constructed largely in the present tense and using present participles too, with lines such as 'the tower blocks are murmuring', in the third stanza; 'we live in all this sin', in the fourth; 'the burn is near celestial', in the seventh; 'this illusion overtakes us', in the thirteenth; and 'behind our backs our shadows laugh', in the seventh, eighth and thirteenth stanzas. Similarly, the majority of actions Tempest describes herself as taking are also positioned in the present tense, for example in, 'I pass out full of madness / And I wake up drenched in thirst', in the third stanza; 'I wake up in the end times' in the seventh; 'I'm telling rhymes', in the ninth; and 'I'm saying', in the thirteenth. Overall, then, the text-world in which the poetic persona is located, her actions and her emotional responses to that world are all given a highly proximal and involving feel. Even when Tempest's frequent uses of modality produce modal-worlds which exist at some distance from the discourse-world, the overall impression she creates in the poem is one of conviction and immediacy.

This is further emphasised by repeated use of other forms of proximal deixis. There are, for example, only four occurrences of the indefinite article throughout the whole text of 'End Times', while the majority of other references are definite in nature. In just the first two stanzas, for instance, we have 'the thunder', 'the rain', 'the only one', 'the flame', 'the others', 'the same', 'the love', 'the heart', 'the floods', 'the badness' and 'the hatches', with forty-two uses of the definite article appearing in total in the poem. Elsewhere, there are multiple uses of the proximal demonstratives 'this' and 'these': 'nights like this'; 'this man', 'this fear', 'this sin', 'these masks', 'this is merely metaphor', 'these people', 'these words', 'these disguises', 'these are whirlpool words' and 'this illusion'. These features make the text-world of 'End Times' seem close up and intimate, particularly for the live audience which shares the same spatio-temporal location as Tempest herself. In both the situation of the live performance and in the split discourse-world of a later viewing of the film or reading of the poem, however, all of these stylistic techniques combine to erase the boundary between the text and the context of its performance, between the experiences and emotions of the poet and those of her co-participants.

### Addresser and addressee

Not all first-person voices, either in poetry or in rap, have a direct addressee. It is perfectly possible for a text to consist of a subjective monologue without the recipient of that narrative being made explicit by the text. 'End Times', however, does contain both a first-person poetic persona and a number of instances of second-person as well as third-person address. Interestingly, though, there are several points of slippage in the poem, where the entities being referred to by the various pronouns in 'End Times' are ambiguous and appear to shift. The second person appears for the first time in the third line of the poem with, 'Look, you're the only one I ever knew / Whose eyes could hold the flame'. This is a clear instance of horizontal second-person address, in Herman's (1994) terms, where 'you' is used to indicate a text-world enactor who exists only within the frame of the fiction. We know, as readers and listeners, that the 'you' here does not refer to us in our discourse-world environment, whether we are co-present with Tempest or not. There is an immediate shift, however, to what appears to be a dialogue between the first-person poetic voice and a third-person text-world enactor, 'she', in the sixth and seventh lines, represented as indirect speech: 'She told me hell's to blame / And I told her hell's a choice we make'. It is not made clear here whether this 'she' is the same text-world entity picked out by the second person in the preceding lines, or a different enactor altogether. Indeed, 'she' only occurs one other time in the whole poem, at the beginning of the third stanza with, 'She's saying "Storm's coming". / 'Course it is', where further ambiguity arises. Here, 'she' would appear to be an anaphoric reference back to 'my goodness' two lines earlier, where the first-person poetic persona's 'goodness' is personified as a figure that 'battens down the hatches' and 'holds on to her partner'. Tempest marks out this instance in her performance as the direct speech of an enactor by raising the pitch of her voice, swaying slightly from side to side and adding a melodic timbre to her delivery. However, the vagueness of the third-person reference to which this direct speech is attached is never resolved, since the pronoun 'she' disappears from the rest of the poem. The second-person pronoun also disappears for twenty-five lines after its first occurrence, eventually resurfacing at the end of the third stanza in, 'I'll love anyone who's near / Enough to looking slightly like you'. Once again, this is a clear horizontal reference to a text-world enactor within the frame of the narrative and with no sense of any cross-world address.

The initially restricted, horizontal nature of the second-person pronouns in 'End Times' changes significantly around the middle of the poem and this shift seems to be connected to a co-occurrence of an increased number of first-person plural pronouns from this point onwards. Instances of 'we' become markedly more frequent in the text in its second half, with only three uses of this pronoun appearing in the first seven stanzas, compared with ten in the last six stanzas. As 'End Times' progresses, Tempest becomes increasingly inclusive in her chosen address forms and 'we' is used collectively to refer to the poet herself, her audience and the rest of humanity in examples such as, 'we can't see the bars', 'we are all in these disguises hidden', 'we sleep through life and live in dreams', as well as repeated variations of the line, 'we wake up in the end times'. Tempest is not just including her immediate co-participants in the discourse-world of her performance in these instances, but she is describing various states of automatised apathy which she perceives across a much larger general population and which also pertain to participants in a split discourse-world of a solitary reading or viewing of the poem. Interestingly, when 'you' reappears at around the same point in the text, it too takes on a broadened inclusivity. In the first line of the sixth stanza, 'you' is used for the first time as a discourse marker in, 'You see, I wake up in the end times'. In this form, 'you' is no longer confined to a within-frame horizontal reference but refers beyond the text-world and into the discourse-world. Discourse markers are commonly seen in linguistics as a means of aiding the flow of a conversation and managing its structure. However, markers which use the second person in this way – 'you see', but also 'you know' – are particularly noteworthy because they foreground the presence and role of the speaker in the discourse, while at the same time making a direct address to their listener. Such markers by their nature make us more aware of the various participants' roles in the discourse. This is yet another technique, then, by which Tempest grounds her poem in the discourse-world and also makes her own subjectivity one of its key points of focus. 'You see' acts to continue the overall informality of the poem, too, and to emphasise its status as a piece of spoken discourse, rather than written text.

Throughout the second half of the poem, 'you' continues to be doubly deictic in nature (see Herman 1994, and Chapters 1 and 2 of this book), although its precise meaning shifts at various points. It is used both to refer to a variety of different text-world entities and often to reach into the discourse-world at the same time. For example, following the discourse marker 'You see' at the beginning of the seventh stanza, the lines, 'life will happen / Whether you dismiss it or expect it' contain another second-person pronoun which seems to address the audience directly in the discourse-world. The 'you' here can equally as easily be read as referring to Tempest herself, though, since this part of the poem is describing her internal thought processes on waking. There is then an imperative verb construction in the fifth line of this stanza, 'So look into my eyes', which makes an unmistakable direct address to the audience. The second-person pronoun which follows this in, 'You'll see your own eyes reflected', shifts in meaning once more. It not only continues the discourse-world reach of 'you', but it could also plausibly be interpreted as including the text-world enactor 'you' who was picked out in the opening lines of the poem (in 'Look, you're the only one I ever knew'). It is worth noting, too, how 'you'll see' here again grounds the poem in embodied experience. Once more, this phrase describes both a possible future sensory perception on the part of 'you' and simultaneously expresses a strong epistemic commitment from Tempest.

Not only is the second person used in a shifting but highly involving way across the text of 'End Times', but the relationships that are constructed between the first-person poetic persona and all of the different text-world enactors in the poem are interesting too. Tempest sticks to a first-person narrating voice throughout, as I have already pointed out. Alongside this, however, she also continuously foregrounds the textuality of the poem, her own performance of it and her role as a writer or 'teller' more broadly. In all of her live work, in both rap and poetry contexts, Tempest describes her performances as 'tellings', and there are multiple references to the acts of writing or telling over the course of 'End Times'. These acts are presented as either being done by Tempest herself or by other enactors in the poem. In the first stanza alone, there are three examples: 'She told me'; 'I told her'; and 'Blake would tell the same'. Later on in the text, further mentions are made of speaking, telling, writing and saying: 'she's saying', in the third stanza; 'All I'm trying to say' and 'all I'm trying to do / Is mark it down and make it true', in the fourth stanza; 'the rhymes will sing in times to come', in the sixth stanza; 'when I'm telling rhymes', in the ninth stanza; 'I'm here to speak for everyone', in the tenth stanza; and 'I'm saying', in the final stanza. Elsewhere, there are several other metaphorical descriptions either of the text of 'End Times' itself, or of Tempest's creative processes. For instance, the line 'I'm crying oceans into paragraphs' is repeated three times across the text, along with similarly figurative depictions of writing in, 'I'm so desperate for beauty / I'll turn scaffolding to mountains, / I'll traffic into breakers', which occur in the final lines. In the fifth stanza, Tempest also draws attention to her own words in, 'this is merely metaphor / But metaphor is flexing jaw', as well as later on in the text at the end of the eleventh stanza in, 'the meaning is the same / No matter which language speaks it', and at the beginning of the final stanza with, 'And that's the real talk. / These are whirlpool words'. Taken all together, these references add up to a heavy meta-textual foregrounding of both the processes and products of literary communication.

Tempest thus establishes a clear position for herself as a poet in the discourse-world, but also carries this across as a defining characteristic of the enactor she creates of herself in the text-world. She not only foregrounds her own emotions and embodied experiences through the physical elements of her performance and her frequent references to her perceptions, but she also produces representations of herself, her writing and her telling at the text-world level. The whole poem centres around her visions of the future of humankind and is full of biblical references to the end of the world. There are mentions of 'hell', 'the floods', 'sin', 'a furnace', 'the burn' which is 'near celestial', 'the new paradigm', and many others, as well as the obvious and repeated 'end times', which also form the title of the text. This prominent biblical register elevates Tempest's status yet further, in the text-world at least, from that of a writer and performer to that of prophet. The prophetic nature of Tempest's words is further emphasised by the parallels she draws between herself and William Blake in the opening lines of the poem. She claims 'hell's a choice we make / And Blake would tell the same', making an intertextual reference, most likely to Blake's (1793) *The Marriage of Heaven and Hell*, and at the same time appearing to position herself on an equal footing to the eighteenth-century visionary. From the outset, then, Tempest institutes a role for her enactor in the text-world as a seer and a role for herself in the discourse-world as a preacher to her audience about what she sees. As the poem continues and the dominant form of address in the text shifts from second to third person, this becomes even more marked. The 'we' pronoun she uses in 'we live in all this sin' and 'we mistake it for normality', in the fourth stanza, 'we have lost our purpose', in the fifth stanza, 'we wake up in the end times', in the eighth stanza, and so on, becomes almost congregational in nature, both through its repetition and its position within the wider biblical theme and register that runs throughout the poem.

However, the barriers of power and authority which one might normally expect to exist between a preacher and a religious gathering are broken down in Tempest's work in many of the same ways that she reduces the formality and distance normally found in traditional poetry readings. She achieves this firstly through her focus on and assumptions about shared experiences and opinions, for example in, 'we can't see the bars', in the tenth stanza, and again in, 'we can't tell the difference', in the eleventh. At the same time, as we have already seen, Tempest creates multiple representations of her subjective, embodied, sensory perceptions and makes repeated use of sensual language, echoing and foregrounding this in the bodily movements of her performance. These techniques combined act to narrow both the epistemological and emotional gap between her and her co-participants in the discourse-world environment in which they are co-located.

By contrast, other entities populate the text-world who are positioned outside the exclusive, intimate relationship Tempest establishes with her audience. These enactors are often nominated using under-specific references too, for example in, 'the others', in the first stanza; 'this man' and 'anyone', in the third stanza; 'these people', in the sixth stanza; and 'shadows', in the seventh, eighth and ninth stanzas. Tempest privileges her audience over these other people, who are presented as lost or unenlightened by comparison with them and with Tempest herself. This privileged position is most acutely felt in the face-to-face discourse-world of Tempest's performance, in which her co-participants are able to identify themselves easily as included within her repeated use of the 'we' pronoun, rather than as one of 'the others' who exist separately from it. The in-group and out-group constructions Tempest creates through her choice of reference, however, also hold in a split discourse-world of a solitary reading. Here, too, the reader is positioned as belonging within an exclusive relationship with the poet, while other, less enlightened people are positioned outside this. This distinction is foregrounded throughout the poem, not only in the instances of inclusive address Tempest employs, but also in the predominant present tense and the repeated proximal deixis which appear across 'End Times', both of which add to the immediacy and intimacy of the text. For instance, I have already pointed out how the majority of nouns in the poem take the definite article and how multiple uses of proximal demonstratives, such as 'this' and 'these' occur alongside them to make the text-world elements they refer to appear close up and current. By comparison, the text-world enactors who are presented as not sharing the perceptions and opinions that 'we' do are positioned at a distance: the 'shadows', for example, laugh 'behind our backs', and the people who 'looked at me with real suspicion' exist in a world-switch situated in the past.

Furthermore, Tempest makes repeated use of negation as she pre-empts and dismisses any potential level of disbelief in her prophecies. In the fourth stanza, she lists a series of opinions which she 'knows' about, framing lines six to nine within an epistemic modal-world, which again expresses her strong levels of confidence: ''Cause I know nothing is eternal / And nothing means a thing / And nobody believes nothing, / That's why we live in all this sin'. These lines also function to create a kind of dialogue between Tempest and an imagined and distant, sceptical interlocutor. As we saw in the analysis of John Burnside's 'Hearsay' in Chapter 4, negation always rests on some form of presupposition and acts to defeat the expectations that accompany it. Each instance of negation here presupposes that a suggestion has been made or could be made that some things are eternal, some things mean something and some people believe some things. The effect is to create a sense that Tempest herself is the one being accused of making such suggestions, an accusation which she is refuting by saying she knows the opposite, negated version to be the case. Line eight of this stanza is also doubly negated, making its rejection of the presupposed counter-argument even more emphatic. On the whole, this stanza further accentuates Tempest's confidence in her view of the world, positioning it as holding water in spite of the potential rejoinders these lines acknowledge and reject.

By contrast with the distant, excluded enactors Tempest creates and the assumed counter-opinions that she negates, the environment and beliefs she constructs as shared between herself and her audience are far more positive, real and proximal. Furthermore, Tempest ensures that the text-worlds she builds which present her vision of humanity are highly cohesive in nature. She uses several stylistic devices which are also typical in rap music in order to achieve this, and chief among them is her use of rhyme. 'End Times' contains a notable density of rhyming techniques, including a number of examples of easily noticeable end-rhymes, for example in 'flame', 'blame' and 'same' in the first stanza. Far more common in the text than these quite obvious rhymes, however, are the numerous instances of internal rhyme which run throughout the poem, alongside multiple occurrences of even more subtly constructed sound patterning. As a typical example, let us look in detail at the sixth stanza of the poem, in particular:

> But we have lost our purpose,
> Hurled into a furnace
> Where the burn is near celestial,

Detestable outside, and yes, my chest is full
Of cider, gin and lightning
And my eyes will dim,
But the rhymes will sing in times to come.
Since I begun,
My head's been filled with end,
'Cause these people wear too many faces,
But I swear the truth will strike again.

This stanza is particularly densely packed with both end-rhymes and internal sound patterning. In the first three lines, for instance, Tempest rhymes the /ɜː/ in 'purpose', 'hurled', 'furnace' and 'burn'. In the third and fourth lines, she rhymes the /e/ in 'celestial', 'detestable', 'yes' and 'chest', while also creating a near end-rhyme with the /ə/ in 'celestial' and the /ʊ/ in 'full'. She repeats an /aɪ/ sound across lines four, five, six, seven, eight and eleven with 'outside', 'cider', 'lightning', 'eyes', 'rhymes', 'times', 'I' and 'strike'. She also creates another near end-rhyme in lines seven and eight with 'come' and 'begun'. Similarly dense rhyming can be found throughout the poem, which seems to rely more heavily on this cohesive device than it does on regular metre as a form of parallelism. This is not to say that there are no metrical patterns to be found at all in Tempest's text, but rather that she prioritises rhyme over metre in both her writing and her telling and that the rhythm of her performance acts in combination with other features of the poem.

On the whole, Tempest sustains a highly conversational metre which shifts and changes frequently throughout 'End Times'. For example, the poem begins with a quite simplistic trochaic tetrameter in the first line, 'I can smell the thunder coming'. The second line is also trochaic and Tempest uses 'Look' as a run-on into the beginning of the third line to close the last of the three metrical feet here. However, elsewhere in this stanza she de-emphasises a number of beats at the ends of lines which might normally be stressed to complete a metrical foot, with the effect of making her delivery feel less poetic and more informal. This happens at the end of the fourth line with 'flame', at the end of the sixth line with 'blame' and at the end of the seventh line with 'make'. Indeed, Tempest's apparent resistance to creating too regular a rhythm in her performance is so prominent and conspicuous that it underlines the artifice of transcribing her poem into a written form in the first place and the limitations that arise from my attempts to do so.

Furthermore, I would argue that Tempest's efforts to transcend the conventions of written poetry and to free her poem from the rhythmical constraints of the metrical line is highly reminiscent of rap style. As Bradley (2009) explains, although beat is of paramount importance in rap music, it is seen as only one component of an overall 'flow'. The achievement of a good flow is prized above all else in rap performance, and it is produced through the fine balancing of rhythm with other stylistic features, such as tempo, accent, pitch, intonation and – most crucially – rhyme:

> Part of the synergy of beats and rhymes is that they protect each other from their own potential excesses. Beats without voices soon become monotonous. Rhymes in isolation expose the frailty of the human voice and the fallibility of the rapper's vocal rhythms. Together, however, beats and rhymes find strength: the voice gives the beat humanity and variety; the beat gives the rhyme a reason for being and a margin for error. This essential relationship is rap's greatest contribution to the rhythm of poetry: the dual rhythmic relationship.
>
> (Bradley 2009: 7)

Bradley goes on to argue that rap's dual rhythmic relationship liberates rappers to produce innovative syncopations and 'an organic unity of rhythm that is more powerful than most literary verses can likely achieve' (Bradley 2009: 7). He also points out that the metre chosen by the majority of rappers is accentual, with stress being placed predominantly on those words that the rap artist deems as most significant in the overall meaning of the piece:

> it is most useful to distinguish between syllables that an MC accords with significant stress and those delivered with less inflection. As a general rule, the more significant the word (or part of a word), the more stress it receives [. . .] The heightened prominence of one syllable in rela-tion to others can be rendered by any number of means, from volume to pitch to length of stress.
>
> (Bradley 2009: 10–11)

Rather than follow conventionally poetic metrical patterns, then, Tempest pursues more accentual and syncopated rhythms in her delivery of 'End Times'. She puts stress on a variety of words which might not necessarily have taken them in a more traditional reading of her poem as a written text, creating a more organic and rap-like flow. She does this in a range of ways. For example, in the fifth stanza of the poem she both places added stress and elongates her pronunciation of the end syllables in three of the first four lines: 'apart', 'masks' and 'heart'. She also picks out 'marks' in these lines in the same way, creating particular cohesion between the /ɑː/ sounds here and making her internal rhyming more noticeable. Elsewhere, however, she creates a more insistent and repetitive effect, for instance where she accentu-ates every word of the last two lines of the eleventh stanza: 'The new para-digm begins / As soon as you're ready to perceive it'. In this case, Tempest's foregrounding is connected more obviously to the overall meaning of the text, as she drives home the core prophetic message of her poem by raising the volume of her voice here and placing equal stress on each word. Once again, her gestures at this point in her performance echo and emphasise her words, as she raises her right hand and makes a repeated downward gesture on each beat, bending her knees and moving her whole body in the same rhythm.

## Poetic performance and the extended mind

Although 'End Times' opens with a regular trochaic metre in its first few lines, rather than remaining constrained by the structure of the poetic line or by the artifice of formal poetic metre, Tempest's flow quickly becomes syncopated, fluid and connected more closely to the body and to the expression of embodied experience than it is to the restrictions of text. Interestingly, recent empirical studies in the cognition of music (Keller and Schubert 2011) have shown that syncopation, which tends on the whole to violate listeners' expectations of where beats should fall in a musical performance, is both perceived as more complex and enjoyed more by audiences. More specifically, music which progressed from simple rhythms to more complicated syncopated beats caused a stronger emotional response in the participants in Keller and Schubert's study than music which did not progress or which took a reverse structure of complexity. Keller and Schubert suggest that syncopation may therefore enhance the processes of internal sensorimotor simulation and online prediction that accompany music listening, and may promote aesthetic enjoyment as a result (see also Kornysheva et al. 2010). They additionally suggest that, when a piece of music begins with a simple rhythmical form, this accesses listeners' existing schematisations of musical structure, which are then challenged or subverted by any movement to more intricate arrangements. Much the same progression occurs in Tempest's performance of 'End Times', which begins comparatively simply before its rhythmical structure deviates from regular metre and Tempest begins using an accentuated metre, underscoring and dramatising the words she chooses to foreground with accompanying bodily movements and gestures.

In employing a style of delivery which is associated more with rap music than with poetry, Tempest preserves the integrity of 'End Times' as a performed, spoken discourse. Alongside this, she retains a consistent focus throughout the poem on her embodied, sensory experience and repeatedly foregrounds of her own creative processes and her position as a teller in the discourse-world. She works to break down the physical barriers of traditional poetry readings and reduce the emotional distance between herself and her audience as well, using proximal deixis and inclusive address as key techniques towards this end. The overarching effect is one by which the poem is not conceptualised by her listeners as a reading or even a telling, but as a shared, embodied and emotional experience. Tempest grounds her words so securely and inescapably in the discourse-world context in which she performs them, tying them particularly to her own bodily movements, that this context becomes an integral and fundamental component in their cognition. From a cognitive science perspective, this could be seen as an example of what has become known in recent years as 'the extended mind' theory of human cognitive processing (see Clark 2008; Clark and Chalmers 1998) in an approach to the mind which can be broadly conceived as 'externalism' (see also Rowlands 2003, 2010). Establishing the extended mind theory as directly opposed to what he calls a 'brainbound' alternative, Clark explains:

> Maximally opposed to BRAINBOUND is a view according to which thinking and cognizing may (at times) depend directly and noninstrumentally upon the ongoing work of the body and/or the extraorganismic environment. Call this model EXTENDED. According to EXTENDED, the actual local operations that realize certain forms of human cognizing include inextricable tangles of feedback, feed-forward, and feed-around loops: loops that promiscuously criss-cross the boundaries of brain, body, and world. The local mechanisms of mind, if this is correct, are not all in the head. Cognition leaks out into body and world.
>
> (Clark 2008: xxvviii)

In other words, then, cognition is essentially and inextricably dependent on the wider physical environment in which human beings exist and interact. Not only do our minds make almost continual use of and refer to the material world around us, but they *think through* that material world, using its physicality as a tool for extended cognition. As Moses puts it, the externalist view sees 'the body and the environment beyond the brain as integral components of cognitive processing' (2018: 309). Clark and Chalmers (1998: 8) acknowledge the apparently radical nature of such an argument but point to the multiple environmental supports human beings use in order to conceptualise complex ideas on a daily basis, such as pens and paper to perform long multiplication, letter tiles to create words in a game of Scrabble, nautical slide rules, as well as language, books and diagrams in general.

Viewing poetry performance from this perspective, it is possible to see how Kate Tempest uses the language of her poetry, her bodily movement and her voice in a polysensual way in order to shape the perceptions and physical experiences of her audience and extend the discourse of 'End Times' far beyond the boundaries of the text. Moses (2018: 309) puts forward a supporting argument that externalist approaches to cognition can help us to rethink and appreciate the mediated nature of all literary texts and the social and environmental conditions that shape our experience of them. He argues that a notion of the mind as extended beyond the brain and the body transforms our understanding of poetry reading as an inward and meditative experience into a collaborative and essentially culturally situated activity. He goes on to explain:

The poem stages an encounter with images taken from ordinary life that are incomplete and yet demand a response. In the absence of full information, we turn to the environment as a parameter that limits the range of outcomes required to deal successfully with the situation. With some precision, we might say that the information about how to interpret the poem is neither in us nor in the world – but rather in the interactive procedures that define the mind's engagement with an environment.

(Moses 2018: 314)

Such a view complements and interlinks perfectly with Text World Theory's notion of the discourse-world as the core foundation of our cognition of all language. It also sits neatly with the view of 'End Times' which I have put forward across the pages of this chapter, as a discourse event that is necessarily grounded both in the physical situation of its delivery and the stylistic techniques that underpin its textuality. It is this symbiotic relationship which allows Tempest to create not just an affecting performance, but a complete poetic and expressive work through which cognition is fundamentally extended and shared. Tempest does not simply tell 'End Times' to her audience, she constructs a physical and conceptual space through which both her own embodied experiences and those of her listeners become distributed, communal and emotionally intensified as a result.

# 6 Metaphor

## Language, metaphor and the mind

The final case study in this book explores the cognition of poetic metaphor. Somewhat unusually, I have left until last the feature of language which has received the most attention from cognitive linguists over recent years and which has been the subject of some of the most influential research in the discipline to date. The work on metaphor and the mind undertaken by academics such as George Lakoff, Mark Johnson and Mark Turner in the last two decades of the twentieth century can be seen to have established and largely defined the discipline of cognitive linguistics as it exists today (see Lakoff 1987; Lakoff and Johnson 1980, 1999; Lakoff and Turner 1989 for key examples of this research). However, metaphor is so deeply connected with and dependent on the other aspects of poetic language I have examined so far that in many ways a discussion of their conceptual operation and effects necessarily preceded this chapter. This is not to say that the preceding chapters of this book have avoided a discussion of metaphor completely. I have already briefly introduced some of the key contemporary ideas about metaphor in cognitive studies in Chapter 2. There, I made use of Fauconnier and Turner's (2002) model of conceptual integration in order to investigate some of the metaphors at work in Simon Armitage's poem, 'Evening'. That discussion was part of a wider consideration of the conceptualisation of time in poetry. In this chapter, however, metaphor forms the main focus of my analysis. For this reason, it is helpful to begin with a fuller summary of some of the most important theories about metaphorical constructions in language which were developed a little further back in the history of cognitive linguistics.

The publication in 1980 of Lakoff and Johnson's book, *Metaphors We Live By*, formed a major turning point in the development of the cognitive approach to language. The book presented a perspective on the operation and purpose of metaphor in the mind, which was not only radically new at the time but which continues to shape cognitivist research across a range of disciplines today. The basic premise of Lakoff and Johnson's work was that metaphor is not solely or simply an ornamental feature of language. Instead, their research revealed that metaphor is an essential aspect of the conceptual apparatus that underpins the architecture of the human mind. Lakoff and Johnson argued that the metaphors we use in everyday speech and writing are surface manifestations of deeper, underlying cognitive structures, which they termed *conceptual metaphors*. They also proposed that many of the idiomatic expressions prevalent in everyday discourse, which had previously been considered as 'dead metaphors', actually reveal the foundation of human thought in embodied physical experience.

We have seen in Chapter 1 of this book how this embodied experience forms the basis of mental patterns known as 'image schemas'. Image schemas are the distillations of everyday encounters around which human knowledge is organised and they provide structured understanding of our physical interactions with the real world (see Johnson 1987). Image schemas also form the basis of what Lakoff and Johnson called *conceptual domains* – coherent segments of human experience stored in the mind. When we produce or receive metaphorical language, we make a connection between a *source domain* – a familiar or concrete area of our knowledge – and a *target domain* – an unfamiliar or abstract concept. According to Lakoff and Johnson, in order to formulate an understanding of the target domain, we superimpose aspects of the source domain onto it in a process they called *conceptual mapping*.

Lakoff and Johnson identified three main types of conceptual metaphor in their early research: *structural metaphor*; *orientational metaphor*; and *ontological metaphor*. The first of these categories, structural metaphor, allows us to understand and express complicated concepts through more simple and specific domains of understanding. One of the most frequently cited examples of this kind of metaphor is the ARGUMENT IS WAR conceptual mapping, which manifests itself in common phrases such as 'She *demolished* his argument', 'He *shot down* all my main points', or 'She *attacked* every point in turn'. Orientational metaphors, by comparison, rely on our knowledge of spatial relationships and arise from our day-to-day experiences of such concepts as UP and DOWN, IN and OUT, and FRONT and BACK. Because of the upright nature of our bodies and the fact that we see, smell, hear and feed ourselves at the top of those bodies, human beings tend to make positive connections with upward orientation, and negative connections with downward orientation. One of the ways this key tendency reveals itself through language is in our frequent use of HAPPY IS UP and SAD IS DOWN conceptual metaphors, present in such surface expressions as 'I'm feeling *on top of the world*', or 'She was *over the moon*', or by contrast, 'He's been *down in the dumps* for weeks'.

The final type of metaphor identified by Lakoff and Johnson, ontological metaphor, enables human beings to conceptualise abstract emotions, ideas and events through their comparison with tangible, material objects and entities. We have already seen how this works in the discussion of metaphors of time in Chapter 2, where I looked at common conceptualisations of time, for example in terms of volume, length, a valuable commodity, a person, and so on. Another common example is the MIND IS A MACHINE ontological metaphor, which is present in expressions such as 'My mind just isn't *functioning* today', or 'The students were feeling *a little rusty*.' In all cases, complex ideas about intangible phenomena are restructured and understood through their comparison with concrete objects or physical sensations.

According to Lakoff and Johnson, in all the different categories of conceptual metaphor summarised above, the cognitive mapping of elements from one domain onto another follows a unidirectional tendency from the concrete to the abstract. This idea supports a wider notion that human cognition of even highly complex, unfamiliar concepts is based on embodied experience in the everyday world. However, several decades later in the development of the discipline of cognitive linguistics, Fauconnier and Turner (2002) revisited and revised the belief that the conceptual processing of metaphor necessarily involves a unidirectional mapping of understanding from one type of domain onto another. As we have already seen in Chapter 2 of this book, their formulation of Conceptual Integration Theory allowed for a more fluid and multiplex perception of the cognition of metaphorical language. Instead of viewing metaphor comprehension as the mapping of elements from a singular domain onto another, the idea of conceptual integration recognises that many metaphors involve the interaction of multiple mental representations in often complicated and mutually expansive ways. In contrast with the two-domain structure of Conceptual Metaphor Theory, Fauconnier and Turner argue that human understanding is based on the conceptual blending of potentially numerous, dynamic packets of knowledge, or 'input spaces'. In the analysis of 'Evening' in Chapter 2, for example, we saw how the line 'Evening overtakes you up the slope' operates through the integration of several input spaces – EVENING, THE HUMAN BODY, AGEING, and WALKING – to form a blended space in the reader's mind. The new mental space which results from this metaphor is more than the sum of its constituent parts and, like all blended spaces, it takes on an emergent structure of its own once conceptualised. In the case of 'evening overtakes you up the slope', the conceptual integration of multiple inputs allows us to personify the passage of time and mentally represent it as a human figure moving rapidly uphill.

The abundant research which has arisen from the camps of both Conceptual Metaphor Theory and Conceptual Integration Theory in cognitive linguistics over the last four decades has shown how fundamental metaphorical language and thinking is in enabling human beings to navigate their way through everyday life and allowing them to interact meaningfully with one another. However, the realisation that metaphor underpins our basic cognition does not mean that it has lost any of its communicative power, nor any of its 'specialness' as a form of language, particularly when used in poetic discourse. The creative use of metaphor still has the potential not only to disrupt conventional modes of expression, but also to present a challenge to established ways of thinking. Throughout the rest of this chapter, I will be examining how some poetic texts can push the boundaries of metaphorical language itself, while at the same time redefining how metaphorical expressions function in the mind. My discussion of metaphor will consider how, in some cases, this particular feature of poetic discourse has the capability to stretch our understanding of language, of the world and of ourselves.

## The poem as an eco-system

So, with a particular focus on the conceptual operation and effects of highly creative metaphor, this chapter will explore the following poem by Alice Oswald:

### Song of a Stone

there was a woman from the north
picked up a stone from the earth.
when the stone began to dream
it was a flower folded in

when the flower began to fruit
it was a circle full of light,
when the light began to break
it was a flood across a plain

when the plain began to stretch
the length scattered from the width
and when the width began to climb
it was a lark above a cliff

the lark singing for its life
was the muscle of a heart,
the heart flickering away
was an offthrow of the sea

and when the sea began to dance
it was the labyrinth of a conscience,
when the conscience pricked the heart
it was a man lost in thought

like milk that sours in the light,
like a vapour twisting in the heat,
the thought was a fugitive — a flare of gold —
it was an iris in a field

and when the man began to murmur
it was a question with no answer,
when the question changed its form
it was the same point driven home

it was a problem, a lamentation:
'What the buggery's going on?
This existence is an outrage!
Give me an arguer to shout with!'

and when the arguer appeared
it was an angel of the Lord,
and when the angel touched his chest,
it was his heartbeat being pushed

and when his heart began to break
it was the jarring of an earthquake
when the earth began to groan
they laid him in it six by one

dark bigger than his head,
pain swifter than his blood,
as good as gone, what could he do?
as deep as stone, what could he know?

Oswald is most often approached by literary critics through the lens of eco-criticism, a logical perspective since she is particularly well known for her writing about the natural environment. Oswald is based in rural Devon, in the south of England, and frequently depicts this countryside in her poetry. Her extended poem *Dart* (2002), for example, represents and explores the River Dart in Oswald's home county, its history, its surrounding landscape and its population. It is one of Oswald's most celebrated texts and won her the prestigious T. S. Eliot Prize for poetry in the year of its publication. However, the natural world, and water in particular, feature prominently in almost all of Oswald's work. Her collection *A Sleepwalk on the Severn* (2009a), for instance, also takes a southern English river as its focus, while *Weeds and Wild Flowers* (2009b) was a collaboration with artist Jessica Greenman to produce a kind of illustrated poetic field guide to the British rural landscape. 'Song of a Stone' comes from Oswald's third poetry collection, *Woods Etc.* (2005a), which is itself populated with numerous poems featuring the natural environment, its flora and its fauna.

Having characterised Oswald as a poet focused on the environment and nature, however, it is important to note, as Middleton (2015) does, that her representation of the natural world in her poetry is far from stylistically conventional within the terms of the pastoral poetic tradition. Instead, Middleton argues, Oswald 'transfers modernist fragmentation to a predominantly rural location' (2015: 160). He compares the tapestry of different voices and perspectives that Oswald creates in *Dart*, for example, with Levi-Strauss's ([1962] 1974) notion of 'bricolage'. Oswald's technique of piecing together existent materials, Middleton goes on to explain, 'corresponds to her use of the river as an overarching structure. Each voice "flows" into the next, as the poem follows the course of the river from its source on Dartmoor to where it joins the sea' (pp. 160–1). Thacker (2015) echoes much of this view of Oswald's methods of poetic collage and montage but places a particular focus on the acoustic dimensions of her poetry. According to Thacker, there is a fundamental connection between the representation of place in Oswald's work and her construction of sound. He argues that, 'Sensitive to the tiniest seeds of sounds, but also to the largest and most complex of rhythms, her verse accommodates the vast range of frequencies found in the environment' (Thacker 2015: 104–5). Thacker also goes on to ascribe both Oswald's acoustic technique and the bricolage-like quality of many of her poems to a desire to subvert anthropocentric poetic tradition. He claims that 'Oswald persistently abstracts the self in relation to nature' (2015: 107), and that this abstraction denies the listener a fully anthropocentric perspective.

Thacker furthermore makes an explicit link between Oswald's work and that of Ted Hughes, a link which has also been made and explored by the poet herself (Oswald, (2005b). In the opening paragraphs of a newspaper article based on the Ted Hughes Memorial Lecture she delivered the same year, Oswald describes the impact Hughes's work had on her on first encounter. Interestingly for the present book, she frames this in terms of a significant cognitive and also physically embodied shift:

> The first Ted Hughes poem I ever read was 'The Horses'. I picked it up one evening after work and I was instantly drawn in. I could feel the poem's effect physically, as if my braincells had been shaken and woken. When I finished reading (and ever since) the world felt different. What struck me straightaway was the real, breathing presence of those horses. They hadn't been described. They hadn't been defined or suggested or analysed or in any way poeticised, but summoned up alive, brought back into being in the medium of language, still 'steaming and glistening'.
>
> (Oswald 2005b)

Hughes's poetry does not simply affect Oswald's conceptualisation of horses, then, but it has a felt impact on her senses which she positions as directly connected to her cognition of the work. Oswald appears to give credence to Thacker's view about the significance of sound in her work too, going on to describe how Hughes's texts inspired her own attempts to layer acoustic patterns in order to capture the real-world experience of nature:

It was a new idea to me – that instead of describing something (which always involves a separation between you and the object) you could replay it alive in the form of sound. You could use poetry to reveal what it sounds like being outdoors: the overlapping of thousands of different noises: the rain's rhythm, the wind's rhythm in the leaves, the tunes of engines, the beat of footsteps.

(Oswald 2005b)

It appears that, for Oswald, poetic discourse provides a unique means of closing the conceptual gap between our physical and sensual experience and its linguistic description; a means of revivifying and reliving the natural landscape, rather than simply representing it.

Baker (2017) picks up on the unique acoustic quality of Oswald's texts as well, arguing that her work suggests that, 'everything in the world is talking, calling and listening, murmuring and counter-murmuring' (p. 100). He also argues that Oswald's texts frequently go one step further than this and that often in her work, 'The usual boundaries of the self are dissolved' (p. 105). This is a perspective which is supported by Goatly (2017) in his stylistic analysis of a number of Oswald's poems, which includes a brief examination of 'Song of a Stone'. Goatly suggests that Oswald frequently blurs the boundary between the human and the natural environment in her poetry and, in support of this argument, provides one of the few linguistic explorations of her work that I have been able to find. In his discussion of 'Song of a Stone' specifically, Goatly points out the high number of nominalisations and the density of personification contained in the text. Both of these linguistic techniques, he notes, have the effect of taking agency away from human beings in one way or another. In the case of nominalisation, processes are represented as nouns, the consequence being that the agent responsible for those processes, whether human or otherwise, is normally made absent from the text. For example, in 'an offthrow of the sea' in the final line of the fourth stanza of 'Song of a Stone', the person who presumably threw something is not nominated in the sentence. Similarly, in 'it was a problem, a lamentation', in the first line of the eighth stanza, the person doing the lamenting is not present in the text-world and only the outcome of this process is described. Personification, on the other hand, repositions agency away from human beings and within objects and entities instead. Goatly notes that, in Oswald's poem, the objects and entities onto which typically human characteristics are bestowed are all elements of the natural environment, in descriptions such as 'the stone began to dream' in the first stanza, or 'the sea began to dance' in the fifth. Overall, then, compared with human activity, there is a much greater focus in 'Song of a Stone' on aspects of the landscape and of nature, many of which are given a special vibrancy and vitality.

Goatly also points out the crucial role that the metaphors at work in 'Song of a Stone' play in further blurring the boundaries between the natural environment and human experience. However, Goatly's analysis of the poem's metaphors is part of a wider survey, not just of this poem, but of several other eco-texts by both Oswald and other writers. My own discussion, by contrast, will take the poem's metaphorical structures as its focal point. Over the coming sections, I will investigate how these metaphors operate in cognitive terms across the whole text and in conjunction with other key features of the poem's language. My aim, as it has been in all the preceding chapters in this book, is to work towards providing a comprehensive and detailed account of the style of the poem and its cognitive consequences. We have seen elsewhere (in Gavins 2016; and in this volume, Chapter 4) how the conceptual effects of contemporary poetic discourse are often interanimative in nature. I have shown that individual features of poetic language are rarely encountered in isolation, but rather exist within a particular reading context and in interaction with the whole of the rest of the poem. Throughout the rest of this chapter, I will provide more evidence that, in order for our conceptualisations of poetry to be fully understood, it is essential to consider how poetic style can develop over the course of an entire text and how the effects of such texts can be incremental and accumulative. I will also suggest that, not only does Oswald reflect an ecological system in her text, she simultaneously creates one through language: an extended community of linguistic features, all of which are interdependent on one another for their conceptual vitality.

This view of poetry as a kind of eco-system is one which has been expressed previously by the poet Gary Snyder, who compares poetic texts with 'climax communities' (Snyder 1980: 116), natural systems which achieve optimum diversity and a steady state through the process of ecological succession:

> When we deepen or enrich ourselves, we become closer to being like a climax system. Turning away from grazing on the 'immediate bio-mass' of perception, sensation, and thrill; and re-viewing memory, internalised perception, blocks of inner energies, dreams, the leaf-fall of day-to-day consciousness, liberates the energy of our sense-detritus. Art is an assimilator of unfelt experience, sensation, and memory for the whole society. When all that compost of feeling and thinking comes back to us then, it comes not as a flower, but – to complete the metaphor – as a mushroom: the fruiting body of the buried threads of mycelia that run widely through the soil, and are intricately married to the root hairs of all the trees. 'Fruiting' – at that point – is the completion of the work of the poet, and the point where the artist or mystic re-enters the cycle: gives what she or he has done as nourishment, and as spore or seed spreads the 'thought of enlightenment', reaching into personal depths for nutrients hidden there, back to the community. The community and its poetry are not two.
>
> (Snyder 1980: 174)

Bate (2000: 247) takes Snyder's ideas a little further in order to note that poetry is an especially efficient system for recycling the thoughts and feelings of a community back into its cultural environment. Unwrapping Snyder's comments on poetry as a climax community specifically, he goes on to explain:

> For Snyder, then, there is a powerful analogy between poetry and climax ecosystem. His own belief in a Zen theory of the interconnectedness of all things means that he does not have to worry that the analogy is *merely a metaphor*. He would reply that metaphor is a way of understanding hidden connections, of reunifying the world which scientific understanding has fragmented. He would argue that the poet is supremely important precisely because he believes in the power of metaphor.
>
> (Bate 2000: 247)

According to Snyder and to Bate, then, poetry is a peculiarly effective means of reunifying the mind and nature. And within poetry, metaphor is the most powerful instrument at a poet's disposal for accomplishing this reunification.

## Textual cohesion and poetic shift

If we are to consider 'Song of a Stone' as a unified communicative system, in which all the features of its language are interdependent and self-sustaining, then it is essential to begin with a whole-text perspective on the linguistic structures and patterns it contains. Looking across the entire discourse, it immediately becomes clear that the poem includes a significant number of repeated stylistic characteristics, which construct both an evolving soundscape and a broader discoursal coherence. These parallel linguistic components act to form cohesive strands across the text, encouraging connections to be made between words, lines and images, as well as drawing attention to the points at which deviations from established patterns occur.

The first thing to note is the overall regularity of the poem's structure: it is made up of eleven stanzas, each of which is four lines long. Many of these lines contain repeated occurrences of sibilance, which again stretch across the whole poem. In the fifth and sixth stanzas, for example, there is a particular density of /s/ and /z/ sounds – in 'sea', 'dance', 'conscience', 'sours', 'twisting', 'was' and 'iris' – although the /s/ phoneme remains consistently present throughout the rest of the text as well. Oswald creates additional whole-text cohesion by using end-rhymes in twenty-two of the poem's forty-four lines. However, this is where her more fluid use of linguistic parallelism, noted by Thacker (2015) and Middleton (2015), can be seen. The end-rhymes are a repeated feature, but they are not full rhymes in the main, with 'break /

earthquake' in the tenth stanza being the only example of a full rhyme in the poem. The rest are slant rhymes, for example in 'north / earth' in the first stanza, 'fruit / light' in the second, and 'gold / field' in the fifth. In most of these examples, only one syllable is rhymed, but this pattern is deviated from too with a single exception with a double syllable rhyme, 'murmur / answer', at the beginning of the seventh stanza.

Where end-rhymes are not used, Oswald employs other forms of stylistic parallelism to form cohesive patterns of repetition across 'Song of a Stone'. Some of this parallelism takes the form of alliteration, in 'cliff / climb' in the final two lines of the third stanza, for instance; while some takes the form of assonance, for example in 'break / plain' in the final two lines of the second stanza; and some is consonance, for example in 'gold / field' in the final two lines in the sixth stanza. There is a clear sense, then, of deliberate, poetic structuring developing across the entire poem. However, this is in the main quite loosely achieved, with suggestions of rhyme being created instead of full rhymes, and with deviations from patterns occurring just as frequently as parallelism itself. For example, along with the sibilance I have already identified, there is a dominance of /f/ sounds in the first four stanzas of the poem, both in the alliteration in 'from', 'flower', 'folded', 'fruit', 'full', 'flood', and so on, and in the consonance of 'cliff', 'life' and 'offthrow'. This dominance gradually shifts as the poem progresses, however, with nasal sounds becoming more abundant in the middle of the text (in 'began', 'dance', 'labyrinth', 'conscience', 'man', 'milk', and so on), and finally plosives becoming more abundant by the end of the poem (in 'buggery', 'appeared', 'heartbeat', 'pushed', 'break').

Metrical patterns are similarly sporadically constructed and then deviated from throughout 'Song of a Stone'. The majority of the poem's lines have either seven or eight syllables, but as quickly as one form of metre in established in one stanza, the text deviates from it again in the next. The metres which do emerge in the poem are also comparatively rare in English poetic discourse and therefore are often difficult to discern at all. In the second stanza, for example, each line has two metrical feet, but in the first line – 'when the flower began to fruit' – the first foot is trisyballic and the second is tetrasyballic, giving seven syllables overall. In the second line – 'it was a circle full of light' – both feet are tetrasyballic, as the line has eight syllables in total. The third line – 'when the light began to break' – reverts to a mixture of trisyballic and tetrasyballic feet, and in the fourth line – 'it was a flood across a plain' – both feet are tetrasyballic again. This means that the first and third lines of the stanza are made up of an anapaest (with the stress falling on the third syllable of three) combined with a much less common fourth paeon (where the stress is on the last syllable of four). The second and fourth lines, on the other hand, contain two fourth paeons each. While this may be an unusual metrical pattern, it is nevertheless definitely present and clearly contrived. However, the stanza which precedes this one has no identifiably regular metre at all, and the one which follows it shifts the metre slightly. In the third stanza, the first two lines have seven syllables and are made up of an anapaest and a fourth peaon ('when the plain began to stretch / the length scattered from the width'), while the second two lines have eight syllables and two fourth paeons each ('and when the width began to climb / it was a lark above a cliff'). In the fourth stanza, the metrical pattern shifts again. Here, every line has seven syllables and each one repeats the pattern of an anapaest followed by a fourth paeon ('the lark singing for its life / was the muscle of a heart, / the heart flickering away / was an offthrow of the sea'), while the fifth stanza makes a more radical break and has no regular metre at all.

Overall, then, Oswald seems to be forging stylistic sequences and a textual architecture which unifies and connects the different stanzas and lines of her poem, while at the same time limiting the extent of these sequences, disrupting and fracturing many of the structures she creates. Middleton (2015) identifies a similar technique to be found in Oswald's longer poem, *Dart* (2002), and comments on the imperfect sound patterning and metre which run throughout that text. In this context, Middleton argues that Oswald's loosely woven parallelisms help to achieve the poem's fluidity and fragmentation, while Thacker notes that 'Oswald's rhythms are incremental, adding depth to her acoustic shaping of her experience working outside' (2015: 111). Both of these critics, then, recognise the importance of the cumulative effect of repeated stylistic techniques, even when one of those techniques might be to break linguistic patterns as much as to initiate them.

The text-worlds that the language of 'Song of a Stone' builds also shift and change across the course of the poem. However, this transformation differs from the repeated world-switches we saw in 'Crates' in Chapter 1, where one image serially replaced another. It also differs from the more mercurial shifts I analysed in 'Evening' in Chapter 2, where the spatio-temporal boundaries between worlds become blurred and disorienting. In fact, in ontological terms, Oswald's poem makes only one shift into a world that is more remote from the initial text-world established in its opening line. The first sentence of the text, 'there was a woman from the north', builds a world with a past-tense time signature, in which the woman nominated as present picks up a stone from the earth. The world-building elements of this initial text-world are vague and generalistic, since both 'a woman' in the first line of the poem and 'a stone' in the second are indefinite references to an entity and an object, respectively, which are difficult to conceptualise in much detail on the basis of such limited information. Although we know they are present, we are not given any additional information on how big or what colour the stone is, for example, or about the age or appearance of the woman. There are also two definite references in these lines – to 'the north' and 'the earth' – but these, too, are very broad in nature. They carry hints of Norse mythology with them as well, which broadens the text's reach yet further, giving these lines a somewhat universal but comparatively indistinct quality. From within this imprecise and generic initial text-world, then, the poem's only shift into a modal-world occurs. In the third line of the first stanza, 'when the stone began to dream', we see the first personification in the text. This gives an inanimate stone the human ability to dream and creates a new, boulomaic modal-world in which this dream is depicted. The language here shifts the poem to a more remote ontological level but, interestingly, the text stays on this plane for the rest of its duration. The fluidity of 'Song of a Stone' is not, therefore, enacted through the repeated creation of ontological movement and distance. Rather, the multiple worlds it contains are all produced through the use of metaphors, each of which remains firmly embedded within the dream-world of the stone.

## Metaphor worlds and Cognitive Grammar

At this point in the discussion, it is useful to recap briefly how Text World Theory handles metaphor and the worlds it creates. As I explained in Chapter 2, the text-world framework borrows Conceptual Integration Theory's core notion that the processing of metaphorical language involves the blending of potentially multiple mental representations into a new and dynamically evolving metaphor world. These blended worlds are necessarily conjoined to the matrix text-worlds from which they are constructed. However, because Text World Theory also adopts the idea that this connection is not unidirectional in nature, it recognises that metaphor worlds can feed back into their matrix text-worlds and have a significant impact on how that originating world is conceptualised. Furthermore, metaphor worlds do not always exist at an ontological distance from their matrix worlds. In the example of 'when the stone began to dream', for instance, a metaphor world is initially created from the personification of the stone. This metaphor involves the conceptual integration of two input spaces, one for HUMAN and one for STONE, but the blending of these mental representations takes place on the same ontological level as the world from which the metaphor springs. It is only once the mental activity of the personified stone is reported that a more remote modal-world is produced in which the stone's dream can be conceptualised. Both of these worlds – the metaphor world and its embedded boulomaic modal-world – have a direct effect on the text-world containing the woman from the north. This originating world becomes imbued with a magical, mythical quality as a consequence of the other worlds which have become embedded within it.

Goatly argues that 'Metaphor is [. . .] a means of undoing the naturalised categories imposed by the languages we speak' (2017: 49). In his exploration of the language of eco-poetry, he is specifically interested in how the metaphorical thinking that underpins all of our day-to-day cognition nevertheless retains the ability to reframe and radically reshape how we conceptualise the world when used creatively. For example, through her use of metaphor, Oswald is able to give life, cognition and volition to elements of the natural world which would not normally possess them, and to take emphasis away from human agents by contrast. The only human figures in 'Song of a Stone' are an indefinite woman in the first stanza, an indefinite man who appears in the fifth, and two ethereal figures who appear in the last three stanzas: 'an angel of the Lord' and, by implication, the Lord himself. There is also a non-specific and indefinite 'they' in the final line of the tenth stanza, but on the whole the humans in the text are under-specified. They are also only responsible for a handful of the processes depicted in the poem (for example, 'picked up' in the first stanza, and 'touched' and 'appeared' in the ninth stanza). Far more often in this text, objects which are normally inanimate and, occasionally, abstract nouns too are placed in the position of agent in the poem's sentence structures. For instance, along with the dreaming stone in the text's opening stanza, light breaks in the second stanza; a plain stretches, length scatters and width climbs in the third; a heart flickers in the fourth; the sea dances and conscience pricks the heart in the fifth stanza; a question changes its form in the seventh; and a heart begins to break and the earth groans in the tenth stanza. Not all of the inanimate objects and animals acting as agents in the poem are doing so in personified form, however: flowers do actually fruit in the everyday world (as in the second stanza), milk sours and vapour twists (as in the sixth) and larks sing (in the fourth stanza). What is interesting about all of the processes which are attached to non-human agents in 'Song of a Stone', though, is that they are all, with only one exception ('conscience pricked the heart'), intransitive verbs.

The framework of Cognitive Grammar (see Giovanelli and Harrison 2018 and Langacker 1987, 1991, 2008 for a useful overview) provides a helpful addition to cognitive theories of metaphor here. It is a means of understanding and describing how grammatical constructions in language, such as the intransitive verbs in 'Song of a Stone', function conceptually and, as such, enables a more fine-grained analysis of key linguistic components of the metaphors at work in the poem. Some of the principal ideas at the core of this grammar have already been introduced earlier in this book, for example in the discussion of image schemas in Chapter 1, and of figure and ground in Chapter 4. These basic building blocks of cognition form the foundations for how we express ourselves and our embodied experience of the world through the language we use. They are also, therefore, at the heart of Cognitive Grammar. Like all other cognitivist approaches, the central view of this linguistic framework is that grammar is a meaningful construct which reflects the architecture of the human mind. Cognitive Grammar recognises, for example, that processes in language express our understanding of energy and motion. We use verbs to describe how things in the world are affected by or responsible for the transfer of energy from one place or item to another, or for physical change achieved through movement. In a transitive verb, for instance, such as 'the woman picked up the stone', energy is transferred from the woman to the stone in a way which alters the stone: it is moved in an upward direction from one place to another as a result of the energy transfer.

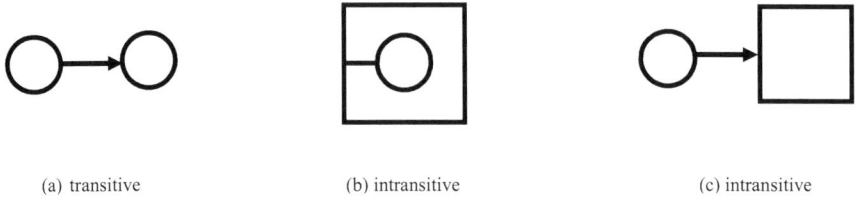

(a) transitive                     (b) intransitive                     (c) intransitive

**Figure 6.1** The conceptualisation of transitive and intransitive verbs, adapted from Langacker (2008: 388)

A process like this one is known in Cognitive Grammar as an 'action chain'. Action chains involve different 'archetypal roles': the 'agent' of an action chain is the participant responsible for wilfully initiating the action, while the 'patient' is the participant who undergoes change as a result of the action. Some action chains also involve an 'instrument', which is used by one participant to affect another, but this is not always the case. From a Cognitive Grammar point of view, focused on energy and movement, the agent in a sentence is the 'energy source', whereas the patient is an 'energy sink'.

Figure 6.1, adapted from Langacker (2008: 388), provides a neat visual summary of how our conceptualisations of transitive and non-transitive verbs differ. In each configuration in the diagram, the circles represent the participants in a sentence and the boxes stand for the settings in which the participants are located. In configuration (a), a transitive verb is depicted in which two participants are interacting. This normally occurs asymmetrically and the arrow in (a) shows how energy is being transferred from one participant to another in an action chain. In (b) and (c), by comparison, two possible conceptual configurations of intransitive verbs are represented. In (b) the participant simply occupies a location, while in (c) the participant moves with respect to a location. In both of these intransitive situations, though, the only participant present is the agent; no patient participant is affected by the actions or location of that agent.

Because the majority of the verbs which are attached to non-humans in 'Song of a Stone' are intransitive in nature, in these examples too there is only an agent present and no patient (as in (b) and (c) in Figure 6.1). For instance, in 'the flower began to fruit' in the second stanza, only the flower is nominated as a world-building element and only the flower is affected by the process described; energy is not transferred from that source to an external sink. Similarly, 'the heart flickering away', 'the question changed its form', 'the earth began to groan' and the majority of other verbs in the text all represent only their non-human agent and no patient. There are some mental interactions described in the poem, too – for example with the dreaming stone – and some movements, such as 'the plain began to stretch' and 'the width began to climb'. These processes do not involve a patient either and most of the agents responsible for the intransitive verbs in the poem are personified, usually inanimate elements of the natural environment.

This has a number of effects across the course of 'Song of a Stone'. First of all, it strongly profiles the agents of the processes depicted in the poem. These agents are not just placed in subject position in their sentences, but they are the only objects, items or animals which are linguistically represented at all, since no patients or instruments appear in their intransitive constructions. Furthermore, lots of research in psycholinguistics has shown that placing an inanimate agent at the head of a clause is difficult for readers to process when compared with animate actors (see Bock 1986; Bock and Loebell 1990; Bock and Warren 1985; Keenan and Comrie 1977; Vernice and Sorace 2018). Weckerley and Kutas (1999), for example, found in particular that sentence-initial inanimate entities occurring in the grammatical role of subject caused significant processing costs in clause comprehension. Sentences with animate agents are simply quicker and easier to read and understand. The majority of the grammatical subjects at the start of the clauses in 'Song of a Stone' are inanimate, meaning that Oswald's choice of sentence structure is likely to be comparatively challenging for her readers to comprehend. Interestingly, the same is the case for the nominalisations the poem contains, since nominalisations too have been shown in eye-tracking studies to take longer to process than other nouns (see Wolfer 2016). In terms of the processing effort required to understand her poem, then, Oswald is placing considerable demands on her readers, disrupting more preferred syntactic structures and opting for non-prototypical syntax which is significantly more difficult to conceptualise.

A further interesting feature of many of Oswald's grammatical constructions reveals itself when we look at tense in 'Song of a Stone'. Oswald does not choose to represent all the processes in her poem as finite verbs carrying tense. Instead, she frequently focuses attention on the very start of a process in time by repeating a 'began to …' construction eight times across the course of the text, followed by the non-finite infinitive form of the verb. This occurs in 'the stone began to dream' in the first stanza; 'the flower began to fruit' and 'the light began to break' in the second stanza; 'the plain began to stretch' and 'the width began to climb' in the third stanza; 'the sea began to dance' in the fifth stanza; 'the man began to murmur' in the seventh stanza; and finally 'his heart began to break' in the tenth. In all but one of these examples ('the man began to murmur'), an inanimate object is strongly profiled in subject position in the clause, and in all cases no participant other than the agent is involved in the sentence and the temporal starting point of the process depicted is a clear point of focus. This leads to a very prominent foregrounding of, in the main, objects and abstract nouns. These world-building elements are all responsible for and at the very start of some sort of activity or event. Overall in Oswald's poem, then, an emphasis is placed on the potency and potential of inanimate items. Crucially, none of the processes represented in the poem through these non-finite, intransitive verbs is ever concluded; their grammatical structure de-temporalises them, giving them an eternal quality. We are never told, for example, whether or when the light stops breaking, or how far the plain stretches, or the width climbs, and so on. No temporal (and, in many cases, spatial) boundaries or limits are imposed on these processes. Each metaphor world is constructed within potentially infinite temporal parameters.

## Metaphor chains

The structure of the poem as a whole adds to the sense of the eternal and infi-nite in 'Song of a Stone', since one metaphor occludes another after another in succession throughout the text. Each new metaphor world, however, remains connected to the last one in some way and this is most often achieved through the use of the temporal connective 'when'. The consecutive continu-ity this establishes adds to the feeling of an ever-extending temporal reach, which builds from stanza to stanza across the discourse. To examine how this functions cognitively in more detail, let us take a closer look at the second and third stanzas of the poem. The first line of the second stanza, 'when the flower began to fruit', takes the form of one of the intransitive, non-finite action chains I discussed in the preceding section of this chapter. It strongly profiles the flower as the subject of the sentence, at the very start of the process of fruiting, for which it is responsible as agent. Although a flower fruiting is not a metaphor in itself, since this is a natural process which happens in the real world, the image is extended in the next line, as additional detail is given about the fruiting, this time in metaphorical form: 'it was a circle full of light'. In the metaphor world which results from this, the input spaces of FLOWER, LIGHT and CIRCLE are integrated to form a new, blended mental representa-tion. However, the LIGHT input space then immediately becomes the subject of the next, connected metaphor worlds in the sequence, which are created across the following two lines: 'when the light began to break / it was a flood across a plain'. In these instances, two closely tied metaphor worlds are built in quick succession. The first takes the structure of LIGHT IS AN OBJECT and is a common conceptual metaphor in everyday discourse. The natural phe-nomenon of the movement of the planet and the consequent change from darkness to light at the start of each day is often described in terms of 'day-break', a metaphor which depicts daylight as a fragile material, and which is commonplace in English. However, this relatively unremarkable metaphor is immediately followed by a second one, which is more creative and unusual in nature. In the final line of the second stanza, the arrival of light at dawn is described as a 'flood across a plain', retaining LIGHT as a key input space, but framing it in a completely different and novel way. Here, LIGHT is inte-grated with the input spaces of FLOOD and PLAIN, which give both a specific, water-like texture and a significant spatial extent to this metaphor world. Dawn here becomes vast, moving and all-encompassing as the blended space created from these different inputs takes on its own emergent structure. In the first line of the third stanza, the string of metaphor worlds continues as this time the PLAIN input space is repeated: 'the plain began to stretch'. Although landscape is often talked about in terms of movement in everyday discourse, this is nevertheless still a metaphor since the plain is not actually moving in any way. Once again, then, a key input space – for the PLAIN – is retained, but reframed, this time taking on the property of pliability along with the movement already established in the previous metaphor in the chain.

In each of these examples, an element of a metaphor in one world becomes actualised in the text-world of the next and subject to metaphorisation itself. So, LIGHT is initially used as an input space for a metaphor for a flower, but then becomes the subject of its own metaphors, 'light began to break' and 'it was a flood across the plain', in the next two lines. Similarly, PLAIN is at first a component of a metaphor world created in order to describe the light, before itself starting 'to stretch' in its own metaphorical construction. This results in a kind of domino effect, with each metaphor world generated in the poem being connected to and having a direct impact on the next. The nature of the connections between each world is important too, since they are all enabled by the temporal connective 'when'. This gives chronology to the sequences of worlds, adding to the poem's coherence and fluidity. The metaphor worlds in 'Song of a Stone' are not discrete: they flow into one another, both through the world-building elements they share and through the temporal cohesion created by 'when'. All of this means that the reader's processing of Oswald's metaphors never really ceases throughout the duration of the text and that the ultimate meaning of each conceptualisation is constantly deferred into the next text-world in the sequence. In this way, Oswald blurs the boundaries between worlds and resists imposing particularly temporal, but also spatial, limits on the metaphors she employs.

There are only a few exceptions to this pattern in the poem; short interruptions where the flow of time and shared world-building in 'Song of a Stone' seems to be disrupted or pauses momentarily. This happens, for example, with the two similes which occur in the first two lines of the sixth stanza: 'like milk that sours in the light / like vapour twisting in the heat'. These similes appear after a chain of a total of seven metaphor worlds connected with 'when' which populate the preceding five stanzas. Unlike these other temporally and conceptually conjoined metaphors, the images of milk souring and vapour twisting lack any world-building connections with the world from which they spring. There is no chronological link specified and the similes do not include any objects, entities or input spaces which have occurred anywhere else in the poem. They appear as entirely separate text-worlds in the discourse. They are used as descriptions of 'a man lost in thought', which appears in the final line of the fifth stanza and is itself a metaphor for 'when the conscience pricked the heart'. The only identifiable stylistic connections they share appear to be with each other, through their common 'like X in the Y' structure and through the parallelism of the slant rhymes which end each line: 'light / heat'. As such, these two images, although linked to each other, create a disconnect with the rest of the poem as a whole, another inter-ruption to an established pattern in Oswald's text. They break the poem's fluidity, its temporal cohesion, and draw attention as a result. Interestingly, the worlds the two lines describe are also characterised by the slowness of the processes the contain. Both milk souring and vapour twisting are not rapidly moving or changing phenomena, causing an overall deceleration of the pace of the poem at this point, both because of the stylistic deviation of the lines and because of the slow nature of the processes they describe. Compare, for example, the pace of 'a flood across a plain', 'the heart flickering away' or 'the sea began to dance' with that established by the images in the opening lines of the sixth stanza. In the final two lines of the stanza and into its seventh stanza, however, 'Song of a Stone' returns to its sequencing of interconnected worlds. After the brief break created by the two similes, 'the thought was a fugitive' picks up 'thought' from the fifth stanza once again, uses it as an input space in a blended world with FUGITIVE, and then creates two further metaphors: 'a flare of gold / it was an iris in a field'.

It is worth noting that the fourth stanza in the poem also does not contain the 'when' connective that is repeated in every other stanza in the first half of the poem. However, the metaphor worlds created in these lines still remain conjoined to the world from which they were produced ('it was a lark above the cliff'), and thus to all the other preceding metaphors in the poem too. This continuation is ensured firstly by the reoccurrence of the LARK input space in the first line of the fourth stanza. In a similar way as we have already seen in other metaphors in 'Song of a Stone', the lark moves from initially being an input space in a metaphor for 'when the width began to climb' to becoming subject to a metaphor itself: 'the lark singing for its life / was a muscle of the heart'. Crucially, the temporal cohesion is retained here by the use of the present continuous tense in 'singing'. The same technique is then repeated in the final two lines of the fourth stanza, where the present continu-ous is used again to position 'the heart flickering away' as happening in the same moment as 'the lark singing for its life'. A temporal chain is thus created again, through slightly different stylistic means.

## World-repair and replacement

The next major disruption in the poem occurs in the eighth stanza, where there is a sudden interjection of direct speech (see Leech and Short 2007), which has been absent from the rest of the text. Although indications of the presence of both human thought and speech have been given elsewhere in 'Song of a Stone', for example in the report that 'the man began to murmur' in the first line of the seventh stanza, this is the first and only direct representation of what is being said or being thought in the poem. Like all direct speech, this instance creates a temporal world-switch, in Text World Theory terms. This is because the tense which has been predominant in the rest of the text, the simple past (for example in 'there was a woman from the north', 'it was a circle full of light', 'the sea began to dance', and so on), shifts to the simple present across three lines: '"What the buggery's going on? / This existence is an outrage! / Give me an arguer to shout with"'. Tense shifts like this one have a kind of 'zooming in' effect. They give the reader closer access to the text-world inhabited by the speaking enactors and represent that world from their deictic zero-point, with a corresponding choice of tense, pronouns, register, and so on. Direct speech thus tends to feel more immediate and involving than, for example, a past tense narrative does. In this particular case, it appears that the speech of 'the man' first mentioned in the last line of the fifth stanza is being represented; however, this is not made linguistically explicit. Furthermore, the interruption to the style of the rest of the poem it creates is jarring, all the more so because of the shift in register it contains as well. The use of exclamation marks reflects the emotional tone of the outburst and the use of the expletive 'buggery', however mild, is nevertheless out of keeping with the much more formal register of the rest of the text. In my own reading of the poem, most likely because of my Northern English background, this usage carried the additional flavour of a Northern English dialect too.

Interestingly, the temporal world-switch into a direct speech text-world with an immediate, informal and exclamatory style, is straight away followed by another significant shift in register. In the ninth stanza of 'Song of a Stone', we are told that 'when the arguer appeared / it was an angel of the Lord'. The tense switches back to the simple past here, but the poem now adopts a marked religious theme. Firstly and most obviously, the ethereal beings, the angel and the Lord, are nominated as present: the angel as an active agent within the text-world and the Lord as more distant, implied figure, somewhere beyond it. Secondly, however, their appearance has a transformative effect on the style of the whole of the rest of the poem, both before and after this point. The angel touches the man who has cried out for him and we are told 'his heart began to break'. Once again, the HEART input in this metaphor becomes part of a metaphor chain and is reframed as an EARTHQUAKE in its own subsequent metaphor world. This is followed up with another event of similarly momentous proportions, as 'the earth began to groan' in the next line. Suddenly, within a whole-discourse context and alongside an emerging religious motif, the repetition of both 'when' and 'and when' at the beginning of thirteen of the lines of 'Song of a Stone' becomes strongly resonant of religious language too. Not only are these two syntactic structures similar in style to verses of the Bible, but their repeated appearance at regular intervals across the whole poem takes on a chant-like and meditative quality.

The scope and scale of the metaphors in the text also increase to biblical levels in the last three stanzas. 'Song of a Stone' moves here from descriptions of the natural landscape – of light breaking, flowers fruiting and the sea dancing – which dominate its first half, to a second half in which an angel of the Lord pushes the man's heartbeat, the heartbeat becomes an earthquake, and the whole earth is personified and groaning. The poem ends with darkness 'bigger than his head', with pain, and, ultimately, with death, adding to the sense that both the grandeur and the solemnity of the language of the text is increasing as it comes to a close. The final stanzas also make apparent a clear lexical field of the human body running throughout poem. Not only are 'chest', 'heartbeat', 'heart', 'head' and 'blood' all present in quick succession in the last dozen lines but, again looking at the whole poem in retrospect, they now seem to echo other instances earlier in the text of phrases such as 'the muscle of a heart', 'the heart flickering away' and 'conscience pricked the heart'. It is even possible, from this more body-centred and whole-text perspective, to read 'an iris in a field', in the last line of the sixth stanza, not as a description of a plant but as one of a human eye.

It is also clear that the human body comes under increasing strain as the poem progresses. The metaphors which populate the closing stanzas of 'Song of a Stone' seem to describe, again in a series of interconnected worlds, a heart attack and a death which results from it: the angel of the Lord pushes the man's heartbeat to the point at which it breaks and kills him. This reading is confirmed in the final stanza by the description of the man being laid in the earth 'six by one'. The final two lines are particularly interesting in this context, since they contain two questions for which neither the addressee nor the addresser are made linguistically explicit. Although it is possible that poetic voice here is the same as that which has run throughout the poem, it is equally possible that the pronouns and punctuation marks in these lines could indicate Free Indirect Discourse and the addition of other voices to the text. To me, the last two lines of Oswald's poem are reminiscent of the murmurings of mourners at a graveside, or perhaps even people ruminating on a life that has passed at a later point in time than the death itself. In fact, in my own experience of reading the text, these closing questions were so strongly evocative of the phatic communion that often occurs at funerals that it led to me to a radical reframing of the whole poem.

In Text World Theory, it is recognised that in all types of language it is quite common for new information to enter into the discourse which can cause the participants in a discourse-world to re-evaluate and sometimes rebuild their text-worlds. The fundamentally dynamic nature of every act of communication means that participants are continuously incrementing incoming knowledge into their mental representations during the discourse process. For example, we often misread, mishear or misunderstand language, but it is also not uncommon for speakers and authors to deliberately misdirect us into constructing text-worlds that are inaccurate or incomplete. When we are forced to rethink our mental representations of discourse as the result of new information, this is known as 'world-repair' (see Gavins

2007: 141–2). In extreme cases, complete 'world replacement' (Gavins 2007: 142) may be necessary in order for sense to be made of the discourse. I have already noted how the introduction of a religious theme in the closing lines of 'Song of a Stone' can lead to similarly biblical language elsewhere in the text becoming suddenly more apparent. However, in my reading of Oswald's text, the last two stanzas of the poem caused me to reconsider my understanding of the whole of the rest of the discourse in a much more profound way. The realisation that the man had died at the touch of an angel and that the disembodied voices asking 'what could he do?' and 'what could he know?' might be mourners at his graveside, led me to replace the text-world I had created at the start of the poem entirely. The 'stone' in the first stanza became a headstone. Furthermore, I then also reframed both the 'song' of the stone and its 'dream' as symbolising the narratives told of an entire life lived, either in a headstone's inscription or in the stories and anecdotes told by those left behind in grief.

### 'that compost of feeling and thinking'

Oswald depicts both human life in general and the specific human life represented in 'Song of a Stone' as an ebbing and flowing sequence of interconnected moments and images. Over the course of this discussion, we have seen how she creates a careful cohesion across the lines of her poem through the use of structural, phonetic and syntactic parallelism. I have outlined the linguistic means through which Oswald connects the multiple text-worlds contained in the poem temporally and stylistically, while at the same time imbuing the text with a sense of elasticity and flux. This looseness is achieved through the use of half-patterns, near-rhymes and almost imperceptible metrical forms, as well as through the balancing of parallelism with an equal amount of stylistic deviation. The discourse of 'Song of a Stone' thus becomes one which is at the same time cohesive and unbound; one which both composes and decomposes order, sequence and shape.

Oswald creates further temporal and conceptual fluidity through the construction of chains of metaphor worlds, which extend across the whole of the discourse. We have seen how each one of these worlds is embedded in the last and how each one is dependent on another for its core imaginary input. Through this technique, Oswald constantly defers the ultimate meaning of the stone's song into the next text-world, and the next, and the next. What is more, the metaphor worlds which form the spine of 'Song of a Stone', its essential composition, are so novel in their architecture that they challenge accepted understanding of how metaphor operates in the human mind. First of all, Oswald's metaphors reach far beyond any notion of a unidirectional mapping of a single area of knowledge onto another, as Conceptual Metaphor Theory would have it. Secondly, however, they also defy even the more multiplex networks of mental spaces proposed by Conceptual Integration Theory. This is because the metaphors in 'Song of a Stone' do not simply involve the blending of multiple input spaces into a new mental representation; they require that each act of conceptual integration is dependent on the last. No single metaphorical mental representation in the poem exists in segregation or disengagement from another, since each new metaphor reframes the dynamic system that has underpinned the metaphor that precedes it.

In this way, the metaphor worlds which predominate in 'Song of a Stone' exist in a state of optimal interdependence, in much the same way as Snyder (1980) describes the organisms at the core of a climax eco-system existing in a self-nourishing interrelationship with one another. Furthermore, although 'Song of a Stone' may not at first glance appear to be so obvious an 'eco-poem' as some of Oswald's other work, it nevertheless enacts the same blurring of lines between elements of the natural world and human beings that characterise Oswald's other environmentally focused poetry. We have seen how the personification in the text, the use of intransitive verbs, and the foregrounding of inanimate objects as agents in the syntax of the poem give a special vitality and potentiality to aspects of the natural landscape. We have also seen that the position of these world-builders in the subject slot in many clauses in the text, coupled with Oswald's use of tense, focuses attention on the very starting point of the specific processes being described. As I have pointed out, research in psycholinguistics shows that such stylistic choices present readers with particular challenges, making conceptualisation and comprehension more difficult and slowing the reading process as a result.

It is useful at this point to revisit Snyder's explanation of how the experiencing of poetry itself allows us to access a different form of consciousness. Snyder recognises the special, decelerated form of reading and cognition poetry demands and argues,

> When we deepen and enrich ourselves, looking within, understanding ourselves, we come closer to being like a climax system. Turning away from grazing on the 'immediate bio-mass' of perception, sensation, and thrill; and re-viewing memory, internalized perception, blocks of inner energies, dreams, the leaf-fall of day-to-day consciousness, liberates the energy of our sense-detritus.
>
> (Snyder 1980: 174)

Not only do the metaphor worlds in 'Song of a Stone' sustain one another in a synergetic system, then, but our engagement with them as readers revivifies our cognition of the world around us. Oswald produces strings of metaphors which impact upon one another in a domino-style chain reaction. However, she also blurs the boundaries between these metaphors by resisting the imposition of temporal and spatial boundaries around the multitude of interwoven text-worlds her poem contains. The whole of the discourse interacts in this way to encourage the interanimation of its stylistic features and to frustrate disconnection and isolation.

Oswald employs all of these techniques in 'Song of a Stone', as Goatly (2017: 49) argues, to 'undo the naturalised categories imposed by the language we speak'. Her creative and experimental use of familiar poetic devices pushes the limits not just of the text-worlds she constructs, but of the very language system through which she constructs them. Only a whole-text perspective on the poem can reveal how these techniques and features interact and accumulate to create 'that compost of feeling and thinking' which Snyder (1980: 174) argues is the essence both of poetic discourse and of our conceptual experience of that discourse. Oswald's poem begins with the foregrounding of a simple stone in a text-world which is vaguely defined yet suffused with mythology. It shifts its reader, line by line, through the multiple, embedded metaphor worlds which delineate the song of a human life, before ultimately returning to the stone that marks that life's passing. Over the course of this journey, the poem's stylistic and conceptual features connect not only individual mental representations, but the very nature of human existence with the inevitability of its extinction, with the potential for its rebirth. As such, 'Song of a Stone' is the very embodiment of the poem as a harmonious and symbiotic system. It is only by recognising how this system creates, sustains and renews itself that the capability of poetry to present the natural world, 'summoned up alive, brought back into being in the medium of language, still "steaming and glistening"', as Oswald herself (2005b) puts it, can be fully understood.

# 7 Poetry in the Mind

I began this book by setting out the five main features of contemporary poetry I intended to explore from a cognitive perspective: time and space; intertextuality; absence; performance; and metaphor. Each of the preceding chapters has dealt with each of these aspects of poetic discourse in turn through the detailed analysis of poems considered in context and in their entirety. I have used Text World Theory (Gavins 2007; Werth 1999) as the central framework underpinning all my explorations, but I have put this analytical apparatus into an interdisciplinary dialogue with other theories and approaches from cognitive linguistics, stylistics, narratology, literary criticism, theology, cognitive psychology and neuroscience. The resulting analyses have not only shed light on how the key dimensions of poetry I have chosen to focus on operate linguistically and conceptually, but they have also revealed interesting connections between the separate poems I have examined and their poetic styles. What is more, it has become evident over the preceding pages that further features of poetic discourse are common across the texts I have explored. In this closing chapter, I review the additional patterns of creative expression which have been revealed over the course of my discussions and examine their relationships with the aspects of contemporary poetic style that I set out to understand at the start of this book.

## Conceptual instability

My analysis of the poem 'Evening' by Simon Armitage in Chapter 2 showed that the process of world-building in this text is nebulous and disorienting. The poem follows a young boy as he walks across a rural landscape, but the temporal parameters of the text-world shift imperceptibly from the start of the text to its conclusion. The boy becomes an adult at a point which is not explicitly signalled in the language of the poem and therefore is not perceived by the reader until after it has taken place. I argued in Chapter 2 that this creates a sense of liminality in 'Evening', since both the 'before' and 'after' states can be seen, but the switch between them is hidden. I also argued that the poem's distortions of time and space echo the visual phenomenon of saccadic suppression, where gaps in perception can result in a feeling of chronostasis. We lose our sense of time in 'Evening' in a similar manner, but with it we also lose our sense of the edges and the stability of the text-worlds we build.

My analyses of other poems across this book have revealed that the disconcerting effects of imprecise or obfuscated world-building are not confined to Armitage's text alone. In the first chapter, for example, I showed how Jo Bell's poem, 'Crates', leads its reader through a kind of conceptual game, constructing a series of text-worlds, each one occluding the last. Although it enacts its instability in a slightly different way from 'Evening', 'Crates' nevertheless foregrounds the volatile nature of the worlds it builds in a playful and meta-textual manner. At the same time, the poem uses second-person address and draws on substantial assumptions about shared discourse-world knowledge in order to sustain a close bond between the reader and the poetic persona. This bond enables a final twist in the poem to be played out, where the reader is suddenly excluded from an intimate scene of which they have previously been to led to feel a part.

John Burnside's poem, 'Hearsay', which I examined in Chapter 4, contains multiple text-worlds which are even more shifting and ephemeral. It is also underpinned by a persistent negativity which has a cumulative effect much darker than that produced in either 'Crates' or 'Evening'. My discussion of this poem focused on how it creates a sense of things absent, half-present, or suggested as present in its text-worlds and how the text as a whole forms a Gestalt – a partial representation that the mind seeks to complete. I looked at how 'Hearsay' becomes populated with echoes, things missing, things barely detectable, or half-seen. I also argued that its gradual build-up of negative tropes becomes apophatic in nature and showed how, in a similar way to 'Crates', Burnside constructs a series of text-worlds in his poem that occlude one another in turn. He also sets up possibilities which are never confirmed, rumours which are never fully realised, and suspicions which play on our darkest fears. In 'Hearsay' too, then, world-building becomes unsettlingly amorphous, as we struggle to establish a mental representation we can believe in or conceptualise fully.

Even in Sinéad Morrissey's poem, '1801', which formed the case study for Chapter 3, text-worlds are not straightforwardly constructed or cognised. Time and space in this poem, although coherently represented by the deictic elements in the text, become intertextually layered, with the worlds and voices of the past being echoed and re-presented through the poetry of the present. Meanwhile, in Chapter 5, we saw how Kate Tempest grounds the text-worlds of her poem, 'End Times', so closely and physically in the discourse-world in which she performs her work that it becomes difficult for her audiences to separate their own embodied experiences from those described in the text. Finally, my analysis of Alice Oswald's poem, 'Song of a Stone', revealed how the interconnectedness and interdependence of the metaphor worlds which constitute the majority of this poem lead to a continual deferral of meaning. My discussion of this text also showed how the text-worlds of 'Song of a Stone' take on a timeless and boundless quality, making the temporal and spatial parameters of the poem almost impossible to pin down.

Each of the texts I have analysed over the course of the book, then, has presented its own particular challenge to any notion that world-building is necessarily based on logical and cognisable spatial and temporal deixis. Identifiable across all of the poems are patterns of slippage, liminality and occlusion, which nevertheless do not prevent readers from conceptualising the worlds of these texts. Rather, these features of contemporary poetic discourse require us to engage more actively in our cognitive processing, to infer and elaborate the details of the conceptual spaces we build just as much as we use the language of the poems as the blueprints for our world-building. It is impossible to say as the result of these few analyses whether the patterns of distortion and confusion I have found in my chosen texts are common in a greater body of contemporary British poetry. However, I would argue that, even if they are present in these poems alone, Text World Theory and cognitive approaches to literary analysis more broadly must have a means of handling and understanding them.

To this end, I have drawn on research from cognitive psychology in particular in this book to help explain how human beings conceptualise time and space and the sorts of cognitive effects their manipulation through language can cause. I have also employed cognitive-psychological theories to consider how the human mind responds when confronted with gaps in information and in its perception of the world. It is my strong belief that Text World Theory needs to remain open to such theoretical borrowing in order to continue to ensure that its account of the cognition of discourse accords with what is known in other disciplines. It also needs to continue to try and explain the readerly *experience* of literature, which my analyses of poetry in these pages have shown is not always confined to the processing of language alone. Text World Theory has, since its inception, aimed to put human beings at the heart of its account of discourse. Remaining true to this aim means holding fast to the idea that the text is only the starting point for our cognition of literature. We need not only to be able to explain how mental representations are formed from textual information, but also what happens in our minds beyond the simple comprehension of words on a page.

## Layering and refraction

My exploration of intertextuality in poetry took place mainly in Chapter 3 through my analysis of Sinéad Morrissey's poem, '1801'. I showed in that chapter how Morrissey's text achieves a complex interweaving of the writing style of Dorothy Wordsworth with that of Morrissey herself. I also revealed various points in the poem where the styles and writing of other authors are made present and considered both my own responses to these intertextual references and those reported by a group of younger readers. However, echoes of other texts, other worlds and other language are not only to be found in '1801'. In Chapter 5, for example, I showed how Kate Tempest makes intertextual references to the work of William Blake in 'End Times', while also adopting the register of religious preaching throughout her poem. Religious discourse reverberates through Alice Oswald's 'Song of a Stone' too. My analysis of this poem in Chapter 6 revealed how the appearance of the Lord and an angel at the end of the text cause an undercurrent of biblical language running throughout the rest of the poem to become suddenly apparent.

Wherever the poems I have examined over the course of this book include language from other texts and other authors, they all do so in a way which either reframes that other discourse or reframes their own. Kate Tempest, for example, establishes a role for herself as a seer and teller in the discourse-world, but at the same time breaks down the social and psychological barriers that would normally exist between a preacher and a congregation. Similarly, the point at which Alice Oswald uses religious language in 'Song of a Stone' triggers significant world-repair in her poem. In '1801', too, Morrissey re-presents the language of Dorothy Wordsworth, but at the same time uses that re-presentation to make her own poetic identity and creativity felt in the text. All of these examples construct a complex layering of worlds, where one text or linguistic style is positioned on top of or seen through another. In Chapter 2, I talked about the palimpsestic effect Simon Armitage creates in his poem, 'Evening', where the world of the boy is viewed through the world of the adult. I would argue that the same conceptual effect is produced in all of the poems I have looked at in this book whenever one style becomes embedded within another. At these moments, both the host text and the embedded text are visible to the reader and their interplay results in an added depth and complexity of expression. Even more crucially, it also results in a refraction of both discourses: not only is the embedded text presented in a new context, but the text in which it is embedded takes on new meaning too.

However, this palimpsestic layering of worlds, along with the refraction of discourses which occurs as a result of it, does not only materialise when intertextual references are made. In my original example, 'Evening', the text-worlds which are layered on top of each other are all generated from within the same textual universe. The poem filters the point of view of a young boy through that of an adult and embeds the voices of parents within the voice of the poetic persona, within the voice of a child. However, no external text is borrowed into this poem and all its text-worlds remain securely positioned within the text's own fictional frame. In John Burnside's 'Hearsay' a similar layering of worlds and voices within the frame of the poem can be seen. In this text, rumours, stories, reports and echoes become laminated on top of one another, producing a disconcerting feel which is all the more accentuated because of the persistent negativity that also runs throughout the text. Once again, the interweaving of competing viewpoints and discourses has a refracting effect, with each world and each embedded voice being reframed as a result of its juxtaposition with another.

Text World Theory's ability to describe and explain the layering of text-worlds in this way has been proven not only across several of the chapters of this book, but also throughout the text-world scholarship that has preceded it. As a framework with an ontological hierarchy at the heart of its analytical architecture, it is ideally equipped to deal with texts that play with the embedding of worlds. Once again, however, I hope to have shown that a full account of the cognition of poetic style must retain a focus on the readerly experience of such techniques. Identifying embedding and layering as present in a text is only the first step in understanding how the worlds of contemporary poetry are conceptualised and the effects they produce.

## Audience

In the first chapter of this book, I introduced some ideas from the field of narratology as a possible new way of thinking about how poetry constructs different audiences through language. I discussed Rabinowitz's (1977) notions of 'the actual audience', 'the authorial audience' and 'the narrative audience'. The actual audience are people in the real world and are different from the authorial audience, a hypothetical construct for whom the author rhetorically designs the text. In Chapter 1, I explained that there always exists some degree of distance between these two audiences, but that the actual audience must come to share at least some of the authorial audience's characteristics if they are to understand the text, since it has been specially structured and composed for this imaginary set of people. The narrative audience, by contrast, is the audience implicitly addressed by the narrator of a text. This audience is afforded an observing position on the text-world and it temporarily adopts the information, beliefs, knowledge and opinions that the author assumes it has. In Chapter 1, I suggested that Rabinowitz's ideas could easily be extended to poetry and the narrative audience reframed as 'the poetic audience'. I also outlined Phelan's (1996) extension of Rabinowitz's model as a means of thinking about how readers are positioned by literary texts. For ease of reference, I reproduce here the quote from Phelan which explains his ideas:

> Even as we participate in the authorial and narrative audiences, we never lose our identities as flesh-and-blood readers, and that fact adds a further layer to our experience. Just as the authorial audience evaluates the narrator's values, so too does the flesh-and-blood audience evalu-

ate the author's. Entering the authorial audience allows us to recognize the ethical and ideological bases of the author's invitations. Comparing those values to the ones we bring to the text leads us into a dialogue about those values. Sometimes our values may be confined by those of the text, sometimes they may be challenged, and sometimes they may be ignored or insulted. When our values conflict with those of the text, we either will alter ours or resist those of the text (in whole or in part). The ethical dimension of the story involves the values upon which the authorial audience's judgments are based, the way those values are deployed in the narrative, and, finally, the values and beliefs implicit in the thematizing of the character's experience.

(Phelan 1996: 100)

I raise these ideas again at this point in my book in order to point out that all of the poems I have analysed over the course of its pages have positioned their audiences in interesting ways, in ethical terms.

All of the poetic techniques I have examined in the preceding chapters, as well as those additional stylistic features I have listed so far in this chapter, create some kind of tension between the actual audience, the authorial audience and the poetic audience. They are all, in one way or another, linguistic features which play with the ethical distance between the different audiences in both the text-world and the discourse-world. The use of intertextuality, for example, can be seen to bring the authorial audience very much to the foreground in the experience of poetry. When Sinéad Morrissey tells her actual audience that her work is based on the writing of Dorothy Wordsworth, she is delineating her authorial audience very clearly for them in the discourse-world. As we take on the position of poetic audience in the text-world of the poem, any distance between each of these three roles will become quickly apparent, and the precise nature of our experience of reading '1801' is highly dependent on whether or not the marked and unmarked references in the text are perceived during its reception. Even if the actual audience encounters '1801' without any introductory framing by its author, the relationship between them, the authorial audience and the poetic audience remains crucial in the processing of this text, as the poem signals its intertextuality through its register, its use of proper names, its poeticism, and so on.

Even when the layering of voices and text-worlds in contemporary poetry happens within the fictional frame of the poem – as it does in 'Crates', in 'Evening', in 'Hearsay', in 'End Times' and in 'Song of a Stone' – the ethical positioning of different audiences still holds an important role. The palimpsestic layering of text-worlds is a poetic technique which plays with ontology, with perspective and with reliability and, in its most extreme form, it can become meta-textual in nature, displaying its own artifice in a way that makes an explicit feature of the manipulation of different audiences. In the majority of literary criticism on postmodernist texts, this sort of meta-textuality would most likely be viewed as a highly self-conscious creative act. However, I would prefer to frame such techniques as 'audience-conscious', since it seems to me that what they actually shape and exploit most knowingly are the distances between the actual audience, the authorial audience and the poetic audience. For example, when Kate Tempest crosses the boundaries between music and poetry, she challenges the actual audience's knowledge schemas for both in the process. She then establishes a position for herself as a teller in both the discourse-world and the text-world, repeatedly foregrounding the acts of seeing, writing and performing in her poem. As she does so, she makes clear her construction of her text around an authorial audience, one which is aware of the genre expectations she is manipulating, but one which is also willing to occupy the position of a congregation, and one which shares her prophetic vision for the end of the world. The emotional impact of her work, however, comes from the intimate and privileged position she reserves for the poetic audience, the embodied experiences she shares with them, and the physically grounded text-worlds she creates. Tempest's poem 'End Times' and her entire performative approach just not simply demonstrate an aware-ness of self but a sensitivity to and control of audience.

Even some of the more subtle techniques of obfuscation that I have exam-ined over the course of preceding chapters, such as the distortion of time and space, or the accumulative deployment of negation, can be seen as examples of an audience-conscious style. When John Burnside fills his poem 'Hearsay' with negative imagery, with ghosts, rumours and gaps, he weaves an unreli-ability through his text which increases the distance between the authorial audience and the poetic audience and which is ultimately estranging for his readers. The same occurs when Simon Armitage builds a text-world in 'Evening' through which time becomes contorted and slippery and in which the liminal spaces where spatial and temporal shifts take place are hidden from the reader. Alice Oswald, too, defeats the expectations of her actual audience in her constant deferral of metaphorical mappings from one world, to the next, and to the next, as well as through her creation of text-worlds that often have no tangible spatial or temporal limits at all. All of the poems I have examined in this book, then, are connected to one another through their common display of an audience-conscious poetic style in one form or another. Each one of them executes some form of manipulation of reader expectations or forges a tension between the ethical positions of its separate audiences. Once again, establishing whether these are stylistic attributes which are shared more widely across contemporary British poetry is beyond the bounds of the present volume. However, again I would argue that their presence in even a small number of texts is worthy of note and of explanation as both linguistic and cognitive phenomena.

## At the boundaries of cognition

The final thread I wish to tease out as one woven through each of the poems I have analysed in this book is that which ties them all to a boundary of some sort. All of the texts I have explored here either build or are focused on some kind of a line. The line itself takes different forms and in some cases is a concrete or physical boundary in the real world and in some cases is an imaginary or conceptual separation. Some of the poems I have explored in this volume play with a boundary between genres, for example in Kate Tempest's 'End Times', where she blurs the distinction between the performance of music and the performance of poetry. Tempest also muddies the lines between herself as a poet and her listeners and readers, as she breaks down physical, social and psychological barriers, using that dismantling to heighten the emotional responses of her audience. In other cases, the boundary around which a text operates is one between worlds, for example the line that exists but is never seen between the world of a young boy and that of his adult self in the poem 'Evening'. This text additionally obscures the divisions between the voices and perspectives of different enactors – between the poetic persona and the boy, between the boy and his parents, and so on. A similar focus on the lines between separate voices and consciousnesses can be seen to be at work in Sinéad Morrissey's '1801'. Here, not only is Dorothy Wordsworth's voice blended with that of Morrissey's, but the voices of William Wordsworth and Samuel Taylor Coleridge are also made present in the text. A particularly poignant blurring of the distinction between Dorothy's and William's selves was explored in Chapter 3, but the boundaries being played with in this poem exist not just between textual entities and real-world entities, but between time periods and between texts too. We have seen, as well, how the poem 'Hearsay' muddies the distinction between presence and absence, between myth and reality, destabilising our sense of what is reliable in that text-world and leaving only further gaps in our knowledge for our fears to fill. Finally, 'Song of a Stone' forges such a tightly knit interconnectedness between the different worlds of its metaphors that we lose all sense of where one conceptualisation ends and the next one begins. Oswald also obscures the distinctions between elements of the natural landscape and the people who inhabit it, giving greater potency to the environment than to humans and underscoring the interdependency of the climax community she creates in poetic form.

I have shown across each of my analyses how all of the poems in this book push at various different boundaries and how they all can be seen to be testing the edges and confines of poetic expression in some way. Each poem has, through its poetic creativity and innovation, presented its own challenge to existing theories of the cognition of literary language. In response, I have sought to bolster and augment Text World Theory in particular through a flexible and receptive dialogue with new approaches from external disciplines and perspectives. I close this volume, therefore, leaving Text World Theory at a boundary in its own way too. Over a decade ago in my book, *Text World Theory: An Introduction* (Gavins 2007), I stated that the limits of the text-world approach to discourse were yet to be established. I suggested that the explanatory capacity of the framework might extend to a much wider diversity of discourse types than had at that point been examined from a text-world perspective. I particularly suggested that expressive arts other than literature, such as painting, sculpture and dance, might one day benefit from a Text World Theory analysis. Over the intervening years, a substantial amount of progress in this direction has been made by an ever-growing global network of text-world scholars (see, once again, Gavins and Lahey 2016 for an indicative selection of this recent research). However, it is clear that there remains a great deal of territory still to be explored. I have aimed through-out this book to continue to push Text World Theory to its limits and to extend its reach further to the outer edges of contemporary poetry and poetic expression. I hope not only to have opened the doors between the text-world approach and other theories of cognition, of language, and of literature, but at the same time to have used Text World Theory to confront the boundaries that exist around language, literature and the mind itself. It is only by making these extremities and borderlands the focus of enquiry that the circumference around our understanding of the cognition of poetic style and of the cognition of discourse more broadly can be drawn. It is only at the boundaries of cognition that the true capabilities of the analytical architecture of Text World Theory can be established.

# References

Allen, G. (2011) *Intertextuality*. London: Routledge.

Armitage, S. (2006) *Tyrannosaurus Rex Versus the Corduroy Kid*. London: Faber.

Baker, R. (2017) '"All voices should be read as the river's mutterings": the poetry of Alice Oswald', *The Cambridge Quarterly*, 46 (2): 99–118.

Baron-Cohen, S. (1995) *Mindblindness: An Essay on Autism and Theory of Mind*. Cambridge, MA: The MIT Press.

Baron-Cohen, S., Leslie, A. M. and Frith, U. (1985) 'Does the autistic child have a "theory of mind"'? *Cognition*, (21): 37–46.

Bartlett, F. C. (1932) *Remembering: A Study in Experimental and Social Psychology*. Cambridge: Cambridge University Press.

Bate, J. (2000) *The Song of the Earth*. London: Picador.

Bell, J. (2015) *Kith*. Rugby: Nine Arches Press.

Bender, A. and Beller, S. (2014) 'Mapping spatial frames of reference onto time: a review of theoretical accounts and empirical findings', *Cognition*, 132 (3): 342–82.

Bengal, R. (2018) 'The Last Poets: the hip-hop forefathers who gave black America its voice', *The Guardian*. Available at https://www.theguardian.com/music/2018/may/18/the-last-poets-the-hip-hop-forefathers-who-gave-black-america-its-voice

Bock, J. K. (1986) 'Meaning, sound, and syntax: lexical priming in sentence production', *Journal of Experimental Psychology-Learning Memory and Cognition*, 12 (4): 575–86.

Bock, K. and Loebell, H. (1990) 'Framing sentences', *Cognition*, 35 (1): 1–39.

Bock, K. and Warren, R. (1985) 'Conceptual accessibility and syntactic structure in sentence formulation', *Cognition*, 21 (1): 47–67.

Bradley, A. (2009) *Book of Rhymes: The Poetics of Hip Hop*. New York: Basic Books.

Bremmer, F., Kubischik, M., Hoffman, K.-P. and Krekelberg, B. (2009) 'Neural dynamics of saccadic suppression', *Journal of Neuroscience*, 29 (40): 12374–83.

Brown, A. (2011) 'Finding "the lit space": reality, imagination and the commonplace in the poetry of John Burnside', *Agenda*, spring/summer: 101–12.

Bühler, K. (1982) 'The deictic field of language and deictic worlds'. In R. Jarvella and W. Klein (eds), *Speech, Place and Action: Studies in Deixis and Related Topics*. Chichester: John Wiley, 9–30.

Burnside, J. (2011) *Black Cat Bone*. London: Jonathan Cape.

Bylund, E. and Athanasopoulos, P. (2017) 'The Whorfian time warp: representing duration through the language hourglass', *Journal of Experimental Psychology: General*, 146 (7): 911–16.

Campbell, J. (1999) *This Is the Beat Generation*. London: Martin Secker and Warburg Ltd.

Carruthers, P. and Smith, P. K. (1996) *Theories of Theories of Mind*. Cambridge: Cambridge University Press.

Clark, A. (2008) *Supersizing the Mind: Embodiment, Action, and Cognitive Extension*. Oxford: Oxford University Press.

Clark, A. and Chalmers, D. (1998) 'The extended mind', *Analysis*, 58 (1): 7–19.

Coussens, C. (2008) 'British national identity, topicality and tradition in the poetry of Simon Armitage', *Cankaya University Journal of the Arts and Sciences*, 1 (9): 17–38.

Cresswell, T. (2014) 'Geographies of poetry/poetries of geography', *Cultural Geographies*, 21 (1): 141–6.

Draisma, S. (1989) *Intertextuality in Biblical Writings*. Kampen: J. H. Kok.

Droit-Volet, S. and Meck, W. H. (2007) 'How emotions colour our perception of time', *Trends in Cognitive Sciences*, 11 (12): 504–13.

Dussol, V. (2011) 'Designating the environment: deixis and nature writing in the poetries of Philip Whalen and Merrill Gilfillan', *Revue Française d'études Américaines*, 129: 100–16.

Emmott, C. (1997) *Narrative Comprehension: A Discourse Perspective*. Oxford: Oxford University Press.

Evans, V. (2004) *The Structure of Time*. Amsterdam: John Benjamins.

Fauconnier, G. and Turner, M. (2002) *The Way We Think: Conceptual Blending and the Mind's Hidden Complexities*. New York: Basic Books.

Franke, W. (2005) 'The singular and the other at the limits of language in the apophatic poetics of Edmond Jabès and Paul Celan', *New Literary History: A Journal of Theory and Interpretation*, 36 (4): 621–38.

Gavins, J. (2007) *Text World Theory: An Introduction*. Edinburgh: Edinburgh University Press.

Gavins, J. (2013) *Reading the Absurd*. Edinburgh: Edinburgh University Press.

Gavins, J. (2014) 'Defamiliarisation'. In P. Stockwell and S. Whiteley (eds), *The Cambridge Handbook of Stylistics*. Cambridge: Cambridge University Press, 126–211.

Gavins, J. (2015) 'Text World Theory'. In V. Sotirova (ed.), *The Bloomsbury Companion to Stylistics*. London: Bloomsbury, 444–57.

Gavins, J. (2016) 'Stylistic interanimation and apophatic poetics in Jacob Polley's "Hide and Seek"'. In J. Gavins and E. Lahey (eds), *World Building: Discourse in the Mind*. London: Bloomsbury, 276–92.

Gavins, J. and Lahey, E. (eds) (2016) *World Building: Discourse in the Mind*. London: Bloomsbury.

Gavins, J. and Stockwell, P. (2012) 'About the heart, where it hurt exactly and how often', *Language and Literature*, 21 (1): 31–50.

Genette, G. [1979] (1992) *The Architext: An Introduction*. Berkeley: University of California Press.

Genette, G. [1981] (1997a) *Palimpsests: Literature in the Second Degree*. Lincoln: University of Nebraska Press.

Genette, G. [1987] (1997b) *Paratexts: Thresholds of Interpretation.* Cambridge: Cambridge University Press.

Georg, K. and Lappe, M. (2007) 'Spatio-temporal contingency of saccade-induced chronostasis', *Experimental Brain Research*, 180 (3): 535–9.

Gibbons, R. (2007) 'On apophatic poetics', *American Poetry Review*, 36 (6): 19–23.

Gibbons, R. (2008) 'On apophatic poetics, part two', *American Poetry Review*, 37 (2): 39–45.

Giora, R., Balaban, N. and Fein, O. (2004) 'Negation as positivity in disguise'. In H. L. Colston and A. Katz (eds), *Figurative Language Comprehension: Social and Cultural Influences.* Hillsdale, NJ: Lawrence Erlbaum Associates, 233–58.

Giovanelli, M. (2013) *Text World Theory and Keats' Poetry: The Cognitive Poetics of Desire, Dreams and Nightmares.* London: Bloomsbury Academic.

Giovanelli, M. and Harrison, C. (2018) *Cognitive Grammar in Stylistics: A Practical Guide.* London: Bloomsbury Academic.

Givón, T. (1993) *English Grammar: A Function-Based Approach.* Amsterdam: John Benjamins Publishing Company.

Goatly, A. (2017) 'Metaphor and grammar in the poetic representation of nature', *Russian Journal of Linguistics*, 21 (1): 48–72.

Gräbner, C. (2011) '"The hurricane doesn't roar in pentameters": rhythmanalysis in performed poetry'. In C. Gräbner and A. Casas (eds) *Performing Poetry: Body, Place and Rhythm in the Poetry Performance.* Leiden: Brill, 71–88.

Green, K. (1992) 'Deixis and the poetic persona', *Language and Literature*, 1 (2): 121–34.

Gross, P. (2013) *Later.* Tarset: Bloodaxe Books.

Habermann, I. and Keller, D. (2016) 'English topographies: introduction'. In I. Habermann and D. Keller (eds), *English Topographies in Literature and Culture: Space, Place, and Identity.* Leiden: Brill, 1–13.

Hartman, D. K. (1995) 'Eight readers reading: the intertextual links of proficient readers reading multiple passages', *Reading Research Quarterly*, 30 (3): 520–61.

Hartman, D. K. (2004) 'Deconstructing the reader, the text, the author and the context: intertextuality and reading from a "cognitive" perspective'. In D. Bloome and N. Shuart-Faris (eds), *Uses of Intertextuality in Classroom and Educational Research.* Scottsdale, AZ: Information Age Publishing, 353–72.

Hasson, U. and Glucksberg, S. (2006) 'Does understanding negation entail affirmation?: an examination of negated metaphors', *Journal of Pragmatics*, 38 (7): 1015–32.

Hedger, K., Necker, E., Barazkai, A. and Norman, G. (2017) 'The influence of social stress on time perception and psychophysiological reactivity', *Psychophysiology*, 54 (5): 706–12.

Hemmer, K. (ed.) (2006) *Encyclopedia of Beat Literature.* New York: Facts On File.

Herman, D. (1994) 'Textual "you" and double deixis in Edna O'Brien's *A Pagan Place*', *Style*, 28 (3): 378–410.

Herman, D. (2002) *Story Logic: Problems and Possibilities of Narrative.* Lincoln: University of Nebraska Press.

Hidalgo Downing, L. (2000a) *Negation, Text Worlds, and Discourse: The Pragmatics of Fiction.* Stamford, CA: Ablex.

Hidalgo Downing, L. (2000b) 'Negation in discourse: a text world approach to Joseph Heller's *Catch-22*', *Language and Literature*, 9 (3): 215–39.

Hidalgo Downing, L. (2002) 'Creating things that are not: the role of negation in the poetry of Wislawa Szymborska', *Journal of Literary Semantics*, 31: 113–32.

Ibbotson, M. R. and Cloherty, S. L. (2009) 'Visual perception: saccadic omission – suppression or temporal masking?', *Current Biology*, 19 (12): R493–6.

Isherwood, C. (2014) 'Mundane, meet dramatic', *The New York Times*. Available at http://search.proquest.com/docview/1941359217/abstract/CD94F781285A4088PQ/1

Jameson, F. (1991) *Postmodernism, or, The Cultural Logic of Late Capitalism*. Durham, NC: Duke University Press.

Jarvella, R. and Klein, W. (eds) (1982) *Speech, Place and Action: Studies in Deixis and Related Topics*. Chichester: John Wiley.

Johnson, M. (1987) *The Body in the Mind: The Bodily Basis of Meaning, Imagination, and Reason*. Chicago: Chicago University Press.

Katz, A. (2013) 'Deconstructing Dickinson's Dharma', *Emily Dickinson Journal*, 22 (2): 46–64.

Keenan, E. and Comrie, B. (1977) 'Noun phrase accessibility and Universal Grammar', *Linguistic Inquiry*, 8 (1): 63–99.

Keller, P. E. and Schubert, E. (2011) 'Cognitive and affective judgements of syncopated musical themes', *Advances in Cognitive Psychology*, 7: 142–56.

Kennedy, D. (1996) *New Relations: The Refashioning of British Poetry, 1980–1994*. Bridgend: Seren.

Knöll, J., Morrone, M. and Bremner, F. (2013) 'Spatio-temporal topography of saccadic overestimation of time', *Vision Research*, 83: 56–65.

Köhler, W. (1970) *Gestalt Psychology: An Introduction to New Concepts in Modern Psychology*. New York: Liveright.

Kornysheva, K., von Cramon, D. Y., Jacobsen T. and Schubotz, R. (2010) 'Tuning-in to the beat: aesthetic appreciation of musical rhythms correlates with a premotor activity boost', *Human Brain Mapping*, 31 (1): 48–64.

Krekelberg, B. (2010) 'Saccadic suppression', *Current Biology*, 20 (5): R228–9.

Kristeva, J. (1980) *Desire in Language: A Semiotic Approach to Literature and Art*. New York: Columbia University Press.

Lahey, E. (2005) Text World Landscapes and English-Canadian National Identity in the Poetry of Al Purdy, Alden Nowlan and Milton Acorn. Unpublished PhD thesis, University of Nottingham, UK.

Lakoff, G. (1987) *Women, Fire, and Dangerous Things: What Categories Reveal About the Mind*. Chicago: University of Chicago Press.

Lakoff, G. (1990) 'The invariance hypothesis: is abstract reasoning based on image-schemas?', *Cognitive Linguistics*, 1 (1): 39–74.

Lakoff, G. and Johnson, M. (1980) *Metaphors We Live By*. Chicago: University of Chicago Press.

Lakoff, G. and Johnson, M. (1999) *Philosophy in the Flesh: The Embodied Mind and its Challenge to Western Thought*. New York: Basic Books.

Lakoff, G. and Turner, M. (1989) *More Than Cool Reason: A Field Guide to Poetic Metaphor*. Chicago: University of Chicago Press.

Langacker, R. W. (1987) *Foundations of Cognitive Grammar*. Stanford, CA: Stanford University Press.

Langacker, R. W. (1991) *Foundations of Cognitive Grammar: Descriptive Application*. Stanford, CA: Stanford University Press.

Langacker, R. W. (2008) *Cognitive Grammar: A Basic Introduction*. Oxford: Oxford University Press.

Leech, G. N. and Short, M. (2007) *Style in Fiction: A Linguistic Introduction to English Fictional Prose* (2nd edition). Harlow: Longman.

Levi-Strauss, C. [1962] (1974) *The Savage Mind*. London: Weidenfeld and Nicholson.

McConnell, J. (2014) '"We are still mythical": Kate Tempest's *Brand New Ancients*', *Arion: A Journal of Humanities and the Classics*, 22 (1): 195–206.

McHale, B. (1987) *Postmodernist Fiction*. London: Methuen.

McLoughlin, N. (2013) 'Negative polarity in Eavan Boland's "The Famine Road"', *New Writing: The International Journal for the Practice and Theory of Creative Writing*, 10 (2): 219–27.

McLoughlin, N. (2019) 'Resonance and absence: a text world analysis of "Tuonela" by Philip Gross', *New Writing: The International Journal for the Practice and Theory of Creative Writing*, 16 (1): 89–99.

Mason, J. (2015) Narrative Interrelation: A Cognitive Model of Intertextuality and its Application to the Study of Literature. Unpublished PhD thesis, University of Nottingham, UK.

Mason, J. (2019) *Intertextuality in Practice*. Amsterdam: John Benjamins.

Matlock, T. (2004) 'Fictive motion as cognitive simulation', *Memory and Cognition*, 32 (8): 1389–1400.

Middleton, R. (2015) 'Connection, disconnection and the self in Alice Oswald's *Dart*', *Green Letters*, 19 (2): 157–69.

Morrissey, S. (2013) *Parallax*. London: Carcanet.

Morrissey, S. (2015) '1801'. Available at http://www.poetryarchive.org/poem/1801

Mort, H. (2014) 'Something Else, Then Something Else Again': Neuroscience and Connection-Making in Contemporary Poetry. Unpublished PhD thesis, University of Sheffield, UK.

Moses, O. (2018) 'Poetry and the environmentally extended mind', *New Literary History*, 49 (3): 309–35.

Moyise, S. (1995) *The Old Testament in the New Testament*. Sheffield: Sheffield Academic Press.

Müller-Zettelmann, E. (2000) *Lyrik und Metalyrik: Theorie einer Gattung und ihrer Selbstbespiegelung anhand von Beispielen aus der englisch- und deutschsprachigen Dichtkunst*. Heidelberg: Universitätsverlag C. Winter.

Nahajec, L. (2009) 'Negation and the creation of implicit meaning in poetry', *Language and Literature*, 18 (2): 109–27.

Novak, J. (2011) *Live Poetry: An Integrated Approach to Poetry in Performance*. Amsterdam: Rodopi.

Núñez, R. and Cooperrider, K. (2013) 'The tangle of space and time in human cognition', *Trends in Cognitive Sciences*, 17 (5): 220–9.

Oswald, A. (2002) *Dart*. London: Faber and Faber.

Oswald, A. (2005a) *Woods Etc*. London: Faber and Faber.

Oswald, A. (2005b) 'Alice Oswald celebrates Ted Hughes', *The Guardian*. Available at https://www.theguardian.com/books/2005/dec/03/poetry.tedhughes

Oswald, A. (2009a) *A Sleepwalk on the Severn*. London: Faber and Faber.

Oswald, A. (2009b) *Weeds and Wild Flowers*. London: Faber and Faber.

Panagiotidou, M. (2012) 'An introduction to the semantics of intertextuality', *Journal of Literary Semantics*, 41: 47–65.

Pate, A. (2010) *In the Heart of the Beat: The Poetry of Rap*. Lanham, MD: Scarecrow Press.

Phelan, J. (1996) *Narrative as Rhetoric: Techniques, Audiences, Ethics, Ideology*. Columbus: Ohio State University Press.

Phelan, J. (2007) 'Estranging unreliability, bonding unreliability, and the ethics of *Lolita*', *Narrative*, 15 (2): 222–38.

Portner, P. (2007) 'Imperatives and modals', *Natural Language Semantics*, 15 (4): 351–83.

Pritchett, P. (2014) 'How to write poetry after Auschwitz: the burnt book of Michael Palmer', *Journal of Modern Literature*, 37 (3): 127–45.

Rabinowitz, P. (1977) 'Truth in fiction: a reexamination of audiences', *Critical Inquiry,* 4 (1): 121–41.

Rauh, G. (ed.) (1983) *Essays on Deixis*. Tübingen: Gunter Narr Verlag.

Reeves, M. (2008) *Somebody Scream: Rap Music's Rise to Prominence in the Aftershock of Black Power*. London: Faber and Faber.

Richardson, G. (2002) 'John Burnside's poetry: no ideas but in somethings'. Available at http://www.aretemagazine.co.uk/10-winter-spring-2002/john-burnside/

Riffaterre, M. (1990) 'Compulsory reader response: the intertextual drive'. In J. Still and M. Worton (eds), *Intertextuality: Theories and Practices*. Manchester: Manchester University Press, 56–78.

Ross, J., Burr, D. and Morrone, C. (1996) 'Suppression of the magnocellular pathway during saccades', *Behavioural Brain Research*, 80 (1): 1–8.

Rowlands, M. (2003) *Externalism: Putting Mind and World Back Together Again*. Chesham: Acumen.

Rowlands, M. (2010) *The New Science of the Mind: From Extended Mind to Embodied Phenomenology*. Cambridge, MA: The MIT Press.

Semino, E. (1995) 'Deixis and the dynamics of poetic voice'. In K. Green (ed.), *New Essays on Deixis: Discourse, Narrative, Literature*. Amsterdam: John Benjamins Publishing Company, 145–60.

Shi, J. and Huang, X. (2017) 'The colour red affects time perception differently in different contexts', *International Journal of Psychology*, 52 (1): 77–80.

Simpson, P. (1993) *Language, Ideology and Point of View*. London: Routledge.

Snyder, G. (1980) *The Real Work: Interviews and Talks, 1964–1979* (edited by W. S. McLean). New York: New Directions Publishing.

Stockwell, P. (2009) *Texture: A Cognitive Aesthetics of Reading*. Edinburgh: Edinburgh University Press.

Stockwell, P. and Mahlberg, M. (2015) 'Mind- modelling with corpus stylistics in *David Copperfield*', *Language and Literature*, 24 (2): 129–47.

Sweeney, M. (2005) *Form and Intertextuality in Prophetic and Apocalyptic Literature*. Tübingen: Mohr Seibeck.

Tempest, K. (2009) 'End Times'. Available at https://www.youtube.com/

watch?v=jYMtmQ_H570

Tempest, K. (2013) *Brand New Ancients*. London: Picador.

Thacker, J. (2015) 'The thing in the gap-stone style: Alice Oswald's acoustic arrangements', *The Cambridge Quarterly*, 44 (2): 103–18.

Thain, M. (2007) 'An "uncomfortable intersection": the meeting of contemporary urban and rural environments in the poetry of Simon Armitage', *Worldviews: Global Religions, Culture, and Ecology*, 5 (1): 58–79.

Theado, M. (ed.) (2002) *The Beats: A Literary Reference*. New York: Carroll and Graf Publishers Inc.

Tottie, G. (1982) 'Where do negative sentences come from?' *Studia Linguistica*, 36 (1): 88–105.

Turner, M. (2006) 'Compression and representation', *Language and Literature*, 15 (1): 17–27.

Van Winckel, N. (2008) 'The apophatic', *Poetry*, 192 (3): 235.

Verdonk, P. (2013) *The Stylistics of Poetry*. London: Bloomsbury.

Vernice, M. and Sorace, A. (2018) 'Animacy effects on the processing of intransitive verbs: an eye-tracking study', *Language, Cognition and Neuroscience*, 33 (7): 850–66.

Wagner, H. (1983) *Phenomenology of Consciousness and Sociology of the Life-World: An Introductory Study*. Edmonton: University of Alberta Press.

Watson, T. L. and Krekelberg, B. (2009) 'The relationship between saccadic suppression and perceptual stability', *Current Biology*, 19 (12): 1040–3.

Weckerly, J. and Kutas, M. (1999) 'An electrophysiological analysis of animacy effects in the processing of object relative sentences', *Psychophysiology*, 36 (5): 559–70.

Werner, V. (2019) 'Assessing hip-hop discourse: linguistic realness and styling', *Text and Talk*, 39 (5): 671–98.

Werth, P. (1994) 'Extended metaphor: a text-world account', *Language and Literature*, 3 (2): 79–103.

Werth, P. (1999) *Text Worlds: Representing Conceptual Space in Discourse*. London: Longman.

Wolfer, S. (2016) 'The impact of nominalisations on the reading process: a case-study using the Freiburg Legalese Reading Corpus'. In S. Hansen-Schirra and S. Grucza (eds), *Eyetracking and Applied Linguistics*. Berlin: Language Science Press, 163–86.

Wordsworth, D. (2002) *The Grasmere and Alfoxden Journals* (edited by Pamela Woolf). Oxford: Oxford World Classics.

# Index